Reform and Reformers
in Nineteenth Century Britain

Edited by
Michael J. Turner

**University of
Sunderland Press**

© The Editor, Contributors and University of Sunderland Press

ISBN 1 873757 94 8

First published 2004

Cover Design by Tim Murphy Creative Solutions
Copy-Editor Felicity Hepburn

Published in Great Britain by
The University of Sunderland Press
in association with Business Education Publishers Limited
The Teleport
Doxford International
Sunderland
SR3 3XD

Tel: 0191 5252410
Fax: 0191 5201815

All rights reserved. No part of this publication may be reproduced, stored in a retrieval system, or transmitted, in any form or by any means, electrical, mechanical, photocopying, recording or otherwise, without the prior permission of the University of Sunderland Press.

British Cataloguing-in-Publications Data
A catalogue record for this book is available from the British Library

Cover image: Copyright permission Mary Evans Picture Library

Printed and bound in the United Kingdom by the Alden Group, Oxford

Contents

Notes on the Contributors   v

Introduction
Michael J. Turner   vii

Chapter 1

   Reform or Repeal? Aspects of Reform in Provincial Ireland, 1829-1835
   Martin McElroy   1

Chapter 2

   The Independent Man: Gender, Obligation, and Virtue in the
   1832 Reform Act
   Matthew McCormack   25

Chapter 3

   Sir Thomas Phillips and the Problem of 'Class-Antagonism'
   Chris Williams   43

Chapter 4

   Reform as Process: The Parliamentary Fate of the Bank Charter
   Act of 1844
   Catherine Molyneux   63

Chapter 5

   Parliament and Free Trade after the Repeal of the Corn Laws
   Michael J. Turner   81

Chapter 6

The Joint Stock Company in Politics
James Taylor   99

Chapter 7

After Chartism: Metropolitan Perspectives on the Chartist
Movement in Decline, 1848-1860
Antony Taylor   117

Chapter 8

The Acceptable Face of Carpet Baggery?
W. H. Willans and Frome's Reformers
Clyde Binfield   137

Chapter 9

Re-thinking Popular Conservatism in Liverpool: Democracy and
Reform in the Later Nineteenth Century
Sandra O'Leary   157

Notes on the Contributors

Clyde Binfield is Emeritus Professor of History at the University of Sheffield. He has lectured and published widely, especially in nineteenth-century British religious, political and social history.

Matthew McCormack teaches modern British history at the University of Manchester. In 2002 he was awarded a PhD in the School of History and Classics for a study of 'the independent man' in Georgian political culture. His recent publications include an article in the *British Journal for Eighteenth-Century Studies*.

Martin McElroy teaches modern British and Irish history at the University of Southampton. He gained his PhD at Queen's University, Belfast, in 2003 for a thesis entitled 'Politics in Munster, 1825-1835', which he plans to publish in due course.

Catherine Molyneux is currently completing a doctoral thesis at St Hilda's College, University of Oxford, on the parliamentary validation of the Bank Charter Act of 1844 and the rhetorical strategies employed by economists, bankers, and politicians in the controversy between the currency school and banking school. Her forthcoming articles include an analysis of the impact of the crisis of 1847 on the introduction of limited liability and a study of Harriet Martineau's political economy novels.

Sandra O'Leary is a PhD student in the history department at the University of Liverpool. Her work represents a groundbreaking reappraisal of the nature of Conservative politics in late Victorian Liverpool.

Antony Taylor is Senior Lecturer in History at Sheffield Hallam University. He has written widely in the field of nineteenth-century popular politics, and is author of *'Down with the Crown': British Anti-Monarchism and Debates about Royalty since 1790* (1999) and *'Lords of Misrule' Hostility to Aristocracy in Nineteenth- and Twentieth-Century Britain* (forthcoming, 2005).

James Taylor is currently the Tawney Postdoctoral Research Fellow at the Institute of Historical Research, London. His doctoral thesis, written while at the University of Kent, is entitled '"Wealth Makes Worship": Attitudes to Joint Stock Enterprise in British Law, Politics, and Culture, c.1800-c.1870'.

Michael J. Turner is Reader in Modern British History at the University of Sunderland. His most recent books are *The Age of Unease* (2000) and *Pitt the Younger* (2003). His research interests relate mainly to reform movements and he is currently completing a book entitled *Independent Radicalism in Early Victorian Britain* (due for publication in 2004).

Chris Williams is Professor of History and Director of the Centre for Modern and Contemporary Wales at the University of Glamorgan. His research interests are in the modern history of Britain and of Wales. He is editor of *The Blackwell Companion to Nineteenth-Century Britain* (2004) and (with Jane Aaron) of *Postcolonial Wales* (2004).

Introduction

Themes associated with reform and reformers have long fascinated historians of nineteenth-century Britain, and remain a staple ingredient of university and sixth form programmes. This volume of essays brings together established names in the field with younger scholars who are in the early stages of their academic careers. It is designed to contribute to and carry forward some of the most interesting recent debates about the nature and scope of reform, the identity, motives and goals of reformers, and the place of reform in the political, social and economic development of nineteenth-century Britain. It reflects the new approaches and directions of current research, while also revisiting older, more familiar questions that have never quite been settled.

This volume contains expanded versions of papers that were originally delivered at a conference hosted by the University of Sunderland, 28-30 June 2001. The conference, 'Varieties of Political Belief in Britain, 1832-1914', attracted considerable attention and was attended by fifty scholars from universities in England, Scotland, Wales and Northern Ireland. It was the most important gathering that year for historians of modern British political history.

Having enjoyed pre-eminence within the historical discipline for so long, the *political* history of Britain fell out of fashion somewhat during the 1960s and 1970s as other topics and priorities came to the fore. But a new generation of historians has returned to the political, and in the 1990s the label 'the new political history' was coined as a result. Studies of reform and reformers are again in vogue. They are essential to 'the new political history', and the success of the Sunderland conference suggests that the revival of interest in political history, broadly defined, can go on to establish even more sturdy roots in the fertile ground of inquiry, discovery and criticism in the new century. The timing of this volume of essays, therefore, could not be better.

In exploring the development of an Irish reform campaign in the era of Catholic emancipation (1829) and the Great Reform Act (1832), Martin McElroy draws attention to the contested meanings of 'reform' and notes the disagreement among reformers on aims and methods. Some activists expected parliamentary reform to pacify the country. Others wanted much more: a whole range of measures designed to assist Catholics in their quest for civil rights. But how best could the desired reforms be achieved? Former allies in the Catholic Association formed opposing camps. Agitation developed for the repeal of the legislative union and re-establishment of a separate parliament in Dublin, on the grounds that only Irish legislators could effectively tackle Irish problems. This was the view of Daniel O'Connell, while other leading Irish reformers such as Thomas Wyse preferred to rely on the Westminster parliament. The dichotomy became obvious in campaigns for municipal and parliamentary reform in the province of Munster. Differing outlooks and tactics prolonged the breach at a time of political fluidity, until a broad pro-reform, anti-Tory front emerged in 1834.

The meaning of 'reform', argues Matthew McCormack, was closely related to the idea of 'independence'. Some reformers upheld the notion of 'the independent man' as a reliable agent of useful improvements and – frequently – their chief beneficiary. 'Independence' denoted virtue, liberty, conscientious judgment and self-control, and in debates about and struggles for a range of reforms the vocabulary of 'independence' played a highly significant role. The conviction that only 'independent men' were legitimate political actors also affected broader opinions about gender, obligation, character, and the nature of the British state.

The state was repeatedly challenged during the nineteenth century by reformist, radical and even insurrectionary groups, and Chris Williams examines responses to one such challenge in a particular time and place. In South Wales a conflict developed between moderate reformers who backed the 1832 Reform Act, and more extreme campaigners who became Chartists and participated in the Newport Rising of 1839. At the root of this conflict, thought Thomas Phillips, Mayor of Newport in 1839, was class antagonism, and he subsequently devoted himself to the promotion of social peace and political consensus. He became a notable champion of moral and religious improvement, following a path that moderate reformers in other regions also pursued.

Phillips decided that political stability was not possible without moral reform, sound religion, social harmony and economic progress. Some of the economic and financial determinants of stability are discussed by Catherine Molyneux, who stresses the importance of currency reform in the early Victorian period. Sir Robert Peel's celebrated Bank Charter Act of 1844 was and is widely regarded as a measure that helped to make nineteenth-century Britain powerful and prosperous, but in fact the arguments for and against Peel's reform continued long after its implementation. Financial crisis promoted its suspension, and there were several official inquiries into its operation and effects. Parliamentary battles over the Bank Charter Act became inextricably linked with a wider contest between the Liberal-free trade and

Conservative-protectionist interests concerning the future direction of Britain's political and economic development.

This wider contest was dramatically affected by the repeal of the corn laws in 1846, and Michael J. Turner investigates the immediate aftermath of repeal to find out why real doubts persisted about the ultimate success of free trade. Opposition to liberal economic reforms was not crushed by repeal. Indeed, the Conservative Party resolutely resisted free trade policies and the party confusion of the time meant that the Liberal majority in parliament was far from secure. On questions relating to commercial duties, the navigation laws and the condition of agriculture, pressure for reform met with an equally well-argued and principled obstruction.

Another important area of reforming activity that directly affected trade, industry and finance was the rise of the joint stock company. As James Taylor demonstrates, Victorian Britain was transformed by the arrival of corporate enterprise on a grand scale, and the need to balance competing interests, not to mention the desire to make sure that economic endeavour would benefit the public, forced governments to pass a series of reforms. But as in so many other contexts, so in this one the meaning of 'reform' was contested. Advocates of economic freedom vied with advocates of regulation, and controversy also raged over business values, practices and structures. The facilitation of joint stock enterprise was usually presented as a natural corollary of moves towards free trade, yet free traders themselves were not of one mind on this transformation, and criticism of the joint stock company was more complicated than has often been supposed.

As many of these problems were addressed, Britain entered a so-called 'age of equipoise', with social and political stability and sustained economic growth. According to this interpretation, the demise of Chartism, the ascendancy of moderate reformism and free trade, relative social mobility and rising living standards made the mid-Victorian generation calm, content and confident. Antony Taylor points out, however, that the end of Chartism masks an essential continuity in popular political militancy. In the reform circles of London, for example, club life, concern for the preservation of open spaces, and a culture of riotous assembly all contributed to ongoing struggles over local government, town planning, poverty relief, meeting places, policing and the franchise.

The diverse nature of reform commitments is highlighted by Clyde Binfield in his study of an electoral contest in the heyday of William Ewart Gladstone. Dissent, radicalism, charities, regionalism and a complex of personal, family and business connections shaped the political identity and electoral rhetoric of many Liberal candidates at this time, and reform became a less contested issue in particular circumstances. The Frome election of 1874 gave added impetus to the consolidation of political beliefs and development of pro-reform perspectives.

The fact that in certain places and periods Conservatives could become reformers is clearly established by Sandra O'Leary in her work on late nineteenth-century Liverpool. Traditionally, political affiliation in Liverpool was explained principally as an offspring of religious sectarianism, and Conservative dominance in the city was assumed to rest on the encouragement and exploitation of rigid denominational loyalty. But an analysis of Conservatism in Liverpool reveals that it was the offer of progressive municipal reform that attracted support, not so much the reliance on sectarian fervour. These provincial urban Tories, it appears, were rather more inclusive and practical than their rivals (and the subsequent historiography) would have us believe.

The insights provided by these essays will certainly deepen our understanding of reform and reformers in nineteenth-century Britain. Discussion ranges over general trends and issues as well as specific events, places, persons and campaigns. There are some revealing case studies. Where appropriate the historiography is critically evaluated (and frequently corrected). High politics and low politics are brought together, as are regions and cities, rulers and ruled, goals and achievements, theory and practice. The topics covered in this volume will have an abiding relevance as future scholars carry forward inquiry and debate on the meaning, nature and reception of reform in a period of remarkable transformation.

Chapter 1

Reform or Repeal? Aspects of Reform in Provincial Ireland, 1829-1835*

The successful achievement of the final Catholic Relief Act in 1829 brought an end to the Catholic Association in Ireland, whose campaign to remove religious disabilities within the United Kingdom was unprecedented in scale. The mass mobilisation of Catholic Ireland in the 1820s created a political movement that incorporated all sections of Irish society from the aristocrat to the humblest labourer, who could join the Catholic Association as an 'associate member' for only a penny per month. There is a general consensus among historians about the impact of the Catholic Association in Ireland. Oliver MacDonagh argues that there was a 'general political mobilisation' in the two decades after 1825 behind the Catholic Association and Daniel O'Connell's various campaigns, resulting in high levels of politicisation. This in turn encouraged lower levels of political violence and diminished the chances of revolution. The age of O'Connell, in summary, witnessed the 'triumph of constitutionalism' in Ireland.[1] Fergus O'Ferrall contends that the Catholic Association's successful campaign, with its high levels of politicisation in large parts of the country, marked the birth of Irish democracy, and that the achievement of 'Catholic Emancipation inaugurated the liberal democratic era' in British politics.[2]

The existing historiography is not as illuminating when dealing with the years immediately following 1829. In other words, what happens to Catholic politics after 1829? Initially, it seemed like it would quietly pass away once the goal of the Catholic Association was achieved. The liberal clubs that formed the basis of the Association's organisation were dissolved as a result of the success of the campaign and the fear of suppression under the act (accompanying the Relief Act) that banned the Catholic Association. The machinery of the campaign rapidly disappeared. An associate of Thomas Wyse wrote prophetically after the dissolution of the Waterford Liberal Club: 'The removal of that weight which pressed against us together will, I fear, soon create divisions amongst those who should be united'.[3] It was new territory for everyone involved in the Catholic Association. Since 1805 an entire generation of Catholic politicians had concentrated on one end: the attainment of Catholic relief in order to overturn the remaining penal laws and allow Catholics to sit in parliament and hold the higher offices of state. This generation included some of the most prominent leaders of the Association, including Daniel O'Connell, Thomas Wyse and Richard Sheil. What happened when the single unifying goal was removed? Would the Catholics remain together as a bloc or would they, as Thomas Wyse's friend feared they would, divide and become enemies over a whole range of issues that affected the United Kingdom at that time? What is clear is that most former members believed that further reform was necessary in order to give Catholics a tangible sense of 'emancipation'. This meant that Catholics would not only in theory have the same political rights as Protestants, but that they would also hold some of the offices from which they were previously excluded. This essay will examine the development of Catholic politics in the province of Munster in the years following 1829 up to the general election of 1834-5.

Munster, the southern province of Ireland, comprises the six counties of Clare, Cork, Kerry, Limerick, Tipperary and Waterford. As with the rest of the country the province experienced a surge in population in the decades leading up to the Great Famine. In Munster the vast majority of the population were Catholic. Though there may be no complete set of reliable figures for the religious demography of pre-famine Ireland, it has been calculated that in the 1820s the Catholic population of Munster outnumbered the Protestant by a ratio of twelve to one.[4] In other words, out of a total provincial population of over two million, around 170,000 were Protestant. Incorporated into this was a great variation in each county. Wakefield, in the first of the great topographical surveys of Ireland in the nineteenth century, concluded that counties Clare, Kerry, Limerick and Waterford were 'nearly all Catholic', with the ratio of Catholics to Protestants being eighty to one. These counties differed sharply from the more densely populated counties of Cork and Tipperary where the ratio was reduced to around twelve Catholics to every Protestant. Within these counties there was also significant local variation. Parts of Cork were selected for plantation in the sixteenth and seventeenth centuries, particularly around the south-west of the county. This meant that the number of Protestants in this area, especially in the Bandon river valley, was much higher than elsewhere.[5]

The main cities of the province also displayed variation in their religious composition. Wakefield calculated that the number of Catholics to Protestants in Limerick city and Waterford city was fifteen to one and ten to one respectively.[6] In Cork city, the provincial metropolis, it was calculated in 1834 that there were 77,500 Catholics, 15,500 members of the Church of Ireland, 384 Presbyterians, and 780 other dissenters.[7] Henry Inglis also noted the numerical superiority of Catholics in the region when he travelled around Ireland in 1834. He recorded that Catholics constituted 25,000 out of Waterford city's 30,000 population. In Clonmel there was a population of around 18,000, of which 15,000 were Catholic. The overwhelming number of Catholics in Munster made it likely that, as a region, it would be supportive of any campaign for further political rights for Catholics.

Though Ireland and Munster can be divided statistically into two broad religious camps, it has not been the intention in the proceeding paragraphs to suggest that each sect was homogenous in terms of class or political outlook. Catholic society in Munster was complex. It included one of the largest landowners in the whole country as well as a wealthy and ambitious urban middle class, and the great body of agricultural workers, both farmers (of various sizes) and labourers. This was a range of groups that in any society could be expected to have a varied political outlook.

Pre-famine Ireland was predominantly a rural society and in Munster the economy was driven by the dairy and provisions trade. The province enjoyed a period of sustained economic success during the Napoleonic wars when the area provided food for Britain, the British army, and such distant parts of the empire as the West Indies. The port of Cork city, supplied mainly from the rich plains of the 'golden vale' that covered areas of Cork, Tipperary and east Limerick, was the source of much of this trade, though Limerick and Waterford were also beneficiaries of the demand for butter and salted meats. The business of buying and exporting these agricultural goods from the ports of the province was dominated by a wealthy Catholic merchant class. This was a group that expanded and developed in the eighteenth century when other professions were barred to Catholics under the penal legislation. Many Catholic landowners had moved into commerce, including the Wyse family in Waterford. The Roches and Arthurs were among the wealthiest merchants in Limerick city.[8] The Callaghan family were amongst the largest butter exporters in Cork. Agriculture and its associated industries were the mainstay of the economy in the province and it has been estimated, in a modern study based on the 1841 census, that at least 60 per cent of the entire workforce in each county was engaged in agriculture. An estimate of the numbers of agricultural workers in each county in Munster is set out in the table below.

Table 1 *Numbers engaged in agriculture in Munster c. 1841*[9]

County	Agricultural Sector (% total workforce)	% Farmers (of Agricultural sector)	% Labourers (of Agricultural sector)
Clare	63.45	17.24 (20,767)	44.62 (53,762)
Cork	63.25	13.28 (40,309)	47.83 (145,173)
Kerry	62.53	16.75 (19,674)	43.50 (51,091)
Limerick	61.07	13.11 (15,056)	46.49 (53,396)
Tipperary	63.67	15.92 (27,344)	46.07 (79,115)
Waterford	67.81	9.78 (7,423)	55.44 (42,061)

These figures also show that the vast majority of those working in agriculture were classed as labourers, that is, those who worked the land and who held very small plots of one to five acres.

The numbers in this class grew dramatically in the years before the famine, subsisting on the amount of potatoes they managed to grow on their small plots. It was this class, with its over-reliance on the potato, that was devastated by the famine. The other major group highlighted here are the farmers. This term obscures the wide variations in the size of land that a 'farmer' could hold. James Donnelly, and subsequently Theo Hoppen, have differentiated between the various size of farmers, ranging from those whose holdings and wealth made them appear to be minor landowners to small farmers who held not much more land than labourers. Some indication of these variations, calculated from the 1841 census for the whole of the country, is shown in the table below.

Table 2 *Adult males and Rural Social Structure, c. 1841*[10]

	No.	Per cent
Rich Farmers (mean holdings 80 acres)	50,000	2.9
'Snug' Farmers (mean holdings 50 acres)	100,000	5.9
Family Farmers (mean holdings 20 acres and rarely employing outside labour)	250,000	14.7
Cottiers (mean holdings 5 acres)	300,000	17.7
Labourers (mean holdings 1 acre, though often without any land)	1,000,000	58.8

In Munster a general profile emerges of the larger portion of the population who were Catholic in religion and who worked predominantly in agriculture. Some could be very wealthy farmers and, in addition to these, a significant number of the old aristocratic Catholic families managed to retain their lands in the province. The most obvious example is the Kenmare family, which owned vast tracts of land (albeit mainly mountainous) in counties Kerry and Cork. This made the Kenmares an important political force in the county after 1793 when the franchise was extended to Catholic 40s freeholders in county elections. Yet the majority of the population in a Catholic province like Munster were likely to be labourers with a small patch of land to work on, as Table 2 would suggest. Therefore, Catholic society in the province was a complex mix of classes and groups and it was this balance that the Catholic Association successfully held together in the 1820s in the campaign for Catholic relief.

Munster was the arena for some of the most critical episodes of that campaign. In terms of the system of collecting the Catholic Rent, Munster was the most organised. Catholic Rent was collected by the Catholic Association to fund its campaign. The amount of money collected by March 1825 showed just how important the Munster counties were to the Catholic organisation overall. Of the four Irish provinces, Munster collected the largest amount of Rent:

Table 3 *Amount of Catholic Rent collected in each Irish Province 1824-March 1825*[11]

Province	Rent collected (nearest £)
Munster	£3,364
Leinster	£3,254
Connacht	£509
Ulster	£446

Similarly, the Association's most successful electoral contests were also in the province. The dramatic Waterford contest during the 1826 general election showed that the Catholic Association had the power to break the traditional deference of tenants to landlords. This was replicated even more spectacularly in Clare in 1828 when O'Connell was elected as MP for the county. The Clare result raised the spectre of numerous Catholic MPs being returned throughout Ireland and it was this that precipitated the final decision by Wellington's government to provide an answer to the Catholic question once and for all.

The excitement and tensions associated with the final months of the campaign for Catholic relief quickly passed away once the Act went through parliament. As it became obvious that the Catholic question would be dealt with by the government, there was a definite shift from concentrating on the national question towards more local ones. Former Catholic Association activists turned their attention to gaining access to local government and to local representation, now that national representation was secured. Specifically this meant reconstructing what many saw as the last bastions of 'Protestant ascendancy', the municipal corporations. Reform of these institutions would allow greater access to Catholics and liberal Protestants who were barred on religious and political grounds. Most of the corporations in Munster were seen as sectarian, self-perpetuating oligarchies (and a subsequent Royal Commission supported this view). Catholics also sought greater access to grand juries and other local government offices. Agitation commenced before 1829 continued as well, notably the petitioning campaign against the Vestry Act.

The movements for *local* Catholic relief or 'emancipation' began even before the passage of the Relief Act in parliament. Tralee corporation was dominated by the Denny family, which determined who was returned as MP for the borough. As a consequence of this, the corporation was criticised for its narrowness, for neglecting the business interests of the town, and for its exclusive, Protestant character. Catholic and liberal Protestant businessmen formed a chamber of commerce to bypass the corporation, and this group was closely connected to Daniel O'Connell and would form the backbone of his electoral organisation in the county in the 1830s. By 1829 these interests had organised themselves to tackle the corporation and extend the business of the town. To air their views they assisted in the establishment of the *Tralee Mercury*. It set out its agenda in its first edition:

> The gross abuses of the Corporation of Tralee should not have been suffered to sink into oblivion; nor the illegal exactions of its underlings allowed to pass with impunity. The trade and commerce of this town should not have been neglected. To give Kerry a journal to suit the exigencies of the times; adequate to the feelings which animate the country, and, as we trust, competent to the advocacy of its best and most vital interests. Independent in every sense of the word, undaunted, unpurchasable and unpurchased – this is the object for which the *Tralee Mercury* has been established.[12]

With Catholic relief secured, the campaign for municipal reform intensified. In the summer of 1829 boroughs with an 'exclusive' character were criticised across Munster. The majority were dominated by a small number of Anglo-Irish families that influenced the voting patterns of the often tiny electorates of the town or city. Cork city's corporation was arguably one of the most exclusive in the province, if not the country. It was an entirely self-perpetuating corporation, dominated by the tightly controlled 'Friendly Club' composed of around 350 freemen.[13] Cities like Cork and Limerick also had large numbers of non-resident freemen, entitled to vote at parliamentary elections and ready to do the bidding of the dominant Protestant cliques. Others corporations in the province were usually under the control of one and sometimes two families. Half of the twelve municipal corporations that were parliamentary boroughs in Munster were closely controlled by the controlling family interest. In three of these constituencies, Bandon, Ennis and Tralee, the right to vote was held by the provost and the burgesses (13 in number) of the corporation. In the other three boroughs (Cashel, Clonmel and Kinsale) closely controlled by an Anglo-Irish family, the franchise was held by the officers of the corporation along with the burgesses and freemen, many of whom were non-resident.[14]

The inhabitants of Tralee met to discuss the issue in 1829 and petitioned parliament for municipal reform, as did the 'inhabitant householders' of Cork city. The inhabitant householders were men of property and a certain degree of wealth. In their petition they asked for the rights and franchise of the city to be extended to them, and, echoing the Catholic Relief Act, submitted themselves to whatever rent or tax qualifications parliament deemed necessary.[15] As in Tralee, the movement for municipal reform in Cork was led by Catholic and liberal Protestant members of the Chamber of Commerce in the city. Again, this body was formed by those merchants and businessmen who were excluded and ignored by the corporation. They developed a concerted campaign in Cork against what they called 'corporate monopoly', and were clear about what they wanted to achieve. Charles Sugrue, a member of the city's liberal Chamber of Commerce, was selected as chairman for an anti-corporation meeting in the autumn of 1829. Sugrue declared that they were gathering 'to achieve another emancipation.' The reasons for meeting were mixed. Some argued that it was a taxation and representation issue, and that wealthy men who contributed so much money and industry to the city should not be barred from office. Many were also angry that they were excluded on religious grounds. Wealthy Catholics felt aggrieved about being overlooked whilst 'every tailor or shaver to an orangeman is thought worthy of being a freeman.'[16]

Elsewhere in the province there were signs that some of the corporations were willing to change and reform themselves, albeit slowly. Responding to the promotion of greater religious toleration by the Catholic Relief Act, the corporation of Youghal, in county Cork, decided to admit Catholics to the privileges of freemen. The corporation of Youghal was controlled by the Duke of Devonshire, the Whig magnate whose estates spread throughout Waterford, Cork and various parts of England. The rumour that the corporation would make a move on the admission of Catholics caused a stir in Youghal and its hinterland. This meant that on the day of the meeting, 3 August 1829, the Court of D'Oyer Hundred at the assembly rooms in the town was attended by a very large number of people. The Court withdrew to hold a private meeting but it made little difference. The result was that at the close of the meeting the by-laws against the admission of Catholics to the freedom of Youghal were repealed, and on that day four Catholics were admitted as freemen. In the context of the entire province this was a small number. Indeed, with some exceptions, very few Catholics were admitted as freemen here or elsewhere before municipal reform. Waterford city, dominated by the Whig Newport family, already had a sizeable Catholic freeman class before 1829. After the Relief Act was passed Thomas Wyse, one of the local leaders of the Catholic Association, was unanimously elected and admitted as a freeman of the city.[17] Wyse would over the next decade come to dominate corporate affairs in the city. These may have been token gestures, yet symbolically it was a sign that things were beginning to change in the province and elsewhere in the country. Catholics were granted local power and privilege in line with the changed political context in the aftermath of the Relief Act.

This initial campaign for municipal reform was, however, short-lived. Like most other political issues, the Catholics' demand for local government reform was sidelined by the campaign of 1830 against the Wellington ministry's tax proposals that suggested the assimilation of British and Irish taxation levels. This issue brought conflicting parties together and revealed the lack of deep sectarian or party division even after almost 10 years of tense campaigning for Catholic Relief. Every major interest group in Ireland rallied and resisted the imposition of the new taxes: Catholic, Protestant, businessmen, landowners, distillers, printers and manufacturers. The issue of the taxes played a prominent role in the election of 1830 in Ireland and few dared openly to support chancellor of the exchequer Henry Goulburn's proposals, which were only partially outlined in the budget.

The government did not continue to pursue the tax issue when parliament resumed in the autumn of 1830 and new issues emerged. In Ireland O'Connell was hinting at a full campaign against the Act of Union. In the United Kingdom as a whole the issue of parliamentary reform was gaining momentum at such a pace that it would shortly topple Wellington. In the wider world France had experienced another revolution and Belgium had revolted against Dutch control. It was a period of change and of optimism in Munster that political systems could be reformed. Consequently the demand for municipal reform re-emerged in Munster. In Cork city a meeting was held at the Chamber of Commerce to consider the most effectual way of proceeding on the issue 'in order that the objects and intentions of the late Relief Bill should not be counteracted by the intolerant monopolising spirit of the corporation.' Organisational machinery for fighting the issue was set up. A subscription fund for 'promoting corporate reform' was opened at the end of the meeting.[18]

Similar meetings took place at this time in Clare and Limerick, where there were calls to 'open' the boroughs of Ennis and Limerick city. In both places, a 'committee of independence' was established to fight the issue. Reformers were determined to see the 'death' of the old order, and in a macabre manner some men of Ennis formed a procession after the election of May 1831, with a mock coffin, representing the funeral of the borough.[19] Ennis was an unusual borough in Munster in the sense that it was controlled by two families, the O'Briens and the Fitzgeralds, who alternatively nominated the member to be returned.[20] Limerick city municipal corporation was dominated by the Vereker family, which also had electoral interests in the county. Like Cork and Tralee, the Chamber of Commerce of Limerick represented the economic and political ambitions of those excluded from local government. They had been instrumental in getting the first 'independent' MP returned for the city in 1820, Thomas Spring Rice. They also backed the two wealthy Roche cousins in the city election of 1832 after the city gained an extra seat from the 1832 Irish Reform Act. The Roches were a family with large banking and commercial interests in Cork and Limerick cities. After 1832 they worked closely with the Limerick Chamber of Commerce to highlight abuses by the corporation to parliament and, after 1833, to the Royal Commission of inquiry into municipal corporations.[21]

Nevertheless, municipal reform was not immediate. Introduced into parliament in 1835, the Whig government's plans to reform Irish municipal corporations were successively defeated in the House of Lords. The 1832 Irish Parliamentary Reform Act was, however, effectively the first step in municipal reform. Overall parliamentary reform in Ireland was not as extensive as it was in England, and the creation of new leaseholder and copyholder franchises had little effect on the political situation in the counties, but the measure would, as Angus Macintyre has stated, give boroughs 'the reform they had hitherto escaped'.[22] Munster had two extra seats after parliamentary reform in 1832. These were additional seats for Limerick and Waterford cities. Each county continued to have two seats each (12) and there were 9 single-seat boroughs. The creation of the £10 householders franchise and the exclusion of non-resident freemen outside the specified perimeter of the boroughs shifted the balance of power in the towns and cities towards the pro-reform side. The non-resident freemen were normally the foot soldiers of the corporation at elections and they were brought in to vote far from the constituency itself. These changes are set out in the table below.

Table 4 *Number of Freemen in Munster Boroughs in 1830 and 1835
Number of £10 Householders registered by 1835*[23]

Borough	No. of Freemen (1830)	No. of Freemen (1835)	No. of £10 Householders (1835)
Cork	c. 1541 (1826)	1244	2263
Limerick	372	285	1574
Waterford	1240	603	767
Clonmel	105	84	601
Kinsale	64	42	222

The table shows that there was a reduction in the number of freemen entitled to vote in these boroughs, indicating the impact that the Irish Parliamentary Reform Act had on the non-resident freemen. This reduction is even more striking when it is compared with the number of new £10 householder voters who were registered between 1832 and 1835. It was this class that had clamoured for the franchise in Cork and elsewhere in the years after 1829. These changes would be fully exploited by O'Connell at the general election of 1832.

The findings of the Royal Commission on Irish municipal corporations upheld the accusations levelled by local reformers: the corporations were sectarian and self-perpetuating oligarchies.[24] The Commission recommended wide changes including a £10 householder franchise similar to the borough franchise. In Munster this recommendation had the potential to create a significant number of Catholic voters in the boroughs, replicating what had occurred after the Parliamentary Reform Act. From 1835 Melbourne's government repeatedly proposed legislation but progress was always blocked in the Lords. The measure was finally secured in 1841. It provided for the household franchise but restricted the number of constituencies in which it was used, since the vast majority of Irish municipal corporations were abolished. Only the corporations of the major towns and cities survived. All other towns had town commissions to look after their affairs.[25] Yet in places in Munster like Cork, Limerick, Waterford and Clonmel, prominent Catholic and excluded Protestant householders gained local power for the first time since 1829. Local 'emancipation' was complete.

The local campaigns for municipal reform in Munster and Ireland had been given direction and focus by Daniel O'Connell.[26] To most people in Munster O'Connell was the hero of the campaign for Catholic relief, especially in the west in his home county of Kerry, and in Clare, the adopted county with which he will eternally be associated. The delight and pride people in Munster had in O'Connell was exhibited everywhere he went. On his journeys through the province to his home at Derrynane or back towards Dublin and, after 1830, Westminster, he was greeted by huge numbers of people. Immediately after the success of the Relief Act, O'Connell's popularity manifested itself in the response to the national testimony to him. In his home county his friends organised a central committee for collecting funds as a sign of their gratitude for his role in the successful campaign for the Catholic Relief Act. This was based in Tralee and it applied to every parish priest in the county, showing that many of the techniques learnt from the previous years of campaigning (using clergymen, for instance) carried on. Similar committees were set up in Mallow and Youghal at this early stage.[27] This was replicated all over the province and formed the precedent for the annual O'Connell Tribute.[28]

During 1830 O'Connell plotted his campaign for the repeal of the Act of Union, and during the general election of that year, following the death of George IV, he became member for county Waterford. The news of the French Revolution and then the Belgian revolt against Dutch rule in the autumn of 1830 acted as the final catalyst, and O'Connell called for the union to be 'agitated in every possible shape'. Munster became the testing ground. O'Connell left his home at Derrynane to attend a public dinner at Killarney that, incidentally, he described as 'the best public dinner' he had ever attended. The next two days saw him at Tralee were he attended another dinner and a meeting in honour of the French and Belgian revolutions. Over the following week O'Connell would attend meetings at Kanturk, Cork, Youghal, and finally Waterford before making his way to London.[29] As he began his campaign, O'Connell unleashed the frustrations and disappointments of certain sections and classes in Munster against the Union. Yet this was no indication at this stage of nationalistic fervour. Rather, the argument against the Union in Munster during the first campaign was purely economic. Repeal was received enthusiastically in Munster because its economic experience was almost the opposite of that of Ulster. With a few exceptions, like the village of Portlaw, Munster's manufacturing base was in terminal decline. Many perceived the Union to be the cause of this decline, as memory dictated that life was better before 1800 or even before 1815 when the war in Europe had stimulated the economy of the region as demand for its goods and food grew.

During late 1830 and early 1831, there were dozens of meetings held across Munster to petition parliament for repeal. The police and stipendiary magistrates' reports from these meetings are all very similar. The repeal meetings quickly took on a distinctive form and were attended mainly by shopkeepers and tradesmen. Virtually all the reports stress the lack of 'gentlemen' present. The meeting at Dungarvan in November 1830 was led by a shopkeeper from the town. At Carrickbeg the chairman was a local farmer, the principal speaker a spirit shopkeeper from Carrick-on-Suir and the audience made up of 'inferior' shopkeepers, mechanics and 'the mob.'[30] At Clonmel a similar meeting took place and once again it was recorded that 'the more respectable classes of society keep aloof from such proceedings.'[31]

These meetings took place all over the province. In the largest cities, Cork and Limerick, the meetings took a slightly different form. They were primarily trades meetings, held by those who felt that they had suffered economically since the Union. Interestingly, it was not just tradesmen who organised to protest against the Union, but tradeswomen also. In one case there was a meeting at Shinkwins Theatre of over two hundred men and women employed in the glove trade in the city of Cork. There were around thirty men present; the rest were women. Both men and women spoke at the meeting. A Mrs Carroll pointed out that 'before the parliament [in Dublin] went away' there were over three thousand females employed in the glove trade in the city, all with full employment and all well paid. Now, since the Union, there were no more than five to six hundred employed and these women could not rely on regular employment.[32] Elsewhere, the tradesmen of Killarney also traced their 'wants and privations' to the legislative union and called for repeal.[33] Extensive as these meetings were, the inspector general of the constabulary in Munster was fearful that the full potential of the campaign had not yet been realised. If an example was set elsewhere in the country of 'obedience to his [O'Connell's] mandates', it could not 'fail to be contagious particularly if the Catholic clergy were to stop being neutral on the issue of repeal'. If this was to happen, wrote Miller, the whole of the population of Munster could be as agitated as they were in other parts of the country, a reference to the tithe disturbances in southern Leinster.[34] Yet the situation in Munster remained calm and O'Connell was able to display 'obedience to his mandates' when he postponed the repeal campaign and switched his attention to parliamentary reform in 1831.

By 1831 agitation was occurring all over Ireland on a number of fronts. Repeal was underway, parliamentary reform was about to get underway, and most dangerous of all was the campaign for the abolition of tithes. The 'Tithe War' began in county Carlow in November 1830. Several reasons have been put forward by historians to explain why the 'war' took place. It was partly to do with the Tithe Composition Act of 1823, which linked tithes in many instances to cereal prices that no longer obtained. It was also partly to do with the 'agitatory vacuum' left after the struggle for Catholic Relief.[35] The sharp economic downturn from mid-1829 was also undoubtedly a factor. The 'war' itself was a campaign of widespread civil disobedience, with farmers, large and small, refusing to pay tithe and boycotting the enforced sale of cattle and other items in order to pay for tithe arrears. Large meetings to petition against tithe were organised in their hundreds. The 'hands on' approach of many established church clerics in pursuit of arrears gave the dispute a sectarian edge. As well as this, the sometimes excessive magisterial use of the police, army and the hated (in Munster at least) yeomanry resulted in bloodshed, as at Newtownbarry in county Wexford where fourteen civilians were shot dead by the yeomanry. This led to a perception of the police and the other forces as being sectarian in nature and as the dispute continued there were further violent clashes. In Carrickshock in county Kilkenny a tithe process server and twelve policemen were stoned and beaten to death by protesters.

With widespread disturbances in Carlow and Kilkenny in south Leinster, it was not long before this disorder moved into Munster. There was always an undercurrent of opposition to tithes in most parts of the province, particularly during the campaign for Catholic relief. County Cork was described to a House of Commons select committee as never being 'quite tranquil on the subject of tithes.'[36] However, organised opposition to tithes in the province did not begin until the summer of 1831, when it moved from the Leinster counties into Tipperary.

The agitation against tithes spread further into the province during 1831 and 1832. By the summer of 1832 the south of Ireland and the midland counties were in 'a perfect state of combination and of the greatest excitement' upon the subject of tithes, despite the economic and agricultural improvements that were taking place and even though rents had never been 'better paid.'[37] The worst of the violence was over by this stage. O'Connell took a firmly constitutional approach and remained aloof from the violent campaign in Ireland whilst he pushed for a general reform of the Church of Ireland in parliament, including a change in the method of paying tithes. He also participated in some of the tithe trials in Cork in the autumn of 1832, showing that he remained the counsellor and defender of the rural poor.[38]

O'Connell was able to demonstrate his knowledge of Munster politics and organisational ability because this was his home area and the main legal circuit on which he had worked. He was also boosted by the wide range of contacts he had across the province. In Kerry his brothers, John and James, served as contacts and organisers. After 1830 he was also backed by the financial and organisational muscle of the Tralee Chamber of Commerce.[39] In Cork he had his relation, Thomas Lyons, to inform him of events there. The Chamber of Commerce in Cork, of which Lyons was a member, also backed O'Connell. Thomas Steele was familiar with his native mid-west area of Limerick and Clare. O'Connell benefited in Tipperary from his friendship and family connection with Charles Bianconi. Bianconi was based in Clonmel and ran the coach system that connected Munster together and linked the province with Dublin. This was a very useful ally for O'Connell to have for rapid movement and mobilisation. O'Connell's main ally in Waterford was the well-informed priest, Rev. John Sheehan, who furnished detailed accounts of local events and acted as a liaison between O'Connell and the Catholic bishop of Waterford.[40] After the dissolution of the Catholic Association, O'Connell continued to use the provincial press to publicise his views, organise his campaigns, and even influence the outcome of elections. He normally advertised in papers that were, in contemporary terms, 'liberal' or 'independent', such as the *Tralee Mercury* in his native county Kerry. The *Tralee Mercury* was paid £11.4s in December 1829 by the former secretary of the dissolved Catholic Association for carrying advertisements and notices, including adverts connected with the opening of the borough of Tralee.[41] For newspapers that operated without government money, continuous advertisements by O'Connell meant a regular source of income and may help explain why they backed him so vociferously.

The result of this organisation and effort was good election results for O'Connell, particularly in the 1832 general election when thirty-nine 'repealers' of various shades of commitment were returned. The majority were elected in constituencies in Munster and Leinster. O'Connell himself had expected Munster to be one of the main strongholds for repeal even before the election.[42] After 1829, he was a serious electoral force and his opinion could determine the outcome of an election in Munster and elsewhere. This was recognised by government and by English MPs. E. J. Littleton felt that when Lord Anglesey returned to Ireland in 1830, his popularity depended on O'Connell's 'will'.[43] As has been shown, O'Connell had the ability to turn the campaign for repeal on or off. The changes were always well received by his supporters in Munster and a deferential attitude was apparent. For example, when O'Connell faced opposition from Feargus O'Connor over the timing of a repeal motion in parliament, a meeting was held in Waterford. The meeting resolved to support O'Connell's decision to postpone repeal and to 'trust in O'Connell's wisdom.'[44]

By such means O'Connell established himself as a major force in elections and politics in Munster in the years following Catholic Relief. The campaign for repeal was well received in Munster, where many blamed an economic downturn on the Act of Union. Yet the agitation was not welcomed by everyone in the province. Among the doubters were some of O'Connell's former Catholic Association allies.

Thomas Wyse was the architect of the 1826 general election success of Henry Villiers Stuart in county Waterford, and a pioneer of some of the Catholic Association's most innovative techniques, such as the liberal clubs. After the success of the campaign he had ambitions to become the first Catholic MP for his native county, Waterford. He quickly realised, however, that this was no easy or straightforward aim, for his broader views clashed with those of O'Connell. In 1830 O'Connell was invited to stand in Waterford after giving up his seat in Clare. Wyse also offered himself as a candidate, but in order to maximise the anti-Beresford vote he stood aside for the more popular O'Connell. Wyse was elected in 1830, but in the neighbouring county of Tipperary, where he had property and family connections. In the autumn of 1830 Wyse endeavoured to consolidate his position in that county by chairing a meeting at Thurles aimed at speeding up the registry of freeholds in Tipperary. A baronial committee was appointed to ensure that this took place.[45]

The embarrassment that Wyse no doubt felt at having to give up his candidacy in Waterford in 1830 may have influenced his future political behaviour in the region. From this point he maintained a single-minded approach that was fiercely independent of O'Connell. Not surprisingly, this led to him being involved in several disputes in Munster. Political conflicts over Wyse's opposition to repeal were the most common. Wyse was essentially a Catholic Whig. He believed in an extensive reform of the main institutions governing Ireland: parliament, local government and the church. He believed that the first step in achieving this would be parliamentary reform 'from whence all other reforms must finally and permanently flow'.[46]

Wyse made himself unpopular in county Tipperary when he called on O'Connell to introduce a motion in parliament to test its support. Wyse was warned by the Catholic bishop of Waterford, Dr. Abraham, that this caused dissatisfaction amongst his constituents because John Doherty, the solicitor-general, called on him to do the same.[47] Doherty had opposed Catholic relief and was seen as a sectarian influence in the Irish administration at Dublin Castle. He was removed when the Whigs came into government. Wyse was a unionist but, like many other Catholics, advocated widespread reform in order to give Catholics greater representation in parliament and in local government.[48]

Wyse attempted to push his reform agenda in Tipperary town as O'Connell's repeal campaign was gathering pace. Conflict inevitably arose. Wyse held a large outdoor 'great reform' meeting in January 1831 to petition parliament for a 'speedy redress of the grievances under which this county still labours'. The meeting favoured a reform of the grand jury laws, a reform of parliament, the extension of the elective franchise and vote by ballot. Thomas Ryan opposed the meeting on the grounds that it was part of a campaign of 'trickery' used by people 'opposed to Mr. O'Connell, for the express purpose of throwing a wet blanket on the question of the repeal of the union, and thereby supporting the shattered reputation of Mr. Wyse'. Ryan's accusation created a furore, and Wyse replied that the meeting did not throw a wet blanket on repeal as the county had already met on that issue, and sent a petition to parliament. This was a separate meeting and should be treated as such.[49] Opposition to Wyse grew, however, and it was feared by some of his allies that he could not win the next election without O'Connell's '*warm* interference'.[50]

Wyse survived the election of 1831, largely because of O'Connell's intervention when gathering support in Ireland for the Whigs' measure of parliamentary reform, but his pro-union views meant that he did not win a seat in the 'repeal' election of 1832 when he failed to take the repeal pledge. Wyse explained to the Waterford Political Union that he could not support repeal at this time because he was 'strongly opposed to everything which can risk the connection between the two countries, upon which, I am convinced, depend the prosperity and safety of each'. He was anxious, however, to secure for Ireland all the advantages of a domestic legislature.[51]

However unlikely it may have seemed, Wyse created an independent opposition to O'Connell in the eastern part of his Munster heartland. This is even more remarkable considering that Wyse had only returned from the continent in the mid-1820s. Yet in the space of a few years Wyse was able to build up a network of contacts in Waterford and Tipperary through his handling of the election of 1826 and his distribution of newspapers and organisation of the liberal clubs. He belonged to an old Catholic family that had moved into commerce in Waterford during the eighteenth century. Therefore his family had a certain pedigree in Catholic politics and was well known in the area. Having a degree of disposable wealth was also beneficial to Wyse's political ambitions. Wyse was advised that for him not to have any doubts about his return for Tipperary in 1831 he would need about £1500, a significant sum. Wyse also had a close network of supporters across the two counties. His brother George acted as one of his main agents and sources of information. Through the family business there were connections in Waterford city. Wyse also had connections in the main towns of Tipperary, including the boroughs of Cashel and Clonmel. In Clonmel he had the support of the editor of the *Tipperary Free Press*, and the town clerk Edward Labarte, who acted as a central agent for Wyse in Clonmel in the elections of 1830-1 and organised a tally room and a committee room as well as his reception.[52]

Wyse also secured the support of some of the most influential Catholic bishops and priests inside and outside the arch-diocese. Wyse had impressed many senior figures in the church with his advocacy of Catholic education. He was backed by Bishop Abraham in Waterford, the influential Bishop Doyle of Kildare and Leighlin, and several local priests in county Tipperary. The latter included Michael Slattery of Thurles, who was subsequently Archbishop of Cashel (from 1833).

Wyse found in 1832 that a network of support like this did not automatically translate into electoral success, especially when up against the popular influence of O'Connell. Over the next couple of years Wyse sought to strengthen his electoral strength in Waterford by making an approach to the Duke of Devonshire. This frightened the repealers of Dungarvan when a by-election took place there in early 1834.[53] Wyse did not stand at this election but he acquired a strong supporter in readiness for the next general election.

Wyse carried on the techniques used by the Catholic Association to move information around as rapidly as possible. This was done through handbills, addresses and printed copies of speeches. Wyse was able to transfer this information to the region with the network of support he had in place. Michael Slattery received and distributed newspapers and printed copies of Wyse's speeches while Wyse was MP for county Tipperary.[54] Similarly, Wyse's brother George, who did extensive electoral canvassing for him, also collected and distributed information and election material.[55] Therefore Thomas Wyse was able to spread and circulate his more moderate reforming political views in the eastern part of the province and beyond. He did so in a manner that was free from both 'Dan' and government. Considering the popular appeal of O'Connell in Munster at this time, it was a remarkable achievement.

The fluid nature of Catholic politics in Munster after Catholic relief changed in the autumn of 1834. Greater polarisation was enforced by expediency as a common enemy emerged when William IV dismissed Melbourne's Whig administration and replaced it with a Tory one led by Peel and Wellington. Melbourne was dismissed for a number of reasons, including the king's opposition to the plan to appropriate the surplus revenues of the Church of Ireland and apply them to secular purposes. Senior Whigs had become more favourable to O'Connell during 1834 after O'Connell's failed repeal motion and Earl Grey's retirement from the premiership. O'Connell was also pleased about the appointment of Lord Duncannon as home secretary and the prospect of several reforming measures. He was in Cork when he heard of Melbourne's dismissal and was horrified.[56] From November 1834 to January 1835 he worked tirelessly to ensure that in Munster and the other two southern provinces there would be little support for the new Tory government. From Cork he went directly to Dublin where he co-ordinated the campaign for the forthcoming election and created the Anti-Tory Association. He made contact with the outgoing Whig chief secretary at Dublin Castle, E. J. Littleton, and assured him that repeal was 'buried' for the present, *and all other questions on which his party might differ from us*. O'Connell also intended to get up a meeting of all parties to co-operate against the common enemy.[57] In Munster the *Tipperary Free Press* called on all classes of reformers to unite against the Tories. To strengthen its case it published a list of all the measures ('Whig claims to national confidence') that the Whig government had proposed for Ireland, including the amending of the Vestry and Subletting acts, changing the grand jury laws and parliamentary reform.[58] Most liberal papers described the events in London as 'The Great Crisis', and carried reports of meetings in every county and major town to address the king on the dismissal of the Whigs. A meeting in Limerick, for example, was addressed by the city's MPs, the Roche brothers, who helped to draw up a 'carefully worded' address to the king that acknowledged his prerogative but stated that the ministers he had chosen lacked the support of the people.[59]

Former members of the Catholic Association put divisions aside, and, in the short term at least, reform displaced the question of repeal. Catholic politicians in Munster had a greater chance of achieving further reform from a Whig government under Melbourne than from the Tories. Political machinery around the province was working at a rate that approached the levels of activity established by the Catholic Association. While meetings like that at Limerick were taking place all over the province and country, preparations for an election were getting underway. O'Connell drew up a circular for the constituencies, seeking to assess the prospects for repeal/liberal/Whig candidates.[60] The circular was probably designed to rally and motivate people as the election approached. It was a mechanism to maintain interest, like the census used by the Catholic Association. The usual team was sent out by O'Connell on the electioneering trail. Maurice O'Connell covered a lot of ground in Kerry, where the threat from the Tories was strong.[61] The Kerry election was particularly important to O'Connell. Originally Lord Kenmare had assured the Whigs that no Tories would be returned in the county. He was appalled, however, by the displays of violence and intimidation at the election, and told his agent Christopher Gallwey to instruct his friends and tenants to vote Tory.[62] This was the outstanding anomaly in this election. Kenmare was a major Catholic landowner, a Whig supporter and an electoral force in the county. He was the most senior Catholic official in the country after the Whigs made him lord lieutenant of Kerry in 1831. Now, shocked by the Whig alliance with O'Connell, he actively worked against them.

Thomas Wyse, though he opposed the change of ministers in London, was wary of openly embracing the Anti-Tory Association. He did not wish to appear to be under the control of O'Connell once again. But the Bishop of Waterford, Dr. Abraham, urged him to get to Waterford immediately. Conservatives, Abraham wrote, were 'inventing and executing every scheme to damp the popular enthusiasm.' Abraham reassured him that he was not perceived to be the pawn of O'Connell: 'The public impression is that you are the nominee of no man, but the ... people's choice'.[63] O'Connell had already decided in conjunction with John Sheehan that Wyse would be one of the anti-Tory candidates in Waterford city. In the end the Beresford interest in the city was easily defeated by the anti-Tory front backed by the Bishop, who had instructed all his priests 'to do their duty against the Beresfords'.[64] The election in Munster returned members that were almost unanimously opposed to the Peel government. Out of the twenty-seven county and borough seats available in the province, all but three were won by anti-Tory candidates. Conservatives were only successful in the boroughs of Bandon and Kinsale and, after petition, one of the county Cork seats.[65] Munster, overwhelmingly supportive of the coalition created by O'Connell, had signalled its appetite for further reform under the Whigs.

The years following the passage of the Catholic Relief Act revealed the extent to which the Catholic Association had been a coalition, representing a broad range of opinion, that put aside all other differences to campaign for one single goal. After the issue was removed the coalition unravelled. Ambitious and wealthy Catholics embarked in a number of diverse localities on a campaign to gain some wider and tangible benefits from the Catholic Relief Act. This was done mainly by targeting for reform the last stronghold of the 'Protestant ascendancy' in Ireland, the municipal corporations. Though this would not come for another twelve years, there were some changes that weakened the power of the corporations, notably some of the provisions of the Irish Parliamentary Reform Act. The conduct of former leaders and members of the Catholic Association based in Munster showed how divided the organisation was in terms of political outlook and tactics. O'Connell, continuing the practices of the Association, used a variety of modern political techniques to build support for repeal, a subject that was popular amongst the workers in the collapsing industries of Munster. O'Connell's popularity and influence after 1829 was huge in Munster. Yet he did not have it all his own way. Many former allies in the province, though they advocated widespread reform to make the political system more equitable for Catholics and liberal Protestants, were unionists, most notably Thomas Wyse. By creating a network of political alliances amongst senior church figures, newspaper editors and influential landlords like the Duke of Devonshire, Wyse was able to exercise a remarkable degree of independence from 'Dan' in the eastern part of the province. In Kerry, at the other end of the province, Lord Kenmare, who acted as a senior patron of the Catholic Association, became a force for moderation against O'Connell. The Whig government made him chief magistrate in the county and he used his vast electoral clout against O'Connell, whom he personally abhorred. In turn, O'Connell feared his influence particularly when Kenmare backed the Tory Knight of Kerry.

It was not until William IV removed Melbourne's administration that common ground was reached once again. With his usual energy and determination, O'Connell worked to ensure that a variety of Whigs, liberals (including Wyse) and repealers were elected in 1834-5. There was a return to single issue politics. Repeal was abandoned for the next five years and a broad anti-Tory front was created, a front that was to be replicated in parliament. The Whig government that was backed by O'Connell from 1835 to 1841 openly spread patronage among Catholics and liberals in this period. For the first time many achieved positions that they had aspired to, particularly in local government. Munster may have had divisions amongst the former allies of the Catholic Association, but this was forgotten as it produced a set of representatives that was almost unanimously anti-Tory in 1834-5.

This indicates a striking fluidity in Munster politics, especially after 1829. On the basis of this study of the development of Catholic politics after 1829, it seems incorrect or premature to argue that the campaign for Catholic Relief in the 1820s created a single unified Catholic democracy or nation. If anything, it reveals how far the Catholic Association was an innovative single issue pressure group. The polarisation of the 1820s along political and sectarian lines had no real short-term impact amongst politically ambitious Catholics. The Association fragmented and local movements for local 'emancipation' emerged, arguing for a reform package to reflect the new situation in Ireland after 1829. On a wider level, there was little support among politically ambitious Catholics like Wyse and his allies for a separate Irish parliament as espoused by O'Connell. This resulted in electoral contests amongst former allies.

Significantly, doubts have arisen as to whether O'Connell was truly committed to repeal of the Union. Repeal has been seen as the highest possible bidding position designed to extract reforms from the government.[66] Certainly, O'Connell's ability to divert support in Munster to repeal, parliamentary reform, repeal again, and then anti-Toryism would support this view. The disputes between O'Connell and Wyse in Munster concerned tactics as well as personality. Reforms for Ireland was the shared goal; how to achieve it was a different matter.

Overall, the years following the passing of the Catholic Relief Act were marked by political fragmentation and confusion. It was not until a common enemy or issue emerged in 1834 that some degree of stability returned and a broad pro-reform front emerged in Munster.

References

*This essay is based on part of my doctoral dissertation, 'Munster Politics, 1825-1835' (Queen's University, Belfast). I would like to thank Professor Peter Jupp for his comments and suggestions.

1. O. MacDonagh, 'Ireland and the Union, 1801-70', in *Ireland Under The Union, 1801-70*, ed. W. E. Vaughan (Oxford, 1989), pp. l-li.

2. F. O'Ferrall, *Catholic Emancipation: Daniel O'Connell and the Birth of Irish Democracy, 1820-30* (Dublin, 1985), p. 273.

3. Robert Cassidy to Thomas Wyse, 4 June 1829, N[ational] L[ibrary of] I[reland], Wyse Papers, MS. 15,023.

4. M. Lenihan, *Limerick: Its History and Antiquities* (Cork, 1967 edition), p. 465.

5. I. d'Alton, *Protestant Society and Politics in Cork, 1812-44* (Cork, 1980), pp. 8-9.

6. E. Wakefield, *An Account of Ireland, Statistical and Political* (2 vols, London, 1812), ii, 623, 630-1.

7. J. B. O'Brien, *The Catholic Middle Classes in Pre-Famine Cork* (Dublin, 1979) p. 4.

8. M. Wall, 'The Rise of a Catholic Middle Class in Eighteenth-Century Ireland', in *Catholic Ireland in the Eighteenth Century: Collected Essays of Maureen Wall*, ed. G. O'Brien (Dublin, 1989), p.79.

9. These figures are taken from alphabetical entries in L. A. Clarkson, E. M. Crawford and M. A. Litirack, *Occupations of Ireland, 1841 (Munster)* (Belfast, 1995).

10. J. S. Donnelly, Jr., 'The Social Composition of Agrarian Rebellions in Early Nineteenth-Century Ireland: The Case of the Carders and Caravats, 1813-16' in *Radicals, Rebels and Establishments (Historical Studies, xv)*, ed. P. J. Corish (Belfast, 1985), p. 152; K. T. Hoppen, *Ireland Since 1800: Conflict and Conformity* (London, 1999), p. 41.

11. O'Ferrall, *Catholic Emancipation*, p. 65.

12. *Tralee Mercury*, 14 Feb. 1829.

13. d'Alton, *Protestant Society*, pp. 90-101.

14. The numbers of electors in each of these boroughs were: Cashel (26), Clonmel (105), Kinsale (64). These boroughs were controlled by the Pennefather, Bagwell and de Clifford families respectively. *Returns of the Number of Persons entitled to vote at the Election of Members for Cities and Boroughs in Ireland*, H. C. 1830 (522), xxxi, 321.

15. *Commons Journal*, lxxxiv, 404-5, 475.

16. *Southern Reporter*, 5 Sept. 1829.

17. Entry for 24 June 1829, NLI, Waterford Corporation Minute Books, p. 5560.

18. *Southern Reporter*, 2 Oct. 1830.

19. Phillips to E. G. Stanley, 21 May 1831, P[ublic] R[ecord] O[ffice], HO 122/15/144.

20. P. Jupp, 'Ennis', in *The House of Commons, 1790-1820*, ed. R. G. Thorne (5 vols, London, 1986), ii, 634.

21. William and David Roche to President and Members of the Limerick Chamber of Commerce, 15 Feb. 1833, Limerick Regional Archives, Limerick Chamber of Commerce letter books, P1.30.

22. A. D. Macintyre, *The Liberator: Daniel O'Connell and the Irish Party, 1830-47* (London, 1965), p. 30.

23. These figures are taken from *Number of Electors who polled at the contested Elections in Ireland, since 1805*, H. C. 1829 (208), xxii, 1; *Number of persons entitled to Vote at the Elections of Members for Cities and Boroughs in Ireland*, H. C. 1830 (522), xxxi, 321; *A Return of the Total Number of Parliamentary Electors appearing, by the Lists or Books of the Clerks of the Peace, registered for each County, City, Town and Borough in Ireland*, H. C. 1841 (240-1), xx, 615.

24. Macintyre, *The Liberator*, pp. 232-5.

25. Town commissions were set up (9 Geo. IV, c. 82) to light, clean and pave towns. They were elected by householders with property worth £20 or more every three years. By 1843, 14 towns across Munster had adopted the provisions of the Act. *Return of the Names of those Towns in Ireland, in which the Act of 9 Geo. 4 has been brought into Operation, wholly or in part; with the Names of the Commissioners, &c.*, H. C. 1843 (632), i, 373.

26. P. Jupp, 'Urban Politics in Ireland, 1801-31' in *The Town in Ireland*, ed. D. W. Harkness and M. O'Dowd (Belfast, 1981), pp. 119-20.

27. *Southern Reporter*, 30 April 1829.

28. O. MacDonagh, *O'Connell: The Life of Daniel O'Connell, 1775-1847* (London, 1991), pp. 296-8.

29. Daniel O'Connell to Michael Staunton, 11 Oct. 1830, in *The Correspondence of Daniel O'Connell*, ed. M. R. O'Connell (8 vols, Dublin, 1977), iv, 1716.

30. Major Miller to William Gregory, 10 Nov. 1830, N[ational] A[rchives of] I[reland], C.S.O.R.P., 1830 O.R./1808/M.138.

31. Major Miller to William Gregory, 2 Dec. 1830, NAI, C.S.O.R.P., 1830 O.R./1808/M.154.

32. *Freeman's Journal*, 10 Dec. 1830.

33. Ibid., 1 Jan. 1831.

34. Major Miller to Lt. Col. William Gossett, 2 Jan. 1831, NAI, C.S.O.R.P., 1831 O.R./1839/M.25).

35. O. MacDonagh, 'Economy and Society, 1830-45,' in Vaughan, *Ireland Under the Union*, pp. 222-3.

36. Evidence of Richard De La Cour, *Report of Select Committee into Tithes*, H. C. 1831-2 (177), xxi, 1.

37. Sir William Gosset to Lord Melbourne, 16 June 1832, PRO, HO 100/241/424-8.

38. Mathew Barrington to Sir William Gosset, 29 Oct. 1832, PRO, HO 100/242/203.

39. Daniel O'Connell to P. V. Fitzpatrick, 15 May 1831, O'Connell, *Correspondence*, iv, 1810.

40. These names have been taken from O'Connell's correspondence. They represent the principal correspondents O'Connell had in these specific areas at this time.

41. Miscellaneous receipts and accounts, NLI, O'Connell Papers, MS. 5241, pp. 13, 103; Receipts section, Dublin Diocesan Archives, D.D.A./C.P./55/2/II.

42. Daniel O'Connell to P. V. Fitzpatrick, 22 Sept. 1832, in O'Connell, *Correspondence*, iv, 1921.

43. E. J. Littleton to Richard Wellesley, 19 Nov. 1830 (Private Possession, Aspinall Transcripts, 1830). I am indebted to Peter Jupp for access to these transcripts.

44. *Pilot*, 10 July 1833.

45. *Tipperary Free Press*, 22 Sept. 1830.

46. *Freemans Journal*, 3 Feb. 1831.

47. Dr. Abraham to Thomas Wyse, 27 Nov. 1830, NLI, Wyse Papers, MS. 15,024 (1).

48. Wyse requires a modern scholarly examination. The main biography remains J. J. Auchmuty, *Sir Thomas Wyse, 1791-1862* (London, 1939).

49. *Tipperary Free Press*, 29 Jan. 1831.

50. James Scully to Thomas Wyse, 2 May 1831, NLI, Wyse Papers, MS. 15,024 (6).

51. Thomas Wyse to the Waterford Political Union, NLI, Wyse Papers, MS. 15,025 (1).

52. Edward Labarte to Thomas Wyse, 'Sunday' (n.d.), c. May 1831, NLI, Wyse Papers, MS. 15,024(11).

53. Rev. John Sheehan to Daniel O'Connell, 19 Jan. 1834, in O'Connell, *Correspondence*, v, 2032.

54. Michael Slattery to Thomas Wyse, 10 Nov. 1830, NLI, Wyse Papers, MS. 15,024 (1).

55. George Wyse to Thomas Wyse (n.d.), c. June 1830, NLI, Wyse Papers, MS. 15,020 (3).

56. *Pilot*, 21 Nov. 1834.

57. E. J. Littleton to Lord Duncannon, 20 Nov. 1834 (Private Possession, Aspinall Transcripts, 1834-5).

58. *Tipperary Free Press*, 3 Jan. 1835.

59. *Limerick Star and Evening Post*, 16 Dec. 1834.

60. Circular of Anti-Tory Association, Dublin (December, 1834), NLI, O'Connell Papers, MS. 5,243.

61. Maurice O'Connell to his wife, 1 Dec. 1834, University College Dublin Archives, O'Connell Papers, P12/4/C/27.

62. Lord Kenmare to Christopher Gallwey (copy), 3 Jan. 1834, Public Record Office Northern Ireland, Fitzgerald Papers, MIC/639/15/8/5/p.15.

63. Dr. Abraham to Thomas Wyse, 26 Dec. 1834, NLI, Wyse Papers, MS. 15,025 (3).

64. Rev. John Sheehan to Daniel O'Connell, 14 Jan. 1835, in O'Connell, *Correspondence*, v, 2197.

65. *Parliamentary Election Results in Ireland, 1801-1922*, ed. B. M. Walker (Dublin, 1978), pp. 56-60.

66. O. MacDonagh, 'Ambiguity in Nationalism: The Case of Ireland', in *Interpreting Irish History: The Debate on Historical Revisionism, 1938-94*, ed. C. Brady (Dublin, 1994), pp. 109-10.

Chapter 2

The Independent Man: Gender, Obligation, and Virtue in the 1832 Reform Act

In May 1797, Charles Grey placed a parliamentary reform motion before the Commons. Charles James Fox spoke in support of his young Whig colleague, and explained the rationale behind the scheme: 'My opinion is, that the best plan of representation is that which shall bring into activity the greatest number of independent voters, and that which is defective which would bring forth those whose situation and condition take from them the power of deliberation.'[1] The motion was lost by 91 votes to 256. Three decades later, Grey and the Whigs would again champion a reform of the representative system, but with greater success. The passing of the Act to Amend the Representation of the People in 1832 – thereafter immortalised as the 'Great Reform Act' – soon came to be regarded as a political landmark. The parliamentary debates on the Bill between 1830 and 1832, and the extra-parliamentary events surrounding them, have long been portrayed by historians as one of the defining episodes in the story of modern Britain: an epic battle featuring heroic protagonists, who steered Britain away from revolution and into an era of democracy and social consensus. One does not have to be a Whig historian to be impressed with the achievement of the Whigs of 1830-2, but the historiography has often missed the extent to which this quintessential 'modernising' measure drew upon habits of thought that were very well established indeed. In particular, the terms in which the parliamentary debates were conducted have rarely been considered in their appropriate cultural context.

This essay will explore how the parliamentary debates on reform in 1830-2 were conducted in strikingly similar terms to those employed by Fox in 1797, and by many other commentators before and since. The key concept in Fox's speech was independence. The ideal voter was 'independent', he argued, because a voter in any other situation was necessarily denied 'the power of deliberation.' This usage of the term 'independence' is alien to the modern reader. Nowadays, the word is entirely used to denote the relationship of persons, institutions, or objects to each other, although it still retains its positive connotations of impartiality (as in 'your

Independent Financial Adviser'). In Georgian English, 'independence' was also used in a relational sense, to denote freedom from obligation (or 'dependence'), but this freedom from obligation was more emotive, and had far greater evaluative implications. 'Independence' connoted not just autonomy, but the condition in which self-mastery, conscience, and individual responsibility could be exercised. Only in this situation of independence, it was argued, could an individual be disinterested, incorruptible, and impartial.

Although some of these relational connotations are still in the language, the implications of 'independence' regarding manners, patriotism, masculinity, and interior character have largely been lost. Personal independence concerned not just freedom *per se*, but a consciousness of liberty, a libertarianism that was supposedly inherent in all true Englishmen. Georgians maintained that 'independent men' were easily identified, because independence entailed an unmistakable forthrightness, assertiveness, and sturdiness of demeanour. In terms of social mores, admirers of independence promoted a pointedly plain model of manliness, emphasising sincerity, naturalness, and straightforwardness. These qualities were all part of the English self-image, but independence came to be regarded as integral to Englishness, and almost patriotic in itself.

Furthermore, because this character type was held to be English in an almost racial sense, the very workings of the political system were believed to be shaped around it. Most Georgians believed in an ancient constitution, a perfect political arrangement that was ratified by generations of usage. For many reformers, political improvement involved overturning centuries of decline in order to return to this ideal state, and 'independence' was the boast of those who claimed to have resisted this corruption. As Marie Peters has noted, independence was 'the only behaviour truly consistent with the theory of the mixed balanced constitution'.[2] Commentators from home and abroad made links between the 'independence' of the English attitude and physique, and the individual freedom upheld by the political and legal systems, attempting to ground England's revered constitution in the character of its people in an organic way.[3]

These interpretations of what it meant to be independent were highly flexible, of course, and we will see how this central marker of personal virtue had been contested for over a century before the opposing sides in the Reform debates attempted legislatively to fix its meaning. Politically speaking, there was much at stake in this contest. Arguably the central question in eighteenth- and nineteenth-century political life was that of who should be given the vote – who should be admitted to full citizenship – and this was commonly negotiated in terms of personal independence. Because of its wide range of connotation, 'independence' cut across many relevant considerations in Georgian political culture, such as respectability, property ownership, and personal character.

All of these qualities related to the issue of manliness in some way, and the concept of 'independence' was almost invariably gendered in the masculine in Georgian discourse. Indeed, the story of the British parliamentary reform movement can be told in terms of how reformers gradually came to associate ever-humbler groups of men with 'independence,' until manhood suffrage made the identification complete: as Anna Clark argues, the history of parliamentary reform is inseparable from considerations of gender.[4] This is not, however, a Whiggish narrative of progress, inclusion, and empowerment. Until the early twentieth century, the notion of independence could be employed to exclude more people than it included from political, legal, and economic entitlement. Its most obvious exclusive implications were for women, and this essay will examine the debilitating cultural association of femininity with 'dependence' in the context of the Reform debates. But supposed *effeminacy* as well as femininity was also politically disempowering: men who were younger, poorer, non-white (or even just non-English), or homosexual were similarly disadvantaged by the cult of the independent man. Understandings of who was capable of 'independence' were constantly being renegotiated, but arguments for empowerment based upon independence always required an 'other' in the form of a disempowered dependant. *In*-dependence is a negative term, so to assert that only *non*-obliged persons should participate in politics is to imply that supposedly *obliged* persons should not.

'Independence' was a question of obligation, and freedom from obligation was understood in terms of a highly gendered conception of personal virtue. The distinction between 'independence' and 'dependence,' and how this was morally evaluated, should be understood in terms of the metaphor of the patriarchal family. Within this model, the male household head controls, protects, and represents the other members of the family who are dependent upon him – his wife, children, servants, and so on, all conceived of in the feminine. Only the householder is 'independent' – that is, free from obligation – and is thus fully in command of himself, and is capable of full self-realisation. All the members of the household may be virtuous, but only the householder is capable of the manly virtue of 'independence.' This notion was derived from the classical understanding of liberty and virtue: only the 'independent man' is fully free and in possession of the manly virtues and thus only he should be admitted to citizenship.[5] Everybody else in the household is in a degrading position of obligation: even if no coercion is exercised, the 'dependent' are fundamentally unfree, and are in a position analogous to slavery.

Throughout the eighteenth century, this familial understanding of gender, obligation, and virtue was applied beyond the confines of the household in order to critique the role of obligation in public life. Thus independent MPs, independent voters, independently wealthy gentlemen, and independent artisans all asserted that they were in a position where full conscientious autonomy could be exercised, and drew upon a common culture of manly virtue and assertive individualism. Anyone who was subject to an influence or obligation that compromised their individual autonomy, on the other hand, was accused of being 'dependent' – a term with considerable force, connoting a degrading lack of manliness, virtue, and free will. 'Dependence' upon a patron, an employer, a landlord, or the parish was enough to call an individual's manliness and freedom into question, and could undermine a claim to political legitimacy. This state of 'dependence' was the polar opposite of masculine 'independence': laudable in females, but contemptible – and supposedly effeminate – in adult men. The Englishman's horror of obligation could result in misunderstandings when he came into contact with other cultures. Sir John Carr, travelling in Spain in 1809, noted the instance of a naval lieutenant who was startled to find that a Spaniard had settled his bar bill, and chased after him to protest:

> He continued, with an oath, that he had never been treated so before, that he had never, hitherto, been under an obligation to any one, and would not put up with it. He then told the waiter, through an Englishman who spoke Spanish, that he insisted upon paying for his punch; the waiter refused to take his money, he remonstrated, the other still refused, and doubtless thought him mad, upon which the worthy, blunt, but mistaken lieutenant threw a dollar into the bar, and ran out of the house, declaring, much as he liked a Spaniard, he would be d–d before he would be under any obligation to him.[6]

In Georgian England, manly virtue was a matter of obligation.

This question of obligation also had important implications for self-ownership, rationality, and subjectivity. As Clifford Geertz has noted, the modern Western notion of the autonomous, rational, sovereign individual is unique among the world's cultures.[7] But not everybody in the modern West was regarded as a sovereign individual: the extent to which persons were fully in control of themselves was hierarchical and evaluative. In Georgian political culture, only 'independent men' were held to possess full political subjectivity, and were fully in control of their homes, their consciences, and their identities. In a sense, the 'dependent' were not held to be subjects at all: they were the objects of political action rather than its originators, the spectated rather than the spectator. Dependent persons may have participated on the margins of politics, but it was seen as desirable to deny them the manly functions of judging and choosing.

This emphasis pervaded political theory throughout the eighteenth-century and well into the nineteenth, and the 'independent man' commonly had a privileged role in political critiques and historical narratives. J. G. A. Pocock has placed great emphasis upon the influence of the Civil War writer James Harrington.[8] Harrington merged Machiavellian republicanism with an idealised vision of rural England, in which he projected a dispersed citizenry of independent arms-bearing freeholders. Skinner and others agree that neo-classical ideas had a profound effect upon eighteenth-century political thought. In particular, the opposition Whigs of the late-seventeenth-century took up this vision and merged it with a belief in an ancient constitution and the national exclusivity of real liberty, so the 'independent man' was re-imagined as one of the constitutional checks and balances that had providentially developed over the centuries.

This conceptual heritage was central to the predominant opposition critique of the eighteenth century, 'Country' patriotism. 'Country' thought maintained the somewhat circular classical dictum that you should only participate in politics if you are virtuous, that you can only be virtuous if you are free from obligation, but that you can only guarantee your freedom if you are politically active. Opposition Whigs and Bolingbroke's Tories maintained that only 'independent men,' uncontaminated by Walpole's formidable networks of patronage, could speak out against the financially and morally corrupt ruling oligarchy. The virtue they claimed to epitomise was 'patriotism,' implying both superior public spirit and supposedly national traits such as boldness and independence. The 'independence' that such gentlemen claimed was underlined by their ownership of substantial landed property. Opposition figures such as Bolingbroke approved of the Qualification Act, which required that

> every Member for a Borough shall have £300 per Annum, and for a County, £600 per Annum; a Law, which was intended to confine the Election to such Persons as are independent in their Circumstances; have a valuable Stake in the Land; and must therefore be the most strongly engaged to consult the publick Good, and least liable to Corruption.[9]

'Country' theorists believed that landed property was more stable and permanent than the moveable wealth accumulated by the beneficiaries of the financial revolution: those who lived off their land were not beholden to the vagaries of patrons, governments, or the market.[10] Furthermore, landed proprietors emphasised their organic relationship with the land and country society, contrasting their (indigenous) rural virtue with the alleged vice of the (alien) metropolis and the court.

This stance was sustained throughout the century by independent country gentlemen backbenchers. In theory, all MPs fitted this description – that is, non-noble landowners who sat on their own interest – but in practice many were not, and it came to suggest a specific social and political type. Sir Lewis Namier brought to our attention the blunt, patriotic country gentleman whose boasted independence enabled him to support the King's government whenever he conscientiously could, but would also lead him fiercely to oppose anything that whiffed of party, centralisation, expense, oppression, or any of the other 'Country' bugbears.[11]

Later in the century, 'Country' patriotism shifted to the left in the hands of radicals and reformers such as John Wilkes, 'Major' John Cartwright, and Christopher Wyvill. From the 1770s, those who criticised the corruption of the establishment no longer placed their faith in the incorruptibility of a handful of country gentlemen who claimed to speak for the nation. Instead, they argued that the very structure of the representative system should be revised – or restored to its 'original' purity – in order directly to ensure that voters could be independent enough to return virtuous representatives.[12] In the mid-century, notions of what property and rank a voter should possess in order to guarantee his 'independence' had been socially exclusive, but radicals and reformers began to conceive of ever-humbler groups of men as having the potential to be independent electors.

In the context of the debate on the French Revolution, the 'independent man' was conceived of in novel ways. Thomas Paine rejected historical and nationally-exclusive conceptions of rights altogether, arguing instead in terms of the natural rights that inhere in all men, but even he was indebted to the neo-classical and 'Country' traditions of independence. He disdained faction and patronage, valorised assertive self-realisation, and conceived of human dignity and liberty in terms of freedom from obligation.[13] As we have seen, moderate reformers among the Foxite Whigs responded to the French Revolution by calling for a domestic parliamentary reform based around the idea of the independent elector.[14] At the other end of the political spectrum, wartime enabled loyalists to draw upon what had formerly been the opposition's patriotic political style, and they too emphasised its socially inclusive implications. From the late 1790s, the establishment promoted an ebullient, active, and participatory notion of national belonging in order to mobilise the population against the threatened invasion from France. Loyalist propaganda reiterated that, in contrast with the Frenchman, the common Englishman possessed a 'high reputation for Greatness, Richness, Valour, Liberty, and Independence'.[15] The 'independent man' was recast as the vigilant loyalist patriot.

When the radical movement revived in the early 1800s – calling first for military and economic, and then for parliamentary reform – the definition of the 'independent man' became an important site of contest, with both the establishment and its critics laying exclusive claims to its legitimising power. Critics of 'Old Corruption' maintained that networks of patronage were emasculating the political system and enriching government 'dependents' at the taxpayer's expense, and called upon 'independent men' to repudiate this state of affairs. In the post-war years, the culture of manly 'independence' was central to the style and political critique of the unstamped press and the 'mass platform' led by radical politicians such as Henry Hunt.[16] By this time, plebeian radicals were conceiving of male political entitlement in the most inclusive terms. The journalist Thomas Wooler employed the argument of natural law in his advocacy of universal suffrage: 'in a natural state, men are all alike; independent of each other, and consequently all alike are equal'. This was emphatically universal *male* suffrage, however: 'the foundation of universal suffrage,' he argued, is 'that men are alone independent by nature, and that idiots, madmen, women, and children, must in all states be dependent.'[17] Plebeian radicals attempted to make gender the sole determinant of independence, in order to undermine the traditional exclusions of property, cultivation, and rank. In identifying 'independence' with maleness itself, however, radicals made political entitlement more insistently exclusive for women, and pursued the claims of working men at their expense.

Importantly, in the late 1810s and early 1820s, reformist Whigs such as Lord John Russell and John Lambton (the future first Earl of Durham) reiterated the place of the independent elector in their reform schemes. Lambton had his reform motion debated in the Commons in April 1821. He began his speech by updating the Whig *raison d'être:* they had no longer to contend with royal prerogative, but with an executive that governed through a corrupt majority in the Commons, to which no effective constitutional check could be posed. The remedy was to ensure that 'the people may be adequately represented in the legislature,' by enfranchising all taxpaying householders, disfranchising decayed boroughs, and establishing triennial parliaments. Taxpayers, he argued, had a right 'to regulate and control' the legislature through their representative, and their modest property was a guarantee of their reliability: 'It affords the best pledge for his conduct, and renders him independent of that commanding and overbearing influence or temptation, which, if exercised against a poor and dependent man, would prevent the possibility of his bestowing a free and unbiased suffrage'.[18] An 'independent' elective body would choose their members with regard to the interests of the country, thus re-balancing the constitution. We will see how this rationale would powerfully bind the Whigs together in 1830-2.

This survey of two centuries of English political culture is necessarily brief, but it is necessary to emphasise several points in order to place the debates on the Reform Bill in context. Firstly, the idea of the independent man was subject to continual redefinition and debate. This contest was far from resolved by 1830, but the fact that the basic elements remained consistent enabled the debate on the nature of citizenship to take place upon common ground: manly virtue and political entitlement were questions of freedom from compromising obligation. Secondly, what started out as an elitist oppositional idea became socially more inclusive. The basis for manly independence shifted from the superficial patrician accomplishments and broad acres accessible only to men of rank, to inner virtues and forms of property that were within the reach of all true men. 'Independence,' indeed, became increasingly equated with maleness itself, and with the masculine stations of father and householder: a shift with important implications for the gendering of political entitlement. Furthermore, it should be emphasised that 'independence' was not merely a tenet of political theory, but played a fundamental part in how Georgian men regarded themselves, and their membership of a society, a political community, or a nation. Sir John Carr's anecdote (related above) reminds us that independence could be a highly emotive aspect of an individual's identity.

In particular, independence was an idea that informed how ordinary Georgians participated in politics, and it is worth focusing briefly upon the culture of the electoral system. Frank O'Gorman has highlighted the phenomenon of electoral independence, whereby voters supported a 'third man' in opposition to powerful interests that sought to control both seats in a constituency. Voters thus protested at the abuse of local power and the devaluation of their electoral privileges, and reminded their betters of their responsibilities, by an assertion of political independence.[19] There were many examples of 'classic' independence efforts in this mould, but independence was a prominent feature of the culture of English elections more generally. It is a striking feature of election speeches that *all* candidates claimed to epitomise the virtue of 'independence,' irrespective of their links to ministers, parties, or patrons. Voters too were conventionally addressed as 'The Independent Electors.' A handbill from the Shrewsbury contest in June 1819 exhorted voters to 'act the part of Honest Independent Men':[20] voters were expected to live up to the assertive, self-governing, and conscientious model of independent manliness. During the canvass, they were permitted to converse plainly with their betters, and at the poll they were required to declare their choice in public, in defiance of drunken mobs or powerful landlords. The riotous mid-Georgian elections immortalised by Hogarth may seem a world away from Victorian equipoise, but we will see how this culture of electoral independence had a profound effect upon Whig conceptions of citizenship.

The language of 'independence' pervaded the Reform debates, and this way of thinking played an important part in the formulation of the Bill. Whenever commentators have noted that the framers of the Bill intended that voters should be 'independent,' however, it has usually been in a limited sense, connoting the amount of property a voter was held to require in order to avoid being bribed or coerced.[21] Little attention has been paid to considerations of gender, respectability, intellectual capacity, or identity; or to the fact that this complex idea had the long heritage outlined above. Only two little-known articles by Richard Davis and Harold Ellis have made the link between the 'independence' discussed in 1830-2, and the eighteenth-century idea of the 'independent elector.'[22] Whig reformers and borough Independents both argued that so long as the Commons was filled with members who were self-interested, incapable, or dependent upon powerful patrons, it could not be expected to provide an effective counterweight to the executive or to legislate for the general good. The return of MPs should rely only upon the free choice of the people: it was the electors who should decide whether candidates for the Commons possessed the requisite ability, manly character, and patriotism. This was not a levelling critique, or an attempt to turn MPs into delegates. Rather, it was an opportunity for the common people to recognise their natural leaders, to express approbation at the just exercise of authority or to protest at its abuse.

As far as the question of 'independence' in English political rationalities was concerned, the Reform Act was not the end of the story, but it was both a culmination and a turning point. For the first time, an opposition had become a government on a platform of parliamentary reform, and was capable of carrying it. From this point, the critique of the political 'outs' informed the governing rationality of the 'ins.' The independent man, instead of monitoring and standing up to the establishment from without, became the preferred unit of political inclusion. By the 1830s, the shifts in the meaning of 'independence' from ebullient libertarianism to responsible respectability, and from social exclusivity to a more accessible conception, had been completed to a sufficient degree to limit official entry to the public political sphere to 'independent men,' and to codify mass participation along these lines. In the Reform debates, 'independence' connoted the qualities of enfranchised citizens, and the electorate was imagined as a polity of 'independent men.'

We get our first systematic view of what the Whigs of the 1830s sought to accomplish in the provisional plan produced by the committee of Russell, Durham, Duncannon and Graham. This document was pervaded by the language of 'independence.' Comprehensive Reform, it was argued, was required to remove 'all rational grounds of complaint from the minds of the intelligent and the independent portion of the community.' The plan included vesting the right of voting in heads of households worth £20 per annum, and establishing vote by ballot. This was impracticable, for in some boroughs the proposed constituency was found to be very small. In the eventual Bill the qualification was set at £10 and open voting continued, but the original plan gives an indication of the Whigs' intention to enfranchise men of standing and means who would vote autonomously rather than with regard to the wishes of a powerful superior, even to the extent of being entrusted with secret voting. The £20 constituency, they argued, would form 'a constituent body including all the intelligence and respectability of the independent classes of society.' It would prevent 'those scenes of corruption and political profligacy which too often occur where the right of voting is vested in those whose want of education and state of dependence render them quite unfitted for its exercise.' Independence may have been quantified in terms of property for the sake of convenience, but it was not just a question of its ownership: the autonomy connoted by 'independence' related to questions of 'education', 'intelligence', 'respectability', and moral fitness. In order to prevent 'corruption and political profligacy', the act was built around a very specific conception of the citizen.[23]

In the subsequent debates in the Commons and the Lords, the nature of the voter was placed under exhaustive scrutiny. A broad consensus emerged that the voter should be 'independent,' and the independence/dependence dichotomy was employed to negotiate the question of who could safely be admitted to the official political sphere. The meanings of this conceptual binary, however, were contested by supporters and opponents of the measure, and a number of positions emerged that were characterised by their takes on 'the independent man': those of the right, the liberals, the radicals, and the Whigs. In general, the parliamentary right – comprehending both the Ultra Tories and those who stuck by Wellington in opposition to reform – were suspicious about independent behaviour among the common people. They were committed to an organic, cohesive, hierarchical, and interdependent conception of the social order, a romanticised vision of rural society in which the squirearchy were the natural social and political leaders of their communities. The right were prepared to accept that 'independence' existed in a safe and laudable form among certain sections of the people, but they had very specific groups in mind. Given their commitment to traditional country society, the right associated independence with the bracing rural virtue and patriotic self-respect of the yeoman, the freeman, or the peasant. The right believed that such men had a natural alliance with the ancient landed aristocracy against their traditional enemies of industrialists, financiers, degenerate city dwellers, non-Anglicans, republicans, utilitarians, and court politicians. In contrast to the 'independent' guardians of the soil, the £10 constituency smacked of the urban petty-bourgeoisie, their other great bugbear: the Earl of Winchilsea enquired whether anyone could be found 'to contend that that class of persons were independent? Surely not. [...] they would be ruled by the worst enemies of the country.'[24] In general – and in marked contrast with the Whigs – speakers of this political persuasion had a low opinion of the people's capacity for virtue. A succession of Tory peers cast doubts on the capacity, responsibility, and disinterestedness of the humble voter. The Duke of Buccleugh reported that the people of Scotland believed Reform meant 'no more excisemen, – no more gaugers; that they should have free trade; that whiskey would be cheap, &c.'.[25]

The right was more confident that voters in counties and rural constituencies would vote for suitable candidates. To the dismay of the Whigs, the Marquis of Chandos appeared to have succeeded in swamping the county electorate with men who were likely to be docile towards landed proprietors, by forcing through an amendment enfranchising £50 tenants-at-will. Milton and Althorp protested that such men would be utterly dependent upon their landlords, but Chandos's supporters responded with the traditional romantic image of the independent man as honest, rustic, loyal, and defiant. In contrast to urban shopkeepers, they argued, 'the franchise could not be trusted to a more independent body than the Yeomen whom the Amendment would include.' In areas such as this, the right hoped that a cohesive, consensual social order – 'where all the relations and dependencies of social life were in a happier state' – would be unaffected by the Bill.[26] Whigs maintained that all the interests of the community would be represented by enabling the people to select enlightened and disinterested governors, while Tories were adamant that the dominant interest in any given constituency would prevail. Therefore, they argued, it was imperative to ensure that there were enough exclusively landed constituencies (that would inevitably return loyal patricians) to counterbalance the urban centres (that would inevitably return demagogues).

Alternatively, the same ethos produced a very different response among Ultras such as the Marquis of Blandford. In order to counter these same forces, it was desirable to enfranchise 'the people' in its broadest sense, trusting in their independence and traditional prejudices to return the sort of MPs who would never have emancipated the Catholics. His own reform plan of February 1830 and his subsequent support for the Whigs' measure were justified in these terms.[27]

The diametric opposite of the right's rationality was that of the liberals. It is difficult to gauge the liberal position on Reform from the parliamentary debates: 'Liberal' was not yet a party label, and those who were committed to a recognisably 'liberal' view of government, economics, and society operated from within the existing parties. Of these, the 'liberalism' of the liberal Tories did not extend to political reform, whereas the liberals in the Reform coalition did not have prominent voices.[28] The liberally inclined 'Young Whigs' like Milton and Althorp tended to toe the Whig line, but in their opposition to the Chandos clause we can get an idea of the liberal conception of independence. They responded to the rustic Romanticism of the right with a dryly-functional consideration: did tenant farmers' agreements with their landlords curtail their autonomy? Althorp sought systematically to debunk independence:

> Few men knew more about them, or had a higher opinion of their intelligence and integrity. But the question was, were they in such a situation as would ensure the same independence as to their votes as might be expected from freeholders? The Committee was not now called upon to decide upon their respectability, but whether they were in that situation which would make them independent county electors.[29]

For liberal Whigs like Althorp, the ideal citizenry consisted of free actors under a uniform franchise, with all the interests of the community amalgamated together. Political economists were inclined to view individuals as functionally equivalent and economically quantifiable, so independence's traditional conceptual baggage was irrelevant. In the liberal view of personal freedom, 'independence' concerned only the individual's ability to resist constraint, and his basic (economic) capacity for self-determination. Failure to meet this second criterion also disqualified an individual from citizenship: significantly, when Althorp was chairing the Committee he allowed the Tory William Praed's amendment excluding those dependent upon parochial relief from the franchise to pass without any debate.[30] The harsher side of liberal self-help played its part in the ethos of the Bill.

Although radical MPs were prepared to unite behind the Bill, it is not possible to talk in terms of a single 'radical' rationality in the parliaments of 1830-2. If radical members had a more populist and zealous personal style, their ideologies were often merely extensions of those of their more mainstream parliamentary colleagues. The most distinctive radical voice in the reform debates was that of Daniel O'Connell, who attuned his radicalism to the pressing needs of Ireland. In May 1830 – before the Reform debates started in earnest – O'Connell took the opportunity to propose his own comprehensive plan. He proposed universal suffrage, and made a case for its constitutionality by citing authorities such as Blackstone. He noted that lawyer's proviso that everyone 'whose wills may be supposed independent' was entitled to vote,[31] and interpreted this in accordance with his own distaste for property qualifications, and with his greater faith in the humble than in the high:

> But even riches were not a sufficient assurance for independence of conduct. If the poor man had natural wants, the rich man had artificial wants – wants that became the more painfully pressing and craving under apparent repletion. Who could look at the opulent classes of society and not see how frequently such was the case? […]

> Who had not frequently been compelled to regard with scorn the creatures who doated on stars, and garters, and ribands, and feathers, and other frippery; – and who for such things sacrificed the noblest possession of a human being – independence.

The only sure way 'of making every man, however poor, independent' was the ballot: 'As the rights of all Englishmen were equal, so also ought to be their votes, and ballot would render them so'.[32] Whilst undoubtedly idealising independence, in common with the liberals he stripped it down to the question of an individual's relation to sources of influence and coercion where political qualification was concerned. Unlike most liberals, though, he saw its egalitarian implications: significantly, the radical-utilitarian *Westminster Review* reached identical conclusions on this issue.[33]

The majority of the political world, however, would not accept the ballot. Open voting was regarded as manly and English, so was successfully defended within the traditional language of 'independence.' In the Manichean moral world of electoral independence, the virtues of openness, sincerity, and defiance – epitomised by the practice of open voting – were diametrically opposed to the vice of secrecy, which was widely seen as suspect in public life and (worse) a characteristic of foreign political systems. Furthermore, the Whigs claimed that the ballot was destructive to character, conducive to perjury, and was ill conducive to the operation of the legitimate moral, intellectual, and social influences that they sought to promote within the electoral system.

The Reform Act was emphatically a Whig measure. As Peter Mandler has argued, the Whig style of government befitted the challenges of the 1830s: aristocratic self-confidence, party cohesion, benevolence, and flamboyance were needed to carry sweeping social and political Reform.[34] The Reform Act, in particular, fitted their self-image and self-appointed role. As 'the people's ancient friends' and the designers of the Revolution Settlement, the Whigs had ensured that the people's political liberty had been kept in trust effectively, until such a time as it could safely be bestowed from above.[35] It was this variety of paternal liberality that informed the Reform Bill.

We have seen how the Whigs had a specific idea of the voter in mind. In particular, the Whig conception of personal 'independence' was more expressly *political* than those of their opponents, and drew connotations from over a century of oppositional critiques and electoral culture. Central to this is the question of how the Whigs used the language of class. The reform debates were pervaded by a three-tiered social vision, to the extent that Dror Wahrman has suggested that the episode was central to the linguistic process by which Britons came to perceive their society as being divided into three classes.[36] The Whigs systematically exploited the common contemporary association of the social middle with virtue and responsibility in their justification of the £10 franchise. Durham, for instance, praised their 'skill, talent, political intelligence, and wealth', and argued that 'the emancipation of the middle classes' was a leading principle of the Bill.[37] The association of 'independence' with the virtues of the middle class was common in contemporary discourse. At Manchester's first election under the new franchise, one of the speakers at the Whigs' celebratory dinner praised 'the virtue, the patriotism, the firmness, and the independence of the middle class of electors'.[38]

The Whigs, however, considered 'independence' and class in political terms. Ellis and Davis go so far as to suggest that they did not use the term 'middle classes' in a sociological sense at all: what Whigs meant by this was the eighteenth-century idea of the 'independent electorate,' positioned between the populace and the nobility.[39] Or, more precisely, between the *dependent* populace on the one hand, and the networks of aristocratic and Crown clientage on the other: the social middle was the stratum that supposedly possessed the greatest independence from compromising obligation. These independent electors, they argued, had the personal qualities and private means to resist bribery and corruption, and were enlightened and responsible enough to select their natural leaders from the ranks above them. The Whigs, of course, had long cast themselves in this role and trusted that 'the independent' would favour *them* with their votes.

This conception of electoral behaviour should be placed in the context of the Whig view of influence and social relations. This contrasted markedly with the automatic community deference (or worrying lack thereof) posited by the right, and with the ideal of unrestrained individual equivalence sought by doctrinaire liberals and radical utilitarians. The distinction between 'legitimate' and 'illegitimate' influence pervaded the Whigs' attempts to justify the Bill. They argued that the influence of bribery, coercion, and 'nomination' was illegitimate: the disfranchisement of 'rotten' and 'close' boroughs, new electoral procedures, and the creation of 'an independent and excellent constituency' would counteract this. Significantly, although all sides denounced the venality of electors, effectual curbs on electoral treating had to wait a further half-century until the Corrupt Practices Act. The Whigs did not seek to end all social and electoral influence. Although electors should be independent, this was in the context of a hierarchical political society where the legitimate influence of intellect, rank, and leadership held sway. As Palmerston argued, the Whigs sought actively to promote 'an influence arising from good conduct and prosperity of demeanour on the one side, and respect and deference on the other; and which was as honourable to those who exercised it, as to those who acknowledged its authority.'[40] This corresponded with the social values of electoral independence: the Whigs realised that this ethos was the best hope for the aristocracy in a changing world, giving them a political role based on their supposed ability and enlightened disinterestedness, and on the mutual respect of elector and elected.

So who was the ideal citizen of 1832? Fundamentally, he was an adult male – the only group held to have the capacity for independence. Although women had long been barred from voting by local custom, the Reform Act formally excluded them for the first time, and it would be a further century before their disqualifying association with 'dependence' was overturned in this respect.[41] This exclusion of women from active citizenship was never discussed in the parliamentary debates on Reform. There is a suggestion that women were not considered to be political beings in a debate on the admissibility of petitions: anti-Reformers insinuated that women had signed certain pro-Reform petitions, thus rendering them unconstitutional.[42] More pervasively, considerations of manliness and patriarchy recur in the debates. As Grey argued, being the man of the household – even a £10 one – entailed a degree of responsibility and respectability:

> they are persons who in my opinion, from the very circumstance of their occupying a £10 house [...] have given a sort of guarantee of their holding a certain station in life – who thereby exhibit an open sign of their possessing some property – who have given a pledge to the community for their good conduct – and who for the most part are married men and the fathers of families.[43]

In a sense, the public role of independent men was predicated upon having people dependent upon them. In common with the Whig view of leadership, the Whig view of citizenship involved manly, enlightened, and disinterested action *on behalf of others*. Householders' mastery over others was testament to their self-mastery, and the fact of their having people to support, protect, and represent was a basic guarantee of their reliability and selflessness. The household – as a unit of the political world, and as a gendered model of obligation, virtue, and power – altered remarkably little from classical republicanism through to Whig reform.

As already noted, the citizen of 1832 supposedly possessed sufficient property and standing to avoid being placed in a state of obligation that would affect his vote. Like O'Gorman's borough Independents, he was also expected to possess a degree of the stoicism and fearlessness of the freeborn Englishman, to resist the intimidation of mobs or overmighty nobles, and to disdain the lure of the demagogue. He was still called upon to cast his vote openly, although new electoral procedures such as multiple polling places and prior registration made this rather less fearsome a task than it had once been. The reformed political world was rendered appropriate for the early-Victorian version of the independent man, just as the unreformed had been for his predecessor.

Lastly, electoral culture's stress on conscientiousness was amplified, but with a new emphasis on intelligence and education. Throughout the Reform debates, supporters of the Bill lauded the moral and intellectual improvement of the people, and the Whigs in particular expressed an active desire that the people should consider and discuss public questions. From 1832, working men who aspired to the franchise were encouraged to elevate themselves, and the culture of autodidacticism and self-improvement would be central to the claims of such men well into the age of Gladstonian Liberalism.[44]

From 1832, independence was the criterion for citizenship, and the state to which disenfranchised men should aspire. Historians such as Catherine Hall and Anna Clark have shown how later Reform Acts gradually expanded the definition of 'the independent' in order to justify entrusting the vote to further groups of people.[45] The reform legislation of the nineteenth century, and the arguments of its proponents and detractors, should thus be seen in the broadest chronological and cultural perspective. In particular, we need to attend to contemporary understandings of gender, obligation, and personal virtue if we are to understand how citizenship was conceived of by nineteenth-century legislators, and experienced by nineteenth-century citizens themselves. The cultural pervasiveness of the idea of 'the independent man' in eighteenth- and nineteenth-century England is a very good argument for the relevance of the history of gender to the study of politics.

References

1. *The Parliamentary History of England*, ed. W. Cobbett (36 vols, London, 1806-1820), xxxiii, 726.

2. M. Peters, 'The *Monitor* on the Constitution, 1755-65: New Light on the Ideological Origins of English Radicalism', *English Historical Review*, lxxxvi (1971), 706-27.

3. P. Langford, *Englishness Identified: Manners and Character, 1650-1850* (Oxford, 2000), pp. 7-9.

4. A. Clark, 'Gender, Class and the Constitution: Franchise Reform in England, 1832-1928', in *Re-reading the Constitution: New Narratives in the Political History of England's Long Nineteenth Century*, ed. J. Vernon (Cambridge, 1996), pp. 239-53.

5. Q. Skinner, *Liberty Before Liberalism* (Cambridge, 1998).

6. Sir J. Carr, *Descriptive Travels in the Southern and Eastern Parts of Spain and the Balearic Isles, in the Year 1809* (London, 1811), pp. 19-20, cited in Langford, *Englishness Identified*, p. 237.

7. C. Geertz, '"From the Native's Point of View": On the Nature of Anthropological Understanding', in *Culture Theory: Essays on Mind, Self, and Emotion*, ed. R. Shweder and R. LeVine (Cambridge, 1984), pp. 123-36.

8. J. G. A. Pocock, 'Machiavelli, Harrington, and English Political Ideologies in the Eighteenth Century', in Pocock, *Politics, Language and Time* (London, 1971), pp.104-47.

9. *The Craftsman*, 8 Sept. 1733.

10. J. G. A. Pocock, *Virtue, Commerce, and History: Essays on Political Thought and History, Chiefly in the Eighteenth Century* (Cambridge, 1985), p. 66.

11. L. Namier, 'Country Gentlemen in Parliament, 1750-84', in Namier, *Crossroads of Power: Essays on Eighteenth-Century England* (London, 1962), pp. 30-45.

12. See, for example, the first parliamentary motion for electoral reform, tabled by John Wilkes in March 1776: *Parliamentary History*, xviii, 1286-98.

13. G. Claeys, *Thomas Paine: Social and Political Thought* (Boston, 1989).

14. H. A. Ellis, 'Aristocratic Influence and Electoral Independence: the Whig Model of Parliamentary Reform, 1792-1832', *Journal of Modern History*, li (1979), On Demand Supplement, pp. 1271-76.

15. *The Warning Drum: The British Home Front Faces Napoleon. Broadsides of 1803*, ed. F. Klingberg and S. Hustvedt (Berkeley, 1944), p. 33.

16. J. Belchem, 'Radical Language and Ideology in Early Nineteenth-Century England: the Challenge of the Platform', *Albion*, xx (1988), 247-59.

17. *Black Dwarf*, 4 June 1817.

18. *Hansard*, new series (25 vols, London, 1803-1820), v, 373-4.

19. F. O'Gorman, *Voters, Patrons, and Parties: The Unreformed Electorate of Hanoverian England, 1714-1832* (Oxford, 1989), pp. 259-85.

20. Handbill (Shrewsbury, 22 June 1819): John Rylands University Library of Manchester, SC12068F, no. 126.

21. M. Brock, *The Great Reform Act* (London, 1973), p. 143.

22. R. W. Davis, 'Deference and Aristocracy in the Time of the Great Reform Act', *American Historical Review*, lxxxi (1976), 532-39; Ellis, 'Aristocratic Influence'.

23. *The Reform Act, 1832: The Correspondence of the Late Earl Grey with His Majesty King William IV and with Sir Herbert Taylor*, ed. H. Grey (2 vols, London, 1867), i, 461-7.

24. *Hansard*, third series (256 vols, London, 1831-91), vii, 1141.

25. Ibid., iii, 1320-21.

26. Ibid., vi, 283, ii, 1316.

27. Ibid., second series, xxii, 678-98; third series, i, 65-8.

28. P. Mandler, *Aristocratic Government in the Age of Reform: Whigs and Liberals, 1830-52* (Oxford, 1990).

29. *Hansard*, third series, vi, 280-1.

30. Ibid., vi, 686.

31. W. Blackstone, *Commentaries Upon the Laws of England* (4 vols, Oxford, 1765), i. 165.

32. *Hansard*, third series, xxiv, 1210, 1214.

33. *Westminster Review*, xxv (July 1830).

34. Mandler, *Aristocratic Government*, p. 8.

35. I. Newbould, *Whiggery and Reform, 1830-41: The Politics of Government* (Stanford, 1990).

36. D. Wahrman, *Imagining the Middle Class: The Political Representation of Class in Britain, 1780-1840* (Cambridge, 1995).

37. *Hansard*, third series, xii, 356, 363.

38. *Report of the Speeches at the Great Dinner in the Theatre, Manchester, to Celebrate the Election of Mark Phillips, Esq. & the Right Hon. C. Poulett Thompson* (Manchester [n.d.]), p. 7.

39. Ellis, 'Aristocratic Influence', p. 1254; Davis, 'Deference', p. 538.

40. *Hansard*, third series, iii, 1326.

41. Clark, 'Gender, Class, and the Constitution'.

42. *Hansard*, third series, ix, 830.

43. Ibid., xii, 19.

44. P. Joyce, *Democratic Subjects: The Self and the Social in Nineteenth-Century England* (Cambridge, 1994).

45. C. Hall, 'Rethinking Imperial Histories: the Reform Act of 1867', *New Left Review*, ccviii (1994), 3-29; Clark, 'Gender, Class, and the Constitution'.

Chapter 3

Sir Thomas Phillips and the Problem of 'Class-Antagonism'*

On 9 December 1839 Thomas Phillips, late Mayor of Newport, was knighted by Queen Victoria 'as a mark of the high sense the Queen entertains of the peculiar merits of [his] individual exertions in maintaining Her Majesty's authority, and preserving the lives and properties of her subjects'.[1] Just over a month earlier, on 4 November, Phillips had led a detachment of regular infantry and a handful of special constables in defeating what has become known as the 'Newport rising': the attack on the Monmouthshire town by at least five thousand armed Chartists led by John Frost, Zephaniah Williams, and William Jones.[2] Phillips had been twice wounded in the 'battle of the Westgate [Hotel]' and was widely hailed as the hero of the hour, being voted the freedom of the City of London and having over £800 raised in his honour through public subscription by a committee of prominent Monmouthshire citizens established for the purpose.[3]

Phillips, born in 1801 in Breconshire, had, from 1819, trained as a solicitor with Thomas Prothero, town clerk of Newport and, at that time, agent to Sir Charles Morgan of Tredegar House, the prominent landowner in the Newport area.[4] In 1824, once qualified, he became Prothero's partner and retained this position until December 1839. He became moderately wealthy very quickly, taking a leading role in the supply of gas lighting for the town, buying a colliery at Cwrt-y-Bella in the Sirhowy valley in 1825, and sometime later opening one nearby at Manmoel. Almost immediately he took over most of the responsibilities of the town clerkship held by Prothero, although his partner retained the office in name until 1836. By 1826 he was skilfully championing the Newport Improvement Act through parliament, and subsequently became one of the town's improvement commissioners.

During the reform crisis Thomas Phillips established a reputation as a parliamentary reformer, if a relatively moderate one. He regularly shared a platform with the Newport radical (and long-time enemy of Thomas Prothero) John Frost, but their opinions on the extent to which reform should be carried, and to what extent it would prove a positive influence on matters social and economic, frequently differed. Frost thought Phillips an 'empty, loquacious' man whose espousal of reform was purely opportunistic: Phillips's association with Prothero was enough to earn him Frost's condemnation. The passage of the Municipal Reform Act in 1835 led to the creation of a new town council in Newport and Prothero at this point stepped down as town clerk. Thomas Phillips was elected his replacement, John Frost topped the poll as a candidate in the West Ward, and the two men were to be at each other's throats for the next four years. By the autumn of 1838, when Frost aligned himself with the local Chartist movement, Phillips had become mayor of the town (a position Frost himself had filled from 1836-7). As Chartism in Monmouthshire became increasingly aggressive, so Phillips acted to combat it. He was involved in assisting the removal of Frost from the magisterial bench; in establishing the anti-Chartist West Monmouthshire Association for the Protection of Life and Property; in banning Chartist meetings from Newport; and in prosecuting Henry Vincent and three other Chartist leaders for having subsequently defied the ban, prosecutions which resulted (in August 1839) in gaol sentences that infuriated the Monmouthshire Chartists and may have helped to provoke the subsequent insurrection. That the rising of November 1839 failed in its assault on Newport was less down to Phillips's personal courage and leadership than to the disorganisation and incoherent leadership of the Chartists themselves. In the trial that followed at Monmouth in January 1840, Frost, Williams and Jones received capital sentences for high treason, commuted to transportation for life, and lesser gaol sentences were passed on eighteen others.

Phillips left Newport in February 1840. Even before the rising he had determined to dissolve his partnership with Thomas Prothero and pursue a career as a barrister. With three terms at the bar already behind him, Phillips was admitted to Gray's Inn later that year and was eventually called to the Inner Temple in June 1842.[5] Before beginning practice he undertook a tour of the Mediterranean and Middle East in the company of the artist Richard Dadd, becoming, in the process, seriously troubled by his young friend's mental state.[6] From 1845 onwards he established his professional chambers at 11, King's Bench Walk, practising on the Oxford Circuit. He developed particular expertise in railway matters, as a Chancery barrister, and in dealing with parliamentary committees. He was made a Queen's Counsel on 17 February 1865 and a bencher of his inn later that year.[7] Ensconced in the capital he became a Governor of King's College, London, a benefactor of and Chairman of the Committee of Management of King's College Hospital, and was prominent in Anglican circles, acting as a Governor of the Corporation of the Sons of the Clergy.[8] His most sustained contribution to metropolitan public life was made through the Society of Arts, on the Council of which he served from 1857.[9] He was Chairman of the society from 1859 to 1862, and from 1866 until his death in May 1867.[10] He acted as Chairman of the Exhibition Committee for the International Exhibition of 1862.[11] According to Sir Henry Trueman Wood, the society's historian, he was a 'very energetic and capable Chairman', 'a man of some character', 'liberal and public-spirited'.[12]

Thomas Phillips was a Welshman who excelled both in his legal career and in more altruistic pursuits. He ended his life a moderately rich man, leaving (as a lifelong bachelor) most of his fortune to his nephews William Page Thomas Phillips (another London barrister) and Thomas Phillips Price (who went on to become Liberal MP for Monmouthshire North, 1885-95).[13] Through the Society of Arts he met Gladstone and both the Queen (again) and the Prince Consort, working with Albert on the preparations for the 1862 exhibition.[14] Yet, in many respects, Phillips's most substantial contributions were made not in London but in the country of his birth. As shall be shown, he was an 'outstanding educational reformer', one of the most active and important members of the Anglican Church in South Wales, and 'a passionate Welsh patriot'.[15] He wrote authoritatively about Wales, served on many committees and in many capacities and gave generously of his own fortune in the service of various good causes. At the time of his death it was noted that he was held 'in great respect ... all over the Principality' and that 'the whole of his life was devoted to the service of the public', that 'he always devoted his services, talents, and great ability to the interests of the county and the cause of science, education, religion etc.'[16] Two decades after his death he could still be held up as 'a remarkable example of self-consecration to duty'.[17]

The twentieth-century was less kind to Phillips, and the place in history and public memory of John Frost and the Chartist movement was subject to a series of revisions that moved the focus of attention and approval away from those in positions of authority at the time of the rising.[18] Phillips's multiple status as a coalowner, landowner, barrister and prominent Anglican was unlikely to endear him to the dominant currents of Welsh historical writing and even his politics were sometimes misrepresented.[19] By the century's end only occasional, often eccentric, voices, were heard to speak up for Sir Thomas Phillips.[20]

Thomas Phillips first came to national prominence as an opponent of Chartism and it is possible to understand much of his life, from 1840 onwards, as both an intellectual and a practical response to what he saw as the movement's origins, particularly as they manifested themselves in South Wales. This essay explores his consideration of what he termed the problem of 'class-antagonism'.[21] It begins by summarising his evaluation of Chartism and the social discontent that he felt had generated the movement. This evaluation he made public first through speeches in the wake of the rising of 1839 and second through a chapter in his book-long reply of 1849 to the 1847 reports of the education commissioners on Wales.[22] In both places, and elsewhere, he commented more widely on contemporary social problems and on the remedies that he felt they demanded. The second half of the essay examines his deeds more than his words: his record as, variously, an educational reformer, church reformer, paternalistic employer and philanthropist. Ultimately, it will be argued, Thomas Phillips merits being remembered as rather more than, as his enemy John Frost would have it, 'a contemptible foe to the industrial classes'.[23] He was a central figure in the liberal reform movement that sought to ensure not only that nothing like

Newport 1839 would be repeated, but that such action should never again be considered legitimate or justifiable by the population of the 'disturbed districts' of Monmouthshire and Glamorgan.[24] He was not alone, nor were either his diagnosis or prescription exceptionally original.[25] He was not a first-rank intellectual. But he was a significant public figure who thought carefully about the world in which he lived and about the responsibilities that should be borne by people of his station. In his combination of philosophy and action, and with his impeccable status as the vanquisher of the Chartist insurrection worn as a constant badge of authority, his views commanded considerable attention.[26]

Phillips's analysis of Chartism was well developed months before the Newport rising. Writing to Lord John Russell in March 1839 he noted that the Chartists, many of whom were colliers and ironworkers in the industrial valleys, looked 'with aversion and dislike on their employers'. Regrettably, he observed, 'the moral influence which ought to belong to government and without which government itself cannot exist is altogether at an end amongst a very numerous class of the community'.[27] For Phillips this meant that whatever the level of physical force applied to hold the Chartists in check, no solution to the general social problem would be forthcoming without more inventive and sympathetic measures. He saw coercion as a short-term measure, effective in suppressing Chartist violence, but irrelevant as means of remedying the profound state of disaffection that appeared widespread in the industrial districts.

This was the view he expounded at length when the guest of honour at a meeting (and subsequent dinner) held in Newport in September 1840. The meeting was called in order to present him with the £862 10s worth of silver plate that had been raised by public subscription between the rising and March 1840. The committees that organised the event and the choosing of the plate themselves included key figures in the political and industrial establishment of Monmouthshire: Phillips's replacement as mayor, Thomas Hawkins; Sir Digby Mackworth of Glen Usk, Chairman of the Newport Poor Law Union; the ironmasters Richard Blakemore, Richard Fothergill and Samuel Homfray (the latter a brother-in-law of Sir Charles Morgan); John Llewellyn, agent to Sir Benjamin Hall; the solicitor and coalowner, Phillips's former partner Thomas Prothero; and Frederick Justice, Prothero's replacement as agent to Sir Charles Morgan.[28] The meeting was held in the Newport National School, the dinner inside the Westgate Hotel, scene of the conflict the previous November.[29] Chairing it was industrialist and banker R. J. Blewitt of Llantarnam Abbey, MP for the Monmouthshire Boroughs and Deputy Lord Lieutenant of the County. In attendance were nearly one thousand of the leading citizens of Newport and district: 'one of the most numerous and fashionable audiences we have ever seen'.[30] On receiving the plate, Phillips was cheered for several minutes. After expressing his gratitude, he gave an account of the progress of Chartism during his term in office, and then asked his audience the following question:

> And as these things happened for our instruction, what is the lesson we derive from them? Do we treat them as accidental occurrences, originating in temporary feelings or causes, or do we view them as warnings, deep and loud-tongued, of dangers by which society is threatened? ... By the great bulk of the community it is believed that Chartism is at an end, because public meetings of Chartists no longer occur, and because those noisy manifestations which at one time marked the progress of Chartist agitation are no longer witnessed; but it would be a great mistake to conclude from thence that the feelings from which Chartism sprang, and by which it was nourished and grew, have experienced any essential change. Impatience of restraint -- discontent with their situation -- a jealously, almost amounting to hatred, of other men -- and a desire to accomplish, no matter by what means, great social and political changes, still animate as powerfully as they have ever done, large bodies of men in this country, and by force alone are those passions prevented from bursting forth into destructive action. ... But although force may restrain violence, and thus afford time for reflection to operate, it cannot change opinion. To influence opinion we require moral agency; and where are the moral agents, in many districts of the kingdom, by which either government or society can be defended from the dangers to which both are exposed.

Phillips noted the rapid growth of population, of urban settlements and of industry locally, but complained that 'so far from the means of sound moral and religious training for the people having kept pace with the growth of population, there are not ... any adequate means of teaching the young or old their duties to God or man'. Given 'political and sectarian divisions', Phillips believed that the state might find it very difficult to 'supply the moral void', in which case individuals had to do 'their duty': 'every man who is placed in the relation of master to others, is bound by the obligation which that relation creates, to see that all in his employment are furnished with the means to obtain sound moral and religious instruction'.

> On the one hand exists the relation of master, on the other that of servant; and that relation presupposes other duties on either side than the performance of a given quantity of work by the one, and the payment by the other of a stipulated price; and unless the moral duties which the relation creates are faithfully discharged, the future condition of this country must be a source of constant anxiety and serious apprehension.

Therefore, with 'a deep sense of duty in our own persons' and 'an abiding sympathy' for 'our poorer neighbours', Phillips asked that 'regardless of all difficulties' and 'according to the measure of our duties and resources' everyone in a position to do so should take responsibility for providing education.

Before an audience that had spent much energy in condemning the Chartists for their criminality, their irreligiosity, their low morality and the absence of any justification for their insurrection, these were striking words.[31] Phillips was throwing down the gauntlet to those who championed him as having defended them from rebellion and anarchy.[32] As Carlyle had written: 'Glasgow thuggery, Chartist torch-meetings, Birmingham riots, Swing conflagrations, are so many symptoms on the surface; you abolish the symptom to no purpose, if the disease is left untouched.'[33] Phillips reiterated his analysis in a memorial to the Lords of the Committee of Council on Education two months later, arguing that the peace of South Wales was still dependent on armed force, but that 'although such a force may restrain violence, and thus afford time for reflection to operate, it cannot influence opinion'. Moral and religious education was the only answer.[34]

If, in 1840, Phillips offered an implicit critique of the failings of local employers, by the time he wrote *Wales* nine years later he was no longer inclined to spare anyone's feelings. Great though the industrial progress of South Wales had been, 'the wealth of the capitalist has ordinarily ministered to the selfish enjoyments of the possessor'. The absence of a middle class in many industrial settlements meant that there was no 'connecting link between the employer and the employed'; employers neglected 'such moral supervision ... as might influence the character of their workmen'; and the communities were lacking in 'institutions for the relief of moral or physical destitution – whether churches, schools, almshouses, or hospitals'.[35]

> Wealth accumulated by the employer, is found by the side of destitution and suffering in the labourer -- often, no doubt, the result of intemperance and improvidence, but not seldom the effect of those calamities against which no forethought can adequately guard: and when no provision is made for the relief of physical or moral suffering, by a dedication to God's service, for the relief of His creatures, of any portion of that wealth, to the accumulation of which by the capitalist the labourer has contributed, it will be manifest that the social and political institutions of our land are exposed to trials of no ordinary severity in these new communities.[36]

The 'antagonism of interests ... between the manufacturer and the operative' was quite unlike anything seen in the past, which had been characterised by greater paternalism, and a greater sense of the mutuality of interests.[37] Phillips lambasted employers who viewed their relations with their employees as purely 'economical' and who took no responsibility for their 'moral condition' as neglecting the 'duties which man owes to his fellow'.[38]

> In our new and neglected communities, Chartism is found in its worst manifestations -- not as an adhesion to political dogmas, but as an indication of that class-antagonism which proclaims the rejection of our common Christianity, by denying the brotherhood of Christians. This antagonism originated, as great social evils ever do, in the neglect of duty by the master, or ruling class.[39]

This 'violation or neglect of duty', Phillips warned, 'works out the appropriate national or individual punishment; and those who sow the wind, will surely reap the whirlwind'.[40]

Phillips was not proposing anything other than a society that would continue to be organised along capitalist lines. He was a defender of economic competition and of free trade.[41] An advocate, indeed an example, of individual upward social mobility, he saw 'equality' as being sought 'in the advancement of the many, and not in the depression of the few'.[42] There were always likely to be rich and poor.[43] 'Labour' was certainly 'the agent of production and the handmaid of progress', yet for 'beneficial employment' it needed 'accumulated capital'.[44] But material progress was not an unalloyed good: the 'eager pursuit of wealth' could lead to 'personal indulgences' and 'a surrender of the powers of the body, and the faculties of the mind to the attainment of transient distinctions, or short-lived gratifications'.[45] 'Happiness' did not necessarily equate to 'prosperity'.[46] A balance had to be struck.

As an employer himself, Phillips felt able to preach on the duties that accompanied wealth and influence.[47] He was quite clear that 'it is the duty of an employer who draws together large masses of the people, and that, too, for his own profit and advantage – to provide, not only for the temporal and material well-being of such people, but also for their moral and spiritual necessities'.[48] All individuals were part of the organic whole that was human society: 'mutual dependence is the social tie by which men are joined together'.[49] Yet, at the same time, individuals, of whatever class, had to take responsibility for their own morality, for 'individual reformation' was 'the root and spring of social and national ameliorations'.[50] Phillips's stress on personal responsibility was paralleled by a preference for voluntarism rather than state intervention or legal regulation.[51]

Ultimately for Thomas Phillips, education was the critical issue. Through appropriate education, moral and religious as well as practical and secular, many benefits would flow. The education of the children of the working classes should be enlightened and sensitive, children being treated 'as beings to be influenced by their affections'. The improvement of moral character and the elevation of social condition was more important than what Phillips called 'mechanical teaching', designed only to increase the skill of the workman 'as a machine for the production of labour'.[52] Phillips felt that education for its own sake was for all, poor and rich, and had expressed such a view as early as 1833.[53] Of course, education could work to improve social cohesion: 'it is by intelligence alone that the classes employed in labour can learn the difficulties by which the masters are surrounded' he told Monmouthshire coalowners and ironmasters in 1857.[54] Ultimately, however, the reasoning was spiritual:

> It is wiser to rest the obligation of educating our poor on the command to employ in God's service the talents He has entrusted to our charge, and of which we are His stewards, than to regard education as the certain and ready means to secure a moral and virtuous people. The highest intellectual cultivation may co-exist with the deepest moral depravity; and no human teaching can eradicate the seeds of evil, or remove the temptations and motives to crime which misfortune, improvidence, intemperance, and evil habits, will ever prompt; but the obligation to teach the

child of poverty its duty to God and its neighbour is not affected by those human results which, in His good providence, may follow the discharge of that obligation.⁵⁵

In Thomas Phillips's views on society and the state, on capitalism and the duties of the capitalist, on the individual and education, on religious duty and on the guiding hand of Providence, it is possible to identify the common ethos of Liberal Anglicanism.⁵⁶ Liberal Anglicans distrusted the idea of progress as merely that of the development of material civilisation, preferring instead to emphasise moral and spiritual growth.⁵⁷ Inspired by a passionate concern for the moral improvement of the people, the role of education was to heal existing social and religious divisions.⁵⁸ Individual exertion was necessary to work God's purpose on earth.⁵⁹ Phillips shared these key tenets of faith and, as a London-based Welshman who maintained strong connections with Wales, he was well-placed to attempt to convert them into practical realities.

Inevitably, on leaving Newport in 1840, Phillips had cut some of his ties with the town. He ceased to act as clerk to the Newport Harbour Commission in March 1840 and he retired as a magistrate and as a town alderman in 1841.⁶⁰ He appears to have given up his house in Newport and instead based himself (with his parents) at Llanellen House, Llanellen, near Abergavenny in Monmouthshire. There he lived in a 'plain and primitive way', prizing Llanellen as a refuge from the 'hustle and excitement of the metropolis'.⁶¹ He remained on generally good terms with Sir Benjamin Hall (later Lord Llanover), whom he had served as election agent in the 1830s, and he attended the *eisteddfodau* staged by the Halls.⁶² Notwithstanding the unhappy experience of travelling with Richard Dadd, Phillips continued to take opportunities to visit Europe.⁶³

Phillips remained a coalowner. By the end of his life he owned, apart from the mines in the Sirhowy valley, concerns in the Cynon valley further west, and in the Forest of Dean.⁶⁴ He owned land in Monmouthshire and in Herefordshire, and wharves at Newport.⁶⁵ He appears to have been a benevolent employer, refusing to allow a truck shop to be established in connection with his collieries and building, in addition to a church and a school (of which more below), a lending library, a co-operative store, and establishing a sick fund.⁶⁶ He played a critical role in the rescue operation that followed the collapse of the Monmouthshire and Glamorgan Bank in 1851, and was active in helping to raise funds for the dependants of the victims of the Risca colliery explosion of 1860 in which over 140 miners had been killed.⁶⁷ He was also Deputy Lieutenant for Monmouthshire, and as such took an influential part in county business at the Court of Quarter Sessions, frequently contributing to and presiding over them.⁶⁸

Beyond his writings in defence of Wales his greatest efforts were in the overlapping spheres of religion and education. As a prominent Anglican benefactor, he built the parish church of Penmaen in 1857, near his colliery at Cwrt-y-Bella, and paid for the restoration of Llanarth parish church.[69] More significantly, he was one of the 'most able and industrious members' of the Llandaff Church Extension Society.[70] He was prepared to be highly critical of the failings of the Anglican Church in Wales, but at the same time passionately committed to its improvement.[71]

Phillips was a benefactor of both Anglican and non-denominational schools, such as Christ's College, Brecon, Howells' School for Girls, Llandaff, and National and British schools at Newport, Llanellen, and Pontygof.[72] Critical in its foundation in 1846, he served on the committee of the (Anglican) National Society in Wales and gave 'generously' to its funds from his private fortune.[73] This involved him in the foundation of Trinity College, Carmarthen, and of what became St. Mary's College, Bangor (initially established at Caernarfon). Phillips himself sent many exhibitioners to Trinity College at his own expense.[74] Notwithstanding his preference for it to be moved to Brecon, he was Sub-Visitor of St. David's College, Lampeter, from 1860 until his death.[75] Phillips was also an advocate of adult education, and acted as trustee and honorary member of the Newport Athenaeum and Mechanics Institute, and served as its president (1857-63) and vice-president (1863-7). As such he regularly chaired meetings, *eisteddfodau* and lectured on a variety of topics.[76] Phillips's most distinctive contributions to the development of education in Wales, however, were in concerns directed towards the working classes. Two stand out: his building of Cwrt-y-Bella (sometimes Court-y-bella) school, and his involvement in the Monmouthshire School Prize Association.

As already noted, Phillips had been owner of the Cwrt-y-Bella colliery from 1825. Early in 1839 he decided to build a school for the children of his workmen and building began that April.[77] Following the Newport rising, Hugh Seymour Tremenheere was given responsibility, amongst other things, for assessing the case for giving parliamentary grant-in-aid to applicants proposing to establish schools. Following up some of Tremenheere's recommendations, the Committee of Council on Education circularised twenty-nine colliery proprietors in Monmouthshire, seeking their co-operation, but only Phillips made a positive and prompt response.[78] Phillips wanted to build a school and a schoolhouse 'for the purposes of affording to the children of the poor a sound, moral, and religious education', hoping that 'the example thus set will be generally imitated by the colliery proprietors of the neighbourhood'. What was the first colliery school in Monmouthshire was opened in 1841, with half the funding having come from the Committee of Council. Workmen contributed one penny in the pound to school funds, for which their children attended free of charge. Children of parents not employed by Phillips were admitted on payment of a small weekly sum. The school could hold over three hundred children, and an adult school was held two evenings per week. The average attendance was between 100 and 150, though few adults used the evening school. Sunday School services were also held in the school, attended by about 220 children.[79] The Newport weekly newspaper, the *Monmouthshire Merlin*, hailed Phillips's efforts:

> Great praise is due to Sir Thomas Phillips ... We trust others of his opulent neighbours will imitate his example. We cannot imagine that children educated like those at Court-y-Bella, with a strong sense of duty and moral obligation, will ever descend to acts of outrage, or become the vile frequenters of the low beer shop. ... Once more we call upon the neighbouring coal proprietors not to allow the founder of Court-y-Bella School to be unaided [in] his well-planned and generous exertions for the instruction of the rising generation.[80]

Phillips was also instrumental in the creation of the Monmouthshire School Prize Association in 1857, copied from a similar scheme established at Tremenheere's bidding by the iron and coalmasters of South Staffordshire. The idea was that elementary school pupils who showed competence in reading, writing, arithmetic and religious knowledge would be rewarded. Three associations were established in South Wales, with Phillips acting as treasurer and honorary secretary in Monmouthshire, often presiding over the annual meetings.[81] More than sixty years after the scheme's establishment, one of its beneficiaries recalled that 'to be able to say that you had been to that examination was equal to saying nowadays that you had been to the University.'[82] All in all, Thomas Phillips's efforts as an educationalist won him praise from many quarters. For Jellinger Cookson Symons he was a 'truly benevolent man'; for Bishop Edward Copleston he provided a shining example with his munificence in the matters of schools and churches; for Hugh Seymour Tremenheere he was 'the most active man in South Wales in promoting all that could improve the conditions and conciliate the minds of the mining people'.[83]

Historians need to exercise caution in taking such assessments at face value. Phillips was no radical in his politics and he did not question many of the orthodox assumptions about the distribution of wealth and property in Victorian Britain. His reforming efforts were confined to a few carefully selected spheres. He inclined more to providing for the working classes than to giving them the means to determine their own destiny. Improvement and progress were conceptualised in essentially middle-class terms. However, none of this should really be surprising. Phillips was a man of his own times. If one compares him with his fellow employers and figures in authority in South Wales, he appears far more impressive than if one measures him against an anachronistic standard of democratic or even socialist values. Ivor Wilks, a historian of Welsh nationalist and socialist sympathies, has argued that Phillips saw 'the problem clearly', the problem being the high level, in industrial South Wales, of 'alienation from English institutions (of Crown, Parliament and Law)'. According to Wilks, in Wales 'the level of hegemonisation into English bourgeois values (of property, trade and empire) was lower'.[84] Viewed from this perspective then Phillips's later career was indeed an attempt to steep the working classes of industrial South Wales in 'English bourgeois values'. They appear to have been values, English or not, to which the vast majority of the Welsh people subscribed enthusiastically.

The 'clear-sighted' Phillips knew that he needed to work with the grain of the system and of conventional attitudes if he was to make a difference. As he explained to his friend Rowland Williams, 'position is the condition of influence, and very often of usefulness also in this perplexed old world in which our lot is cast'.[85] His motives we have no reason but to take in good faith: a profound religious commitment, a sense of duty and public service, appear to have been central forces in his life.[86] It is difficult to find evidence for the cynical response that his religious belief was merely a veneer applied to a secular, pragmatic, and essentially selfish set of motivations. For later generations he has been a figure whose reputation has been difficult to embrace. However, given the combination of conscientious analysis, planning, and action, by which his public life in Wales was characterised after 1840, it is possible to comprehend why, on the day of his funeral, the shops of Newport were closed in honour of 'a great man in all the walks of this life'.[87]

References

*I should like to thank Patricia Allderidge, Andy Croll, John Elliott, Jonathan Osmond, Jennifer Ridden, Miles Taylor, Olwen Williams and Siân Rhiannon Williams for their advice and encouragement, and the staff of Newport Reference Library for their unstinting assistance.

1. B[ristol] M[ercury], 16, 23 Nov. 1839; *Times*, 22 Nov., 14 Dec. 1839; M[onmouthshire] M[erlin], 23 Nov. 1839.

2. See D. Williams, *John Frost: a Study in Chartism* (Cardiff, 1939); I. Wilks, *South Wales and the Rising of 1839: Class Struggle as Armed Struggle* (London, 1984); D. J. V. Jones, *The Last Rising: The Newport Insurrection of 1839* (Oxford, 1985).

3. *BM*, 9, 30 Nov. 1839; *MM*, 23 Nov. to 7 Mar. 1840 *passim*; *Times*, 29 Nov. 1839.

4. For a detailed study of Phillips up to 1839, see C. Williams, '"The Great Hero of the Newport Rising": Thomas Phillips, Reform and Chartism', *Welsh History Review*, xxi (2003), 481-511.

5. *Times*, 18 Feb. 1840; *MM*, 12 Dec. 1840.

6. P. Allderidge, *The Late Richard Dadd, 1817-1886* (London, 1974). Shortly after their return, Dadd murdered his father. See also Sir T. Phillips, *Wales: The Language, Social Condition, Moral Character, and Religious Opinions of the People, Considered in their Relation to Education* (London, 1849), pp. 590-2.

7. S[tar of] G[went], 16 Mar. 1861; [The] L[aw] T[imes], 1, 22 June 1867; J[ournal of the] S[ociety of] A[rts], xv (1867-8), 494; *Masters of the Bench of the Hon. Society of the Inner Temple, 1450-1883, with biographical notices by J. E. Martin* (1883), i, p. 118; J. Morgan, *Four Biographical Sketches: Bishop Ollivant, Bishop Thirlwall, Rev. Griffith Jones, Vicar of Llanddowror, and Sir Thomas Phillips Q.C.* (London, 1892), pp. 171-2; *The Dictionary of Welsh Biography Down to 1940* (London, 1959), p. 762; *Dictionary of National Biography*, ed. S. Lee (London, 1896), xlv, 218; letter from Adrian Blunt, Deputy Library, The Honourable Society of the Inner Temple, 24 Mar. 1997.

8. King's College, London, In-Correspondence, 1855-65, Files P/32, P/33, P/34, P/35, P/41, P/45, P/46; *SG*, 31 Oct. 1863; *MM*, 1 June 1867; *Usk Gleaner and Monmouthshire Record*, ii (1875); W. D. Wills, 'The Established Church in the Diocese of Llandaff, 1850-70: a study of the evangelical movement in the South Wales Coalfield', *Welsh History Review*, iv (1969), 242-3.

9. R[oyal] S[ociety of] A[rts], *Minutes of Council*, xi (1860-1), 48.

10. RSA, *Minutes of Council*, x (1858-60), 137; ibid., xi (1860-1), 53; *JSA*, viii (1859-60), 623; ibid., x (1861-2), 519; D. Hudson and K. W. Luckhurst, *The Royal Society of Arts, 1754-1954* (London, 1954), p. 355.

11. RSA, *Minutes of Council*, xi (1860-1), 50, 95; J. Hollingshead, 'A Concise History of the International Exhibition of 1862', in *The Official Illustrated Catalogue of the International Exhibition*, i, 179; Sir H. T. Wood, *A History of the Royal Society of Arts* (London, 1913), p. 417.

12. Wood, *A History of the Royal Society of Arts*, p. 360. For a tribute from his successor as Chairman, William Hawes, see *JSA*, xvi (1867-8), 5: 'He was a judicious adviser and a sincere friend, and earned, by a long and consistent course, in public and in private life, the esteem and respect of all who enjoyed his friendship.'

13. *MM*, 1 June 1867; *SG*, 20 July 1867; *Gentleman's Magazine and Historical Review*, ccxxiii (July 1867), 107; J. Morgan, 'Sir Thomas Phillips', *The Red Dragon: The National Magazine of Wales*, ix (Jan. - June 1886), 320.

14. RSA, *Minutes of Council*, xi (1860-1), 32.

15. J. Wilson, *Art and Society in Newport: James Flewitt Mullock and the Victorian Achievement* (Newport, 1993), p. 35; *LT*, 22 June 1867; G. A. Williams, *When Was Wales? A History of the Welsh* (London, 1985), p. 204.

16. *LT*, 22 June 1867; *SG*, 6 July 1867. See also N[ational] L[ibrary of] W[ales], MSS 11427B, Alderman John Davies, 'Monmouthshire Worthies: paper read before the Newport Cymmrodorion Society', (n.d., prob. 1895).

17. Morgan, 'Sir Thomas Phillips', p. 321.

18. C. Williams, 'History, Heritage and Commemoration: Newport,1839-1989', *Llafur: Journal of Welsh Labour History*, vi (1992), 5-16.

19. A lifelong Whig-Liberal, he was termed a 'Conservative' by J. G. Williams, *The University Movement in Wales* (Cardiff, 1993), p. 13.

20. See Williams, 'History, Heritage and Commemoration', p. 12; and *South Wales Argus*, 2, 4, 7, 8, 9 Sept., 8 Nov. 1999.

21. Phillips, *Wales*, p. 50.

22. Ibid. For the controversy surrounding the 'Blue Books' see P. Morgan, 'From Long Knives to Blue Books', in *Welsh Society and Nationhood: Historical Essays Presented to Glanmor Williams*, ed. R. R. Davies et al. (Cardiff, 1984), pp. 199-215.

23. *Western Vindicator*, 3 Aug. 1839.4

24. For the phrase, see G. S. Kenrick, *The Population of Pontypool and the Parish of Trevethin: Situated in the So-Called 'Disturbed Districts'; Its Moral, Social, and Intellectual Character* (London, 1840).

25. For other key publications on the state of South Wales at the time, see *(inter alia)* *Minutes of the Commitee of Council on Education: With Appendices, and Plans of School Houses, 1839-40* (London, 1839-40), Appendix II: *On the State of Elementary Education in the Mining District of South Wales. Report of Mr. Seymour Tremenheere*, pp. 155-72 (henceforth *Tremenheere Report I*); E. Dowling, *The Rise and Fall of Chartism in Monmouthshire* (London, 1840); Kenrick, *The Population of Pontypool*; Parliamentary Papers 1842, xvii, Commission on the Employment and Condition of Children in Mines and Manufactories, *Report of R. H. Franks* (henceforth *Franks Report*); xxiv, Mining Commission, Monmouthshire and Breconshire, *Report of H. S. Tremenheere* (henceforth *Tremenheere Report II*); *Reports of the Commissioners of Inquiry into the state of Education in Wales*, especially parts 2 and 3 (London, 1847) (henceforth *Blue Books*); H. A. Bruce, *The Present Position and Future Prospects of the Working Classes in the Manufacturing Districts of South Wales* (Cardiff, 1851).

26. As G. T. Roberts, *The Language of the Blue Books: The Perfect Instrument of Empire* (Cardiff, 1998), p. 212, has noted, Phillips was able to write 'from the standpoint of a Welsh-speaking Welshman whose allegiance to the political and social *status quo* was beyond suspicion'. For instance, at Phillips's first address as Chairman of the Society of Arts, the proposer of the vote of thanks reminded the audience that 'it was Sir Thomas Phillips who distinguished himself in suppressing the Frost rioters at Newport some twenty years ago': *JSA*, viii (1859-60), 9.

27. Public Record Office, Home Office Letters and Papers 40/45, letter of 12 Mar. 1839.

28. *MM*, 23, 30 Nov. 1839, 21 Mar., 29 Aug., 15 Sept. 1840; *Times*, 29 Nov. 1839; M[onmouthshire] A[dvertiser and] N[ewport] M[ercantile] P[resentment], 22 Sept. 1840.

29. Initially the plan had been to hold the dinner in a marquee in Westgate Square 'on the immediate spot where the Rioters halted' (*MANMP*, 22 Sept. 1840), but it was decided that the weather was too unfavourable.

30. For the meeting, see *MM*, 26 Sept. 1840; *MANMP*, 29 Sept. 1840.

31. For such condemnation see Jones, *Last Rising*, p. 37.

32. The candelabrum that was the centrepiece of the service of silver plate had engraved, on its pedestal, five figures, representing wisdom and valour defending Britannia from rebellion and anarchy.

33. T. Carlyle, *Chartism* (London, 1839), p. 4. Phillips cited Carlyle directly in *Wales*, pp. 493-7.

34. Memorial to the Lords of the Committee of Council on Education, *Minutes of the Committee of Council*, 12 Nov. 1840, p. 16.

35. Phillips, *Wales*, p. 47.

36. Ibid., pp. 47-8.

37. Ibid., pp. 48-9.

38. Ibid., p. 49.

39. Ibid., p. 50.

40. Ibid., p. 51. See also pp. 222-7.

41. Sir T. Phillips, *The Industrial Progress of England: A Lecture* (London, 1851), pp. 46, 49-50; see also W. J. Morgan, 'County Elections in Monmouthshire, 1705-1847', *National Library of Wales Journal*, x (1957), 181.

42. Sir T. Phillips, *The Life of James Davies: A Village Schoolmaster* (London, 1850), p. 177.

43. Phillips, *Industrial Progress*, pp. 50-1. Phillips recognised, in *Wales*, p. 57, that 'but few, and those the product of peculiar native energy or great self-culture ... rise from the lowest to the highest steps of the social ladder'.

44. Phillips, *Industrial Progress*, pp. 8-9.

45. Phillips, *James Davies*, p. 179. See also *MM*, 1 Oct. 1852 for his speech at the Newport Athenaeum and Mechanics' Institute *Eisteddfod*.

46. Phillips, *Industrial Progress*, p. 48.

47. Ibid., p. 50. See also 'Paper contributed by Sir Thomas Phillips', in W. J. Copleston, *Memoir of Edward Copleston, D. D., Bishop of Llandaff, With Selections from his Diary and Correspondence* (London, 1851), p. 246.

48. *MM*, 29 Aug. 1846.

49. Phillips, *Industrial Progress*, p. 17.

50. Ibid., p. 51.

51. Phillips, *Wales*, ch. 9.

52. *Franks Report*, p. 540. He did, though, suggest that girls' education should at least include needlework, knitting and sewing. See Phillips, *Wales*, pp. 482-3.

53. *MM*, 12 Jan. 1833.

54. *SG*, 25 July 1857. See also Phillips, *Wales*, pp. x-xi, 296.

55. Phillips, *Wales*, p. 81.

56. For the influence of Thomas Arnold on Phillips, see *MM*, 1 Oct. 1852, and *JSA*, viii (1859-60), 8.

57. D. Forbes, *The Liberal Anglican Idea of History* (Cambridge, 1952), pp. 4-7.

58. Ibid., p. 118; see also R. Brent, *Liberal Anglican Politics: Whiggery, Religion, and Reform, 1830-1841* (Oxford, 1987), pp. 17-18, 57-8, 220.

59. Forbes, *Liberal Anglican Idea of History*, p. 99.

60. *MM*, 9 May 1840, 13 Nov. 1841; *The Newport Harbour Commission (founded 21 June 1836): Centenary* (Newport, 1936), p. 35.

61. *LT*, 22 June 1867; *Dictionary of National Biography*, xlv, 218; Morgan, 'Sir Thomas Phillips', p. 320; NLW Llangibby Papers MS17106D, A.242, letter to William Addams Williams, 5 July 1862.

62. Bodleian Library, Phillipps-Robinson MS, c.488, fols.220-23, letter from Sir Thomas Phillipps (of Middle Hill), 7 Mar. 1844. Phillips and Hall did not see eye-to-eye on the matter of St. David's College, Lampeter, however: see *The Life and Letters of Rowland Williams, D. D., With Extracts From His Note Book* (London, 1874), pp. 197, 207-8.

63. Bodleian Library, Phillipps-Robinson MS, c.548, fol.228, letter to Sir Thomas Phillipps (of Middle Hill), 9 Oct. 1858; Ibid., d.196, fol.32, letter to Sir Thomas Phillipps (of Middle Hill), 3 Oct. 1866.

64. *SG*, 20 July 1867.

65. *LT*, 22 June 1867; J. H. Clark, *History of Monmouthshire* (Usk, 1869), p. 196; G[went] R[ecord] O[ffice], Prothero MSS, Malpas Estate, D.501.1311.

66. *Franks Report*, p. 541; Morgan, *Four Biographical Sketches*, pp. 170-1; J. H. Morris and L. J. Williams, *The South Wales Coal Industry, 1841-1875* (Cardiff, 1958), p. 225.

67. *Times*, 6, 8, 16, 20 Oct., 3, 7 Nov. 1851; GRO, M000545, M000546, Monmouthshire and Glamorgan Banking Company: Settlement Indenture 1851; *MM*, Oct. 1851 - Jan. 1852, *passim*; *SG*, 29 Dec. 1860, 6 July 1867; NLW Llangibby MS17106D, A.238, letter to William Addams Williams, 26 Feb. 1862; *Usk Gleaner and Monmouthshire Record*, iii (1875); Morris and Williams, *South Wales Coal Industry*, pp. 144-5; Cefni Barnett, 'Bankrupt banks', *Presenting Monmouthshire*, xviii (1964), 19-21.

68. See, for example, *SG*, 31 Jan., 24 Oct. 1857, 9 Jan. 1858, 8 Jan. 1859, 5 Jan. 1861, 18 Oct. 1862, 28 Mar., 4 July, 24 Oct. 1863, 9 Jan., 19 Mar., 2 July 1864, 1 July 1865, 24 Mar. 1866, 5 Jan., 23 Mar. 1867; *South Wales Times*, 23 Oct. 1858; Morgan, *Four Biographical Sketches*, pp. 173-4.

69. *The Church Builder: A Quarterly Journal of Church Extension in England and Wales*, xxiii (July 1867), 119-20; Rev. W. A. Evans, 'Sir Thomas Phillips, of Llanellen, Monmouthshire (1801-1867)', *Presenting Monmouthshire*, xv (1963), 45; *Monmouthshire: A Green and Smiling Land*, ed. A. Mee (London, 1951), p. 59.

70. Wills, 'The Established Church in the Diocese of Llandaff', pp. 242-3, 266.

71. See particularly Phillips, *Wales*, ch. 6, and 'Paper contributed by Sir Thomas Phillips', p. 250.

72. *MM*, 12 Jan. 1833; NLW, Tredegar Estate Papers, Box 57/250, 279, letters of 5, 4 May 1841; Morgan, 'Sir Thomas Phillips', p. 319; *Kelly's Directory of Monmouthshire*, 1901; Mee, *Monmouthshire*, p. 62; Evans, 'Sir Thomas Phillips', p. 45; L.W. Evans, *Education in Industrial Wales, 1790-1900: A Study of the Works Schools System in Wales during the Industrial Revolution* (Cardiff, 1971), p. 176.

73. *Report from Select Committee on Education* (1866), pp. 268-81; Appendix 4, p. 312; Morgan, 'Sir Thomas Phillips', p. 319; Davies, *Monmouthshire Schools*, p. 100; Evans, *Education in Industrial Wales*, p. 177.

74. Phillips, *Wales*, pp. 416-20, 481; Morgan, *Four Biographical Sketches*, p. 176; E. T. Davies, *Monmouthshire Schools and Education to 1870* (Newport, 1957), p. 87; F. Smith, *The Life and Work of Sir James Kay-Shuttleworth* (Bath, 1974 edition), p. 203; H. G. Williams, 'Longueville Jones and Welsh Education: The Neglected Case of a Victorian H.M.I.', *Welsh History Review*, xv (1991), 416-20.

75. *Life and Letters of Rowland Williams*, pp. 157-9, 164, 188, 206-8, 228-9; D. T. W. Price, *A History of St. David's University College Lampeter, vol. 1: to 1898* (Cardiff, 1977), pp. 74, 91, 94, 204.

76. *MM*, 9 June 1849, 20 Apr. 1850, 1 Oct. 1852, 5 Apr. 1856; *Illustrated London News*, 2 Oct. 1852; *SG*, 18, 25 Apr., 24 Oct. 1857, 17, 24 Apr., 23, 30 Oct. 1858, 22 Oct. 1859, 5 May 1860, 27 Apr. 1861, 26 Apr. 1862, 25 Apr. 1863, 23 Apr., 22 Oct. 1864, 22 Apr. 1865, 13 July 1867; *Rules and Regulations of Newport Athenaeum and Mechanics' Institute, Great Dock Street, Newport, 1859* (Newport, 1859), p. 10; *Newport Athenaeum and Mechanics' Institute Monthly Journal*, ii, 17 (May 1865); *Newport Gazette*, 1 June 1867.

77. Davies, *Monmouthshire Schools*, pp. 109-10.

78. For general comment see R. Johnson, 'Educational Policy and Social Control in Early Victorian England', *Past and Present*, xlix (1970), 98-9.

79. *Tremenheere Report I*; Minutes of the Committee of Council on Education, 1840-1, p. 15, Appendix II: Statistics of Applications for Aid from the Parliamentary Grant, pp. 48-9; Memorial to the Lords of the Committee of Council on Education; *MM*, 29 Aug. 1846; Report of the Commissioner Appointed under the provisions of the Act 5 & 6 Vict., c99, to Inquire Into The Operation of That Act, And Into The State of the Population in The Mining Districts, 1846, p. 34; *Blue Books*, Part II, pp. 280, 285; Davies, *Monmouthshire Schools*, pp. 94-5; E.L. and O. P. Edmonds, *I Was There: The Memoirs of H. S. Tremenheere* (Eton, 1965), p. 37; Evans, *Education in Industrial Wales*, pp. 174-6; D. C. James, 'Hugh Seymour Tremenheere and Educational Provision in South Wales, 1839-1861' (University of Wales, M.Ed., 1977), pp. 4-6, 74, 85.

80. *MM*, 24 Aug. 1844. The school closed in 1901 and was demolished in 1949.

81. *SG*, 25 July 1857, 14 Aug. 1858, 20 Aug. 1859, 10 Aug. 1861, 9 Aug. 1862, 1 Aug. 1863, 30 July 1864, 5 Aug. 1865; *Newport Gazette*, 1 June 1867; James, 'Hugh Seymour Tremenheere', pp. 66-74, 84.

82. Councillor Alfred Jones of Ebbw Vale, writing in the *Ebbw Valley Weekly News and West Monmouthshire Advertiser,* 19 Sept. 1919.

83. *Blue Books*, Part II, p. 285; Copleston, *Memoir of Edward Copleston*, pp. 200-202; Edmonds, *I Was There*, p. 39. Such views have generally been echoed by Welsh educational historians: see Davies, *Monmouthshire Schools*, pp. 94-5; Evans, *Education in Industrial Wales*, p. 174.

84. Wilks, *South Wales and the Rising of 1839*, pp. 236-7.

85. *Life and Letters of Rowland Williams*, pp. 260-1.

86. Brent, *Liberal Anglican Politics*, pp. 104-5.

87. *SG*, 8 June 1867.

Chapter 4

Reform as Process: The Parliamentary Fate of the Bank Charter Act of 1844

Reform is a process, not a moment.[1] The process of entrenching the currency principle into the management of the Bank of England extended beyond the passing of Peel's Bank Charter Act of 1844. Despite the conventional representation of 1844 as a revolutionary moment, at which the currency school – banking school controversy was resolved, the parliamentary history of the Act reveals sustained opposition to the principle and its implications for the management of the Bank of England. That the Act survived the scrutiny of select committees in the late 1840s and 1850s has been misinterpreted as indicative of parliamentary acquiescence.

Select committees were not fora of objective investigation established with the purpose of seeking to determine the truth of the subject at hand. Their primary purpose was to remove the subject from public parliamentary discussion to the more private confines of the committee rooms. In the case of the committees pertaining to the Act, the appointment of the committee also delayed discussion of currency issues until such time as the economy had recovered from the financial panics of 1847 and 1857. By selecting a majority of MPs and witnesses known to be in favour of the legislation, a report endorsing the Act was guaranteed. The appointment of a committee thus allowed for the representation of the government's endorsement of the Act as arising from laboured, objective consideration rather than political bias. By controlling the representation of economic phenomena, the currency principle and the Bank Charter Act could be represented as the optimal form of currency management.

The purpose of this essay is to reconstruct the parliamentary validation of the Bank Charter Act prior to and following its suspension in October 1847. The discussion of the Act in 1847 and 1848 was conducted along party lines; and a parliamentary majority was used to preserve it.

Parliamentary discussion of the Bank Charter Act and the currency principle resumed within the context of the Whig government's distribution of the Irish loan.

On 26 April 1847, debate over the proposed loan of £620,000 to three Irish railways – Great South Western Railway, Waterford and Kilkenny Railway, Dublin and Drogheda Railway – intended to maintain employment and enhance Irish productivity, provided the opportunity to initiate discussion of the monetary pressure and the ramifications of the government proposal. Between January and April 1847, large corn imports had been paid for by substantial net exports of bullion.[2] Despite reserves declining by £6.2 million between 23 January and 10 April, the Bank held its rate constant at 4 per cent. The rate of interest in New York increased in this period, inducing a speculative outflow and further depleting the Bank's reserve. The need to accommodate the government with deficiency bills in late April forced the Bank to borrow on the market, restrict its discounting severely, and raise the rate to 5 per cent. This prompted a number of failures in the north, primarily of firms engaged in the East India trade.

For the first time, discussion of the Act and the currency principle pertained to current events and the impact of decisions made by real economic agents, rather than the hypothetical expositions of the functioning of an abstract, self-regulating machine. The debate was dominated by the criticisms of Bentinck, Spooner, Newdegate, Hume, Muntz and Cayley, with Wood and Peel leading the defence of the government and the Act. Party divisions were obvious. Concern over the wisdom of the timing of the loan, its potential effectiveness, and the appropriateness of the government effectively competing with the money market by loaning funds to the companies was supplanted by debate over the purpose of the Act and its relation to the current state of the market. Opponents of the government had four main criticisms of the Act: its theoretical basis, that it failed to meet its practical objectives, the role of the Banking department proscribed by the Act, and how the relationship between the Bank and the government influenced current market conditions.

As the debate continued, two versions of the state of the money market came to be defined. That presented by supporters of the government also defended the Act by taking its operation for granted. The increase in interest rates arising from the limits on note issue were treated as its natural consequences. Wood chose to minimise the extent of the market distress. Such problems as were conceded were blamed on overtrading and on the mismanagement of the banking department of the Bank by its directors.[3] Peel's strategy to defend the Act centred upon denying that it was ever the intent of the Act to prevent such market conditions.[4] The preservation of convertibility was its sole object. It was not intended to relieve the Bank of responsibility towards the public, or to teach people to be cautious. The Act and the concept of the self-regulating principle pertained only to the issue department. By defining the purpose of the Act narrowly, and the duties of the Bank broadly, Peel could exonerate the former whilst blaming the latter. It was not the rationality of the system that created problems, rather the irrationality of individual agents within the system. Therefore, a suspension of the Act could not solve the problem, and would only depreciate the currency.

In contrast, Cayley argued that the market problems were severe, and had been caused by the Act's restrictions on note issue. The publication of declining reserves had served to demonstrate the Bank's inability to accommodate customers under the new regime and inspired panic and hoarding.[5] This reduced the supply of funds to the discount market and intensified the upward pressure on interest rates. The transmission of information that was theoretically necessary to make the Act work was shown to undermine confidence and stability. This prevented his adversaries from directly engaging in debate over the causes of the distress, as to criticise the effectiveness of the signalling function of the published accounts would be to concede a weakness in the Act's potential efficacy.

Richard Spooner addressed the socio-political consequences of adhering to the Act.[6] First, the assistance recently given to the Bank by the 'ambitious' Russian Emperor was cited as evidence of the vulnerability of the nation under the existing currency regime. Deposits made could as quickly be withdrawn, allowing a foreign government to threaten the nation without the burden of raising an army. Second, he warned that the shortage of money had led manufacturers to suspend orders, as they feared that they would be unable to find money with which to pay their workers. This decline in production implied that more gold would have to leave the country, as imports would not be paid for with goods. Maintaining a currency system that would seek to keep gold in the country would deter the import of enough corn to feed the people and risk social unrest.

The speeches of Cayley and Spooner (and of the Act's opponents generally) sought to represent the options available as limited to either abandoning the Act or destroying market stability, starving the people, and falling prey to the whims of foreign governments. In their arguments, Irish hunger was caused by the Act, not by a potato blight, and market conditions were caused by the Act's institutional arrangements, not by the actions of people within the system. By associating the repeal of the Act with other political issues, they could create an identity of interests with other politicians, and gain support in the House for their position.

The pressure continued, and deputations approached the government seeking the suspension or repeal of the Act. The Act's opponents prepared to continue their fight, with Joseph Hume seeking information from the Governor of the Bank with which to defend the Bank's management. The Governor maintained his loyalty to the Government and the Act by declining to provide information, and warned Wood of Hume's request. Wood remained in frequent contact with the Governor regarding the state of the market, and with Russell's consent sought the counsel of Peel. Wood had also been informed that the belief that the government would suspend was sustaining the pressure, as borrowers were not decreasing their engagements in anticipation of continuing pressure and high rates. A public declaration of the government's intention to uphold the Act was necessary.[7] On 7 May, Wood announced a plan to restore market order.[8] The government would not suspend or repeal, but would increase the rate of interest on Exchequer bills and offer an inducement to the contributors of the Irish loan to pay in their instalments early. The details of the plan were announced three days later. The new issue of Exchequer bills was to pay 3 per cent interest. Contributors to the loan would receive higher interest by way of discount for paying prior to June 18, the day of bill exchange.

Wood's formal statement of the particulars of the inducement were prefaced by an explanation of how it and the increased rate of interest on the Exchequer bills would both alleviate the distress in the money market and improve the government's credit. Wood now listed the cause of the alarm as the withdrawal of funds from the discount market in response to the earlier alarm, and claimed his plan would release these hoards. The provincial merchants and manufacturers, he reported, were unable to carry out their business as they could not have bills discounted by their banks, as the banks were unable to rediscount in London. A substantial reduction in the amount of funds available for use in discounting had been withdrawn in order to make advances on railway shares. The increased practice of placing money at call with London bill brokers instead of investing in securities had earlier led to an increase in the amount of bills discounted and rediscounted. However, the alarm motivated the lenders to recall their monies, causing a further reduction in funds available for discount and increasing the market pressure. This recall was enhanced by the unsalability of Exchequer bills rendering recall the only means of raising cash. The increase in interest on Exchequer bills would restore their market and allow the withdrawn call money to be returned to the discount market. The second aspect of this plan, the inducement to early payment of instalments of the loan, would provide the funds necessary to pay the increased interest on Exchequer bills without the assistance of the Bank of England.

Wood then defended the government's practice of receiving assistance from the Bank. He denied (correctly) that it had been expected that the passing of the Act would mark the end of this practice.[9] The equalisation of the dividend payments across the four quarters had been intended to minimise the demands upon the Bank. That these demands were easily foreseen would allow the Bank to adjust their business accordingly. Wood's defence thus tacitly underscored his earlier blame of the Bank's management for the current alarm while neglecting to admit that the restraints of the Act would exacerbate the influence of such assistance on markets. The plan and his representation of the distress tacitly took the Act's influence on institutional arrangements for granted. At no point was the contingency and changeability of these arrangements acknowledged, nor was it explicitly mentioned that his plan amounted to an attempt to manipulate market behaviour in order to save the Act. For Cayley, the central problem was that the Act's limits on note issue had inspired a cycle of hoarding and distress that could only be broken by suspending the Act. In Wood's view, the central problem was the illiquidity of Exchequer bills motivating the withdrawal of call money, with the obvious solution being the restoration of the market for the bills. Rather than intervening by allowing the Bank to increase its issue, intervention was to originate in the Exchequer's policies. What was an equally conscious attempt to manipulate market conditions in response to the result of the interaction between the limits on note issue and other economic conditions was thus represented as mere Exchequer policy: a matter of government finance, rather than a concession to the weakness of the existing system and legislation. It is also worth noting that Wood did not publicly acknowledge the existence of problems in the market until he had prepared a plan by which to restore order.

Hume, Newdegate, and Bentinck aggressively attacked the plan, and Wood's defence of the government's reliance on the Bank for assistance. Hume facetiously defended the Bank's behaviour as merely the logical, profit maximising conduct implied by the Act, while claiming that in 1844 it was understood that the Bank would no longer be called upon to make advances to help the government meet dividend payments.[10] Sound management on the part of the Exchequer should be enough to ensure payment. Newdegate echoed Hume's 'approval' of the Bank's management, and declared the existing currency system incompatible with free trade.[11] The failure of the system, and of the concept of the self-acting principle, was evidenced by the government's need to have the Bank intervene through the banking department in order to support the currency.

Bentinck used the market problems as an opportunity to attack free trade.[12] The government's plan to stabilise the market could work only temporarily, he argued, as the combination of free trade and the currency principle would eventually lead to the collapse of the Bank. The poor cotton crop and resultant decrease in cotton imports and manufacturing implied that the increased corn imports would need to be paid for in bullion rather than goods. There was little hope of a reduction in the tariffs faced by British manufacturers in America while the Mexican war continued; and the Prussian and Russian tariffs were equally unlikely to change. The necessary export of bullion and resultant increase in discount rates would not – as the Act's creators claimed – merely punish overspeculators. The increase in rates would fall upon all industries, leading to a further decrease in production and the bankruptcy of solvent houses. He concluded by proposing that the Act be suspended.

The calmness of the markets throughout the summer appears not to have placated the Act's critics. The City interest prepared a petition opposing the Act, while Bentinck's correspondence reveals the existence of organised opposition to the Act.[13] Cobden and the Anti Corn Law League were apparently involved, leading Bentinck to believe that the Act would be brought down and Peel's reputation ruined.

The calm gave way. As it became apparent that harvests were good and that large imports would not be necessary to meet the demand, the corn houses and their creditors began to fail and confidence declined. By late September the Bank was forced to increase its interest rate to 6 per cent and to refuse advances on Exchequer bills. The cash shortage led to a large selling of stocks and commodities, driving down their prices. Failures of banks and other credit institutions left the Bank as one of the few suppliers of money. The early failures included that of Robinson, the Bank of England's Governor. This necessitated his replacement (with James Morris), and raised concerns about the stability of management at the Bank. Peel and Wood again mooted the prospect of making the governorship a permanent post.[14] As in 1844, the same problems remained: the means of selecting a governor, and whether or not public support existed for the idea. The imperfection of the current system was, however, openly acknowledged between them.

As the problems increased, politicians and Bank directors discussed amongst themselves the best course of action to take. As early as 5 October, Wood solicited F. T. Baring's advice about the possibility of suspending the Act. Wood also claimed to be at a loss over whom to trust in such matters.[15] While he valued the judgement of Thomas Baring, he knew him to have always opposed the Act. He was similarly concerned that the advice of Loyd and Norman was biased in the opposite direction.

By mid-October, it was becoming increasingly obvious that something would have to be done. Correspondence between Wood and the Bank continued, and more deputations were received requesting the Act's suspension. All involved, including Loyd, began to believe that a suspension of the Act was inevitable.[16] The crisis culminated on 24 October. At a cabinet meeting attended by Loyd and Norman, the decision was taken by Russell and Wood to write a letter authorising the Bank to issue notes against securities in excess of the £14 million limit, at a rate of interest of no less than 8 per cent. For the Bank to violate the restrictive clause of its charter would require a bill of indemnity. Thus Parliament was reconvened.

The resolution to appoint a select committee was introduced by Wood on 30 November. He began his speech by defending the Act and the principle against the charge that the suspension had proven them invalid.[17] The problem that had led to the suspension was the irrationality of borrowers' hoarding, not other underlying economic conditions. Loyd and Huskisson were quoted as having earlier written that such hoarding could be anticipated. Thus Wood identified suspension as part of the currency school's theory, representing it as consistent with their views, rather than as a concession to the discretionary issue advocated by the banking school. His account of the events of 1847 emphasised the Bank's mismanagement, railway investment, and the unsound credit practices of the East India merchants as destabilising factors.

James Wilson spoke critically of the Act and the government's representation of the causes of the crisis.[18] In response to the government's attempts to minimise the claims that the Act would deter speculation, Wilson cited Loyd and Torrens as having stated in 1844 that it would. He further argued the Act had in fact increased speculation, as those who had fallen during the panic had believed that the self-acting principle would prevent the 'revulsions' of previous times and therefore did not decrease their borrowing. Wilson also denied the desirability and possibility of the

Bank regulating the currency according to the foreign exchanges: currency should serve the needs of trade, while the Bank operations that were said to regulate the currency affected only deposits and reserves leaving notes in the hands of the public unchanged. If notes were taken out of circulation, they would be replaced by cheques. Wilson argued that the underlying problem with currency school theory was its emphasis on currency rather than capital, as represented by the deposits in the Bank of England. The Act's theoretical basis was unsound.

Thomas Baring and Cayley blamed government policy for contributing to the crisis. The overtrading that Wood had cited as a cause of the crisis was, Baring argued, also undertaken by the government, as the Exchequer's need to borrow from the Bank in April could be described.[19] Furthermore, the 'overtrading' undertaken by importers of corn and colonial produce had been undertaken at the suggestion of the government and facilitated by their decisions to alter the corn and navigation laws. To this Cayley added that the speculation in railways persisted because of Peel's rejection of Lord Dalhousie's recommendations of greater governmental involvement in the planning of railway construction. The government's own policies were at odds with the Act.

Cayley continued his attack on the government by refuting Wood's account of the causes of the panic. First, he argued that railway investment had not caused a deficiency of capital. Railway construction did not involve a conversion of floating capital to fixed.[20] The floating capital was merely transferred from the company to those that constructed the railway, and it was labour that was fixed within the railway. Had railways taken capital from manufacturing, then the quantity of goods produced would have decreased and prices increased. Cayley argued that the collapse in prices observed over the last year implied that there had been no decrease in production arising from a shortage of capital.

An alternative account of the events of the previous year was then presented, in which the primary cause of the crises of April and October was the loss of public confidence in the ability of the Bank of England to support the system. Cayley did not alter his views on the panic of the spring. The accommodation of the Exchequer, not the export of bullion to pay for corn, had dangerously reduced the Bank's reserves. The public's learning that the Bank was forced to borrow had destroyed confidence in the Bank's ability to support mercantile credit and caused panic. In May, the drain and the panic were subsiding, but the prediction of a good harvest led to a collapse of corn prices over the summer. The good weather thereby caused the failure of the corn houses. As confidence had not yet been restored, bills of exchange, accounting for, Cayley claimed, eight tenths of the nation's 'circulating medium' became unsalable and bank notes were hoarded in anticipation of future contingencies.

In mid-December, the selection of committee members led to further parliamentary discord. Two themes dominated the debates: the motives for the government's examination of the topic by a committee, and the biases of those members chosen to sit. Opponents of the government stated their belief that the appointment of the committee was merely an attempt to remove the discussion of the crisis and the currency from the public domain.[21] Bentinck and Cayley claimed that the government had deliberately weighted the committee with supporters of the Act. Bentinck noted that the committee did not include any MPs who had voted against the Act in 1844. He further argued that it lacked representation from important interests, such as the Scottish commercial community, and accused the government of excluding Muntz because of the 'shrewdness with which he can cross-examine a bullionist theorist'.[22] Cayley claimed that the government had constructed the committee so as to render the question one of party.[23] Twelve or thirteen members were in favour of the government; six or seven were Peelites, while only six were Protectionists. Wood defended the objectivity of the committee, saying that of the twenty-five, nine were likely to be in favour of the Act (himself, Peel, Russell, Goulburn, Labouchere, Graham, Cardwell, Ricardo, Clay), ten were likely to oppose (Bentinck, Herries, Thompson, Thomas Baring, Spooner, Cayley, Hudson, Hume, Wilson), and six had not previously expressed any opinion (Cobden, Beckett, Glynn, Thornely, Home Drummond, Tennent).[24] Wood ignored the support that he was likely to receive from Cobden, as the Manchester Chamber of Commerce had approved of the Act in 1844. Beckett and Home Drummond were also identified with the Peelites, and unlikely to oppose the Act. Whilst Wilson's opposition to the Act was well known, so was his support for free trade. He had just begun his parliamentary career as a Liberal. It was unlikely that he had been asked to stand without first agreeing to support the government on the currency question. The potential for party interests to determine the outcome was certainly present. That the debate had thus far revealed adherence to party interest suggested that Cayley was right.

In the months between the appointment of the committee and its first meeting, the politicians corresponded on how best to ensure that their views would prevail. Wood and F. T. Baring strategised as to the best order in which to have witnesses appear, with Wood expressing concern as to the impact of the opposition witnesses testifying first.[25] Bentinck received advice from Henry Burgess about manipulating the outcome by introducing evidence about the Bank's assistance to the Union Bank of Newcastle at the prompting of Wood, which he felt would be enough to discredit the man and the Act.[26] This correspondence reveals the politicians' appreciation for the importance of matters other than the objective evaluation of evidence to their success.

The committee met twenty times between February and May. Seventeen witnesses were examined, of whom four were involved with the management of the Bank (John Horsely Palmer, William Cotton, James Morris, and Henry James Prescott), four were merchants and manufacturers (Charles Turner, Thomas Clutton Salt, P. H. Muntz, Robert Gardner), six were engaged in finance (Adam Hodgson, Samuel Gurney, Robert C. L. Bevan, Joshua Bates, Joseph Pease, Thomas Birkbeck). Lord

Loyd, Thomas Tooke, and John Taylor were called to testify before the committee as political economists. The relationships between witnesses and committee members were not mentioned in the sessions, thus preserving the image of objectivity. Joseph Pease identified himself to the committee as not being connected with any bank – 'acting treasurer of some considerable railway companies, but not taking out a licence as a banker' – although all present knew of his background as a banker and railway entrepreneur.[27] Similarly, P. H. Muntz described himself as a general merchant, while all present knew that as a member of the Birmingham Political Union and brother of G. F. Muntz, he had long opposed the Act.[28] That such statements went unchallenged is suggestive of the extreme influence of gentlemanly norms of conduct over the proceedings. As in the parliamentary debates, party interests were reflected in the questioning of witnesses. Whig and Peelite members asked questions leading witnesses to give answers supporting the Act and Wood's interpretation of the events of the previous year. Protectionist and Radical members sought to elicit evidence in support of their arguments.

The committee had been declared a committee of secrecy. The minutes of the evidence would not be released, only the report. This was a well-known strategy of concealment, allowing the prevailing faction to prevent opponents from demonstrating inconsistencies between the report and the evidence. The assumption that the government had adopted this strategy prompted one witness, Thomas Clutton Salt, to publish a pamphlet before the committee had completed its deliberations.[29] A Birmingham lamp manufacturer, Salt had long been a leading member of the Birmingham Political Union. Like Attwood, P. H. Muntz, and G. F. Muntz, he endorsed a paper currency.[30] Salt prefaced his pamphlet with the claim that the committee had been rendered one of secrecy in order to 'delude the operatives'.[31] Whilst claiming to be a transcript of his evidence before the committee, the pamphlet was in fact a restatement of his arguments that the distress had been caused by the Act and the gold standard. He advocated, not surprisingly, a return to a paper currency, and suggested that the ensuing stability and prosperity would neutralise 'all calls for such organic changes as those sought by the Chartists, by leaguers, and by Repealers'.[32] Like Spooner, he associated paper currency with social stability.

From the testimony of the witnesses, two distinct lines of argument may be discerned. The supporters of the Act – Loyd, Morris, Prescott, and Cotton – described the events of the previous years and the functioning of the Act in terms consistent with currency school theory, taking the consequences of the Act for granted. The problems in the money market were minimised, to the point of denying the existence of any serious threat to convertibility. Such problems as were acknowledged were blamed on poor management on the part of the Bank or overtrading on the part of investors. The people had not responded rationally to the conditions created by the Act.

The Act's detractors, led by the questions of like-minded parliamentarians, presented a fundamentally different view of the economy and of the Act's efficacy in maintaining stability. Therein, the Act was described as distorting the system by placing unnecessary and damaging limits on the Bank's ability to issue that were incompatible with the motivations and needs of borrowers. The lack of discretionary note issue had created conflicts of interest between the Bank's obligations to the government, the public, and its proprietors. This was observed in the cheapening of money immediately after the passing of the Act. The expansion of its discount activities in order to maximise profit for its proprietors had suited the interests of the merchants who constituted the Court of Directors. The April pressure arose from the need to fulfil its duties to the government (the Irish loan, deficiency bills, payment of dividends) whilst being unable to accommodate the public with discretionary note issue.

The lack of discretionary note issue was also incompatible with the functioning of commodity markets. The term structure of debt and anticipated profit margins implied that the demand for money was interest-rate inelastic, in direct contrast to currency school reasoning. The consequences of this theoretical shortcoming were most readily apparent in the corn market. The increase in Bank rate brought about by the need to import corn did nothing to decrease borrowing for the purposes of import. Nor was it desirable that the rate increase should have such an effect. The magnitude of the bullion efflux had been increased by the relaxation of the corn laws. Peel's greatest legislative achievements were therefore incompatible. Furthermore, the rate increases created by the currency rule, or the promise thereof as indicated by the publication of accounts, would not have the stabilising effect promised by the Act's supporters.

In fact, the transmission of such information, combined with the knowledge of the Bank's inability to issue at its discretion, had inspired hoarding. This had turned the pressure arising from the autumn corn failures into a panic. That market order had been restored by the suspension of the Act proved the necessity of allowing the Bank to function at its discretion. Such evidence should have been enough to convince the committee that the Act could not deliver the stability it had promised.

To be sure, the criticisms of the role of the Bank may be interpreted as a vaguely dishonest attempt to discredit the Act. Bank intervention in the economy, to assist government or industry, was by no means anathema to the banking school. The ultimate object of these criticisms was to oppose the limits on note issue. It was the interplay of these interests and the limits on note issue that were represented as detrimental to stability and equity. In the critics' view, the Bank and currency should adjust to the economy; the Act's supporters continued to argue the opposite.

The process of preparing the report involved the collision of these conflicting views. Meeting over five days, the committee members debated the final version of the committee's conclusions. Charles Wood, Edward Cayley, and Richard Spooner, each prepared alternative versions for the approval of the committee. The Cayley and Spooner versions, condemning the Act, were rejected. Cayley had argued that the Act had either caused or exacerbated the crisis: the need to import food did not imply that a monetary crisis was inevitable, railway investment had caused no capital shortages, and stability, confidence, and prosperity could not be maintained under the existing legislation. Spooner also blamed the Act for the crisis, and advocated the introduction of 'National Paper Money' for domestic use and a 'Mint Bank' to accommodate foreign trade.[33]

It was Wood's version that formed the basis of the report that was eventually submitted for the consideration of Parliament. Committee members were required to vote their approval of each paragraph, and from the minutes of this part of the committee meetings one finds evidence of distinct factionalisation between committee members. Consistently supporting the views of Wood were Peel, Graham, Cobden, Herries, Beckett, Goulburn, Cardwell, Labouchere, Ricardo, Thornely, Wilson, Clay, and Home Drummond. Those generally in opposition were Bentinck, Thomas Baring, Disraeli, Spooner, Herries, Thompson, Hudson, Cayley, Hume, and Glyn. Thus these factions confirmed the suspicions expressed earlier by Cayley, that the committee was weighted in favour of the Act's supporters and that party interests abounded.

Wood's (brief) report presented a selective view of the evidence that absolved the Act of causing or exacerbating the problems of 1847.[34] The April pressure was blamed on the management of the Bank. The October distress, it was claimed, was caused by the deficient harvest and the subsequent need to export gold to import food. Secondary causes included the deficient supply of cotton, the diversion of capital into railway construction, over-trading in the East India trade, and 'exaggerated expectations of enlarged trade.' The report acknowledged the Bank's special position in the economy, but denied the existence of any conflict of interest between the Bank's proprietors and the public. The suspension of the Act was deemed a success in restoring order to markets, but it was labelled impossible to give a relaxing power to the government, as the enumeration of the circumstances that would justify relaxation was impossible. Tellingly, no mention was made of any suggestion to give the Bank such a power.

Voting on the paragraphs of the report took place over three days. Hume, Herries, Spooner, Cayley and Disraeli proposed amendments to the report which would have fundamentally altered its meaning. Herries was the most aggressive, suggesting that Wood's report be replaced with a declaration that Wood's version was not in accordance with the evidence received by the committee.[35] Resolutions claiming that the report did not reflect the evidence were also put forth by Cayley and Spooner.[36] Cayley also vainly attempted to have a clause inserted blaming the East India failures on 'Acts of the Legislature, which had so depressed the price of Colonial produce, and with it the value of property in part of our Eastern possessions, that the East India Houses were disabled from sustaining the monetary pressure of 1847.' Disraeli also set forth a resolution may be interpreted as an attack on free trade: 'that in consequence of the habitual over-trading of this country, it is not expedient to pass any further laws to stimulate commercial enterprise.'[37] The majority of the committee members being in favour of the Act precluded the inclusion of such resolutions.

The committee was reconvened in order to examine the distress in Scotland and Ireland, and the effects of the Acts of 1845 thereupon. Meeting on seven occasions between 20 June and 18 July, the committee heard testimony from five Scottish and two Irish witnesses. Five were bankers (James Andrew Anderson, managing director of the Union Bank of Glasgow; John McDonnell, Governor of the Bank of Ireland; Robert Murray, director of the Provincial Bank of Ireland; Robert Bell, manager of the City of Glasgow Bank; James Bristow, managing director of the Northern Bank of Ireland), whilst two were representing the views of the Edinburgh and Glasgow Chambers of Commerce (J. F. MacFarlan and John G. Kinnear, respectively). Questioning was largely confined to the impact of the Acts in Scotland and Ireland, and was primarily concerned with the bullion reserve requirements and the prevention of new banks of issue.

All witnesses agreed that the bullion efflux arising from the need to import corn had been the primary cause of the pressure. Two witnesses – Kinnear and Murray – cited the impact of railway investment in withdrawing funds from commercial purposes as a secondary cause. All but three members (McDonnell, Bristow, and McFarlan) cited speculation, particularly in railways, as a secondary cause. Only the Irish witnesses endorsed the Acts of 1844 and 1845. Of the Scottish witnesses, only Bell felt that the Acts of 1844 and 1845 had aggravated the panic. The remainder believed that only the Act of 1844 had aggravated the panic, by forcing up interest rates.[38]

The committee heard mixed opinions as to the expediency of the clause that prohibited the establishment of new banks of issue. Both of the Irish witnesses agreed that it had been beneficial. Murray claimed that it had succeeded in discouraging banks from issuing their own notes, while Bristow claimed that new banks would have led to wasteful competitive practices. Only one of the Scottish bankers, Robert Bell, advocated the restriction, claiming that it had prevented the creation of banks that would have surely contributed to the speculation of the previous years. Kinnear and Anderson felt it unnecessary. The secretaries of the chambers of commerce also disapproved, with MacFarlan claiming that giving the existing banks a monopoly had led them to impose new transactions costs on customers, and Kinnear arguing that the impossibility of over issuing notes rendered the restriction unnecessary.[39]

There were also differences of opinion as to the consequences of the bullion reserve requirements introduced by the Acts. McFarlan told the committee that the costs of holding the bullion had been passed on to the consumer in the form of higher discount rates. Bell claimed that the costly reserves did nothing to increase the public's confidence in convertibility, as a run would inevitably be initiated by deposit, not note holders. To this Anderson added that the withdrawal would be from London, not Scotland. The gold was therefore of no use in Scotland, and could better serve the needs of the system if held in the Bank of England.[40]

As in the earlier committee, the members convened to vote on the report to be submitted to parliament. Wood's proposed report was extremely brief, only six sentences.[41] Wood made no attempt to discuss the contents of the evidence, stating quite dishonestly that in the opinion of the witnesses, the Acts of 1845 had produced 'no material effect'. He declined to relate their views on the Act of 1844, stating that the committee had already expressed their views on the subject.

Spooner proposed nine resolutions in response to Wood's report.[42] He claimed that the Scottish witnesses claimed that the Act had aggravated the monetary pressure, that the gold held in Scotland was unnecessary and of better use in London. The legislation had increased costs to the public through increased discount rates and transactions costs. The confidence needed to return Glasgow and Edinburgh to prosperity would not be restored until the Acts of 1844 and 1845 were repealed. The Irish witnesses were cited as having approved of the restriction of new banks of issue, but Spooner noted that all had testified as to the necessity of a relaxing power. That the system required that a drain of gold to respond to a famine to reduce the paper currency was, Spooner wrote, unsound.

Hume's alternative report centred upon the irrelevance of the Acts of 1845 to the Scottish and Irish banking systems.[43] Therein, he provided a lengthy description of the functioning of the systems in order to demonstrate that the Acts did nothing to enhance their stability. The public had always had confidence in their system, the Act was merely costly in its reserve requirements and unfair in its granting of a monopoly to existing banks of issue. Hume's description of the Scottish system, while extracting information from the minutes of evidence, was largely a restatement of well-known facts. He concluded that the crises had been commercial, not monetary. The problem had been a shortage of credit and security, not notes. That the circulation had increased during the peak of the pressure demonstrated as much. The Acts of 1844 and 1845 exacerbated the crises, by obligating banks to lock up part of their capital in gold, thereby limiting their ability to lend. The Act should remain suspended.

Voting to reject the proposals of Spooner and Hume saw Wood, Peel, Russell, Graham, Cardwell, Cobden, Clay, and Labouchere in the affirmative, and Hume, Spooner, Herries, and Glyn in the negative. The partisan divisions thus paralleled those of the earlier committee. Whigs and Peelites supported the Act, Protectionists and Radicals opposed.

Despite securing the support of the majority of the committee, the Act's supporters remained concerned over the fate of the Act. Concerns that Herries would attempt an overthrow of the Act whilst its supporters were out of the House led to great effort on the part of Peel to ensure that the House was adequately attended.[44] Parliamentary discussion of the reports was brief, lasting only one day. Herries led the attack, telling the House that only four of the witnesses had supported the Act, and demanding that parliament re-examine the currency question at the next session.[45] Wood defended his report, and its heeding of the minority of the witnesses. It was thoughtful analysis of evidence, not the views of the majority of the witnesses, that should determine the conclusions, 'otherwise the only thing necessary would be to appoint a shorthand writer to take down the evidence'.[46] Herries' resolution was negatived and the matter was not discussed again. Parliamentary majority, rather than a preponderance of evidence preserved the Act.

The modern and Victorian interpretations of the crisis are similar in their fundamentals. The need to import corn due to the potato blight led to massive exports of bullion, which necessitated a contraction in the currency. The increase in interest rates and fear of a lack of discounting facilities inspired a panic that induced hoarding. This persisted until the government suspended the Act, restoring confidence and market discipline. What is missing from both views is a consideration of the Act and its influence as arbitrary and contingent.

Whilst it is neither possible nor profitable to engage in 'what if...?' history and ask if the crisis and its resultant failures, loss of capital, and unemployment could have been averted under alternative currency regimes, certain conclusions about the validation of the Act in 1848 emerge. The endorsement of the Act involved deliberately ignoring strong evidence that the theory underlying the Act was flawed. Pressure and hoarding could not be avoided as long as the Act was in place. The separation of departments which allowed the Bank to enter into the discount market had had unforeseen consequences. There can be no doubt that the Bank of England had market power, either through the magnitude of its discounting or through its position of social influence over other discounters. The management of the Bank for the benefit of its proprietors undeniably had the potential to conflict with the interests of the public and the government. The existence of conflicting interests and motives between sectors and institutions called into question Loyd's vision of a self-regulating machine. As currency school theory left the meeting rooms of the Political Economy Club and the Houses of Parliament and entered the real world, its once compelling simplicity deteriorated.

The Whig-Peelite coalition had succeeded in preserving the Act and the reputation of free trade. The appointment of a select committee was not motivated by a desire objectively and thoroughly to investigate the subject. Rather, it served the political interests of the government. First, it allowed for the removal of the discussion of the Act from the more public forum of parliament until the economic recovery was underway and public anger over the panic had subsided. Second, by controlling the membership of the committee, the government could ensure that a majority would vote in favour of a report exonerating the Act. Majority voting, and not quality of evidence, was again used when the discussion of the matter was returned to parliament in August. Party loyalties on the committee and in the House ensured the Act's survival.

The creation of a report exonerating the Act and the retention of the existing legislation carried with it the connotation of the currency principle's validity as the optimal form of currency management. By representing the (mere) preservation of note convertibility as the primary objective of the Act, and ignoring the broader objective of ensuring systemic stability, the Act could be deemed a success. No amount of losses or failures could be used as evidence of theoretical or legislative inadequacy.

Nonetheless, the investigation had revealed the flaws in the currency principle and the institutional arrangements mandated by the Act. The phenomenon of hoarding, the unresponsiveness of borrowing to an increase in interest rates, and the conflicting roles of the Bank of England implied that in the absence of discretionary note issue, crises would recur.

References

1. This essay is based on a chapter in my forthcoming University of Oxford doctoral thesis, 'Quality, Currency, and Credit: politicians and economists in the validation of the Bank Charter Act of 1844'.

2. H. M. Boot, *The Commercial Crisis of 1847* (Hull, 1984); C.N. Ward-Perkins, 'The Commercial Crisis of 1847', in *Essays in Economic History*, ed. E. M. Carus-Wilson (3 vols, London, 1954-63), iii, 358-80.

3. *Hansard*, third series, xci (1847), 1423-35.

4. *Hansard*, third series, xcii (1847), 213-33.

5. Ibid., 213-48.

6. Ibid., 260-6.

7. Hickleston MS, University of York, A4/130.

8. *Hansard*, xcii, 529-30.

9. Ibid., 602.

10. Ibid., 605-7.

11. Ibid., 609-15.

12. Ibid., 618-27.

13. Portland MS, University of Nottingham, Pwl 417.

14. Hickleston MS, A4/122.

15. Hickleston MS, A4/54/1.

16. Grey MS, University of Durham, GRE/V/C3/13.

17. *Hansard*, third series, xcv (1848), 374-414.

18. Ibid., 421-6.

19. Ibid., 437-8, 469-70.

20. Ibid., 473-7.

21. Ibid., 1031-4, 1038, 1043, 1134-7.

22. Ibid., 1035-7.

23. Ibid., 1043-4.

24. Ibid., 1132.

25. Hickleston MS, A4/54,156.

26. Portland MS, Pwl 55.

27. Irish University Press, British Parliamentary Papers, *First and Second Reports from the Select Committee on Commercial Distress with Minutes of Evidence: Part One* (Shannon, 1968), Q. 4575.

28. Ibid., Q. 1250.

29. M. Taylor, *The Decline of British Radicalism, 1847-60* (Oxford, 1995), p. 95n.

30. M. Hovell, *The Chartist Movement* (Manchester, 1918), pp. 93-103, 241.

31. T. C. Salt, *Breach of Privilege: Being the Evidence of Mr. John Bull, Taken before the Secret Committee on the National Distress in 1847 and 1848* (London, 1848), p. 5.

32. Ibid., passim, p. 32.

33. *First Report of the Secret Committee on the Commercial Distress*, ix-xi.

34. Ibid., iii-iv.

35. Ibid., xii.

36. Ibid., xiii, xiv, xvi, xviii, xxi.

37. Ibid., xiv.

38. *Second Report of the Secret Committee on the Commercial Distress*, Q. 6022-4, 6220-2, 6618, 6705, 6707, 6711-12, 6803, 6817-18, 7542-3.

39. Ibid., 6038-41, 6327, 6714-17, 6807-10, 7404-10, 7238.

40. Ibid., 6255-6, 6969-72, 7430.

41. Ibid., iii-iv.

42. Ibid., v-vi.

43. Ibid., v-xii.

44. J. B. Conacher, *The Peelites and the Party System, 1846-52* (Newton Abbot, 1972), p. 43.

45. *Hansard*, third series, xcvi (1848), 392, 394.

46. Ibid., 402.

Chapter 5

Parliament and Free Trade after the Repeal of the Corn Laws

The repeal of the corn laws has been described as 'the central rite of passage of mid-Victorian politics' and 'a decisive step in the process of reform'. A truly 'pivotal' event, repeal has been taken to signify the ascendancy of free trade, and in its wake Britain followed 'an unprecedented course' in trying to persuade the rest of the world to abandon protection. At home free trade 'won persistent endorsement', and it became perhaps 'the single most distinctive characteristic of the British state' for almost a century.[1] Nevertheless, the continuing vitality of protectionism cannot be denied. Although it was a minority creed, reluctantly abandoned as a party platform by the Conservatives after the 1852 general election, protectionism was not destroyed by the repeal of the corn laws. A coherent approach to perceived economic, social, and political problems, protection still appealed strongly to influential groups in this period.[2] Protectionists were unwilling to accept the policy and practice of free trade, and their dogged resistance after 1846 meant that the ultimate victory of free trade was no foregone conclusion. The struggle continued. This essay will focus upon the parliament of 1847 to 1852 in order to reveal more about the protagonists and what they thought was at stake.

The parliament of 1847 to 1852 was the first to be elected after repeal. Free trade appeared to have gained considerable prestige among newspapers, voters and politicians, and in July 1847 many free traders were successful at the polls. Conservatism had been fractured and there seemed to be little chance of reconciliation between Peelites and protectionists (who retained the 'Conservative' party label). Free traders might have expected to carry all before them in this parliament, but it was to be a battleground, not the arena for an impressive victory flourish.

A unique insight into parliamentary proceedings is provided by the activities and observations of Thomas Perronet Thompson (1783-1869), and these will form the basis for what follows. Thompson, a former soldier who had risen to notoriety as a political economist and contributor to the *Westminster Review*, had been a prominent campaigner for reforms since the late 1820s. As the new MP for Bradford, from 1847 to 1852 he lived up to his reputation for independence and outspokenness, and his published and unpublished writings included regular (often day-by-day) accounts of clashes in parliament involving advocates and opponents of free trade.

A determined champion of free trade, Thompson was to find that many of his fellow radical MPs failed to assist him as he wished. He became ever more insistent about the dangers posed by a protectionist revival, and increasingly contemptuous towards radical leaders in the House of Commons. Free trade did not advance as expected in the aftermath of repeal, Thompson thought, because of the negligence and inactivity of its adherents. This was not an ideological failure, for the credibility and force of free trade arguments were incontestable. Rather, this was a political failure of the first magnitude.

In the months leading up to his election in Bradford, Thompson was preoccupied most of all by the decision to disband the Anti-Corn Law League, and by the ease with which other issues, notably education, superseded free trade in extra-parliamentary politics. In the summer of 1845 he had eagerly anticipated further reforms for which the League could campaign. A year later he was incensed to hear of resolutions approved in Manchester (2 July 1846), the effect of which was to dissolve the League. He took little consolation from undertakings expressed at the time that the council of the League would reassemble should the Conservatives take office and attempt to reintroduce protection. Thompson visited Manchester in August 1846 and reported to his closest political ally, John Bowring (who had been returned as MP for Bolton in 1841), that the League would soon be dead. The battle for free trade and reform was not over, he protested, and the disbandment of a tried and tested political organisation, the loss of the League's influence and campaigning zeal, and the retirement of seasoned agitators would make a protectionist revival inevitable.[3]

With this matter preying on his mind, Thompson also had to contend with demands from his prospective constituents in Bradford that he clarify his position on certain issues. He realised that it was education rather than free trade that most interested Bradford's active liberals, many of whom were Dissenters. They opposed a plan for increased grants and teacher training because it entailed professional examinations and government inspection. Dissenters saw this as an attempt to increase the influence of the Established Church. As the general election approached in 1847, candidates in many constituencies were pressed to condemn the education plan and to state their commitment to religious liberty.[4] Thompson was frustrated because the Bradford election was not the straightforward plebiscite on free trade for which he had hoped.[5]

There were other hindrances. Unfortunately for Thompson, the clarity of purpose to which he was accustomed as an extra-parliamentary campaigner contrasted sharply with the party disarray and confusion of goals in parliament. Many of the problems of subsequent years can be traced directly to the 1847 election and the nature of the government's unwieldy coalition, which consisted of Whigs, Irish, moderate reformers, and radicals. The 1847 election was an untidy affair,[6] and when the new parliament assembled it became clear that Lord John Russell (prime minister since July 1846) had no secure majority in the lower house. The Conservatives were incapable of forming a viable administration, but they were the largest single group in the Commons with about 243 MPs. There were 89 Peelites, who refused to ally themselves with any other group, although their desire to frustrate the Conservatives made them favourably disposed towards Russell's ministry. The government coalition consisted of around 324 MPs, but this was no united voting bloc. Dependent on their allies, the Whigs had to govern as best they could in a period characterised by disorganised parties, executive weakness, cross voting, and general indiscipline in the Commons.[7]

The government pursued a course of Whig centrism, a moderate approach designed to give ministers broad appeal by demonstrating administrative competence and resisting extreme or sectional claims. This not only failed to secure permanent Peelite support; it alienated many radical and Irish MPs. Ministers were uneasy because Peel and his followers held the balance in the Commons, and because radical numbers had been increased by the 1847 election. Nor could ministers control even their own Whig supporters. It proved impossible to predict the mood of the Commons on any given question. Peelite voting patterns were inconsistent, while radicals argued among themselves on education, finance, factory reform, and foreign policy. In April 1848, about sixty radical MPs formed themselves into a separate party committed to financial retrenchment and parliamentary reform. They joined with extra-parliamentary activists to establish the Parliamentary and Financial Reform Association. Discord persisted on the government side as Whigs, moderates, and radicals failed to work together.[8] There was also tension on the Conservative side. Personal and political differences ruled out reunion with the Peelites, though Conservative leader Lord Stanley (who succeeded as fourteenth Earl of Derby in June 1851) tried several times to win over individuals. Most Conservatives were still committed to protection, and Stanley retained it as party policy. But Benjamin Disraeli, the party's chief spokesman in the lower house after the death of Lord George Bentinck in September 1848, decided that protection was unpopular with voters and that the Conservatives would not be able to form a strong and lasting administration until it was discarded. This crisis of Conservatism was only a little less debilitating than disunity on the government side.[9]

Thompson was dismayed by the prevalent confusion, but it also increased his determination to combat error and promote reforms. He hoped to enhance radical influence and to secure from all non-Conservative groups in the Commons an unequivocal commitment to free trade. From February 1848 he published 'letters of a representative' addressed to the secretary of the Bradford Reform Association. These first appeared in the *Sun* on Mondays and Wednesdays. In commencing the series,

Thompson suggested that the distance between parliament and public was growing and that reform initiatives could no longer originate in parliament. He pointed to the League's agitation as proof of this, and to the recent platform appearances of Richard Cobden, MP for the West Riding. Cobden had the right idea, Thompson argued, for speeches outside parliament were more effective than speeches delivered inside, and influence built up outside was the best kind that could be used inside.[10] Thompson kept up a regular contact with allies and supporters through these open letters, and as public interest in his reports spread, more newspapers made use of them for comment and agitation. During 1849 the letters were addressed to the secretary of the Metropolitan Reform Association, a sign that London radicals had become as concerned as their northern counterparts about what Thompson had to say.[11]

Thompson regularly addressed the Commons. He had an excellent attendance record, and in 1848 his name appeared in every division list except a few for which only the minority was listed (because it was so small).[12] He remained thoroughly independent, but a sense of isolation occasionally crept in, as when Cobden and others tried to dissuade him from speaking in particular debates. Thompson was annoyed to find that certain colleagues, assuming that he would be too confrontational and that this would upset their plans and damage their reputations, expected him to remain silent. This he refused to do. He used the Commons and the reform press to argue for free trade at every opportunity, regardless of friend or foe.

Economic and financial matters loomed large in the parliament of 1847 to 1852, and there were three main subjects that came to the fore: tariff and taxation policy, the navigation laws, and the condition of agriculture.

In February 1848 Conservative MPs made plain their intention to press for the reversal of liberal measures. Led by Bentinck, they challenged the government on the vexed question of the sugar duties. Reformers were cheered by the remarks of Charles Wood, the chancellor of the exchequer, who explained that ministers did not intend to depart from the policy implemented in 1846: gradual equalisation of duties on foreign and colonial sugar, to be accomplished by 1851.[13] Thompson stressed the need for the antislavery movement to take up a more active role (the sugar duties had long been controversial, not only as a matter of trade and revenue but also in connection with slave labour systems in Asia and the Americas). By June 1848, however, with no firm line being taken by ministers, support for a liberal policy began to splinter. According to Thompson the real issues at stake had not been clearly established: that free trade was universally advantageous, that all restrictions on trade were harmful, that the West Indian interests had only survived at the expense of the rest of the community, and that they wanted to restore the slave trade.[14]

A deepening commercial crisis and pressure from the City of London, West Indian lobby, and protectionists (who opposed the reduction of sugar duties) prompted the government to allow a longer time for equalisation. Radical MPs complained about this retreat, and on 30 June John Bright, MP for Manchester, insisted that the sugar duties of 1846 should not be altered. Bright's motion was heavily defeated,[15] and Thompson feared that Russell's government would compromise further if the West Indies persisted in complaining about the principle of equalisation. This strengthened the argument that the 1846 duties ought to be left alone, yet on 10 July the proposal to amend the duty on muscovado was carried by 180 to 124 votes.[16] On 22 August 1848 Bentinck tried and failed to force ministers to allow the home consumption of sugar refined in bond for exportation. He pointed out that this would help English sugar refiners in competition with their Dutch rivals. Some free traders, including Thompson, voted with Bentinck because they saw that consumers would benefit by having sugar at the lowest possible price (consumers had to pay more when English importers sent their sugar abroad to have it refined).[17]

Already, three significant trends were becoming apparent: a weak government's willingness to compromise, criticism of government measures by advanced radicals and free traders, and the Conservatives' ability to exploit divisions within the government's broad coalition.

Thompson often drew attention to the justice and policy of commercial regulation, and its implications for social welfare and public finance. He became interested in the tea duties following a Commons debate of 10 February 1848 on economic relations with China. Thompson held that any increase in charges on the poor ought to be balanced by an increase in charges on the rich.[18] Two years later, in his correspondence with Bowring (now consul-general at Canton), he analysed the proposition that a remission of duties on tea would cause a price increase in favour of the Chinese grower. In other words, the duty only affected the grower and here was a tax that the British government collected but nobody in Britain paid. Thompson dismissed this as nonsense.[19] He linked the question of commercial duties with the need to ensure that taxation should not press more heavily on the lower classes than on the wealthy, and he advocated a reform of the income tax in order to make the wealthy contribute more towards the national burdens.[20]

Income tax was one of the most sensitive issues of this period. Conservatives knew that if the government was forced to do without income tax, it would have to rely more on revenue from import duties and halt the dismantling of protection (which might make possible the re-imposition of a corn duty). Most radicals liked the idea of cheaper government and tried to limit expenditure so that indirect taxation could be reduced. Yet radicals were by no means united on this question, and there was strong disagreement on income tax between Cobden and another leading radical, Joseph Hume, MP for Montrose. Peelites also wanted tax cuts, since economical administration was central to their agenda. Income tax was renewed for three years in March 1848, but the government's attempt to increase the rate (from 7d to 1s in the pound) was defeated. This necessitated a series of awkward financial expedients that did little to raise the Whigs' reputation for financial management. Defence costs, famine relief in Ireland, tariff reform, and the difficult economic conditions of the late 1840s brought budget deficits, and Wood had persistently to advise caution as Russell proposed further tariff reductions and more spending on social policies. Eventually the situation improved and there was a healthy budget surplus in 1850, but ministers then argued about how to protect the revenue and how best to employ the surplus. Cabinet divisions developed alongside further quarrels among the radicals, with Hume and Bright regarding parliamentary reform as the essential precondition for genuine retrenchment, and Cobden arguing that financial reform should come before parliamentary reform (Cobden wanted to change the whole nature of Britain's government and external relations, not just the electoral system).[21]

Worried about the possible repercussions of financial and economic problems, Thompson continued to condemn protection in parliament and out of doors. Discussion of income tax and commercial duties during March 1848 prompted a diatribe against 'the spirit of inaccuracy and unreason which possesses the Protectionist benches'. Disraeli and others had asserted, despite evidence to the contrary, that tariff reform did not lower the price of goods to consumers and that import duties on foreign products were paid by the foreigner. Thompson published long essays repudiating these 'fallacies', and noted with incredulity 'that men so incompetent to explain the simplest phenomenon of trade should maintain pretensions to make the Government of a commercial country'. In May he ridiculed Bentinck's suggestion that Queen Victoria should be advised to appear in public wearing only British-made dresses. Here was further proof of the protectionists' determination to reverse free trade.[22] Thompson followed this up by supporting a reduction of the duties on copper and lead.[23]

Intense disagreement about commercial duties continued throughout the life of this parliament, and Thompson became increasingly concerned about protectionist influence and assertiveness. The danger became all the more palpable in May 1851 when Lord Naas, Conservative MP for Kildare, proposed that the Commons should take into consideration the duties on spirits in bond. Whig ministers opposed, arguing that some duties had to be retained so that others could be lowered. But the motion was carried by the casting vote of the speaker, Charles Shaw-Lefevre. The radical MP for Sheffield, J. A. Roebuck, then raised the possibility that ministers might resign because of this defeat.[24] Thompson was appalled by these developments: 'the Protectionists are so strong that whoever chooses to join with them, as in the actual case the representatives of Irish and Scottish distillers, may show a powerful front. Thus at the present time, the fates of Europe and perhaps the world hang upon whisky'.[25] Three weeks later Thompson voted against a motion to reduce the excise duty on hops. Along with other free traders he wanted the duty abolished, not merely reduced. Leave to bring in a bill was refused by 88 to 27 votes. In July the Commons debated the matter again, and Thompson repeated that all such duties harmed trade and prevented foreigners from buying British manufactures. The tax on foreign hops was especially galling because it allowed British hop growers to enjoy undeserved profits, and inflate beer prices, at the public expense.[26]

Thompson sought assiduously to publicise all debates on commercial questions, frequently drawing his readers' attention to the benefits that particular reforms would bring to manufacturing regions in general and to Bradford in particular. He welcomed Wood's plan to lower the duty on chicory, for this would facilitate the mixing of chicory with coffee. Those with economic privileges in the Far East would resist, as would some beverage manufacturers and retailers, but coffee would be cheaper for West Riding operatives. The Commons subsequently rejected a move to prevent the mixing of chicory with coffee (30 June 1851) by 199 to 122 votes. Thompson was also pleased to report that an attempt to bolster the agricultural interest by lowering the malt tax was lost by a margin of more than two to one in the Commons on 17 June 1851. Yet free traders could not afford to be complacent. On 15 July Naas moved for a committee on the milling interest in Ireland. This provided an opportunity for Conservative MPs to demand the return of the corn laws. 'All parties evinced the usual horror of principles', Thompson informed his readers. 'The Government replied to small details by smaller. No word of defence from the Free Trade benches. Such folly has not been seen since the day Eve ate the apple. You are let down, you are surrendered; never was a gained cause so thrown away.' Although the motion was lost by 128 to 93 votes, the protectionists were getting stronger. Thompson was mindful of the ministerial crisis of February 1851, when Russell had resigned following the government's defeat on a motion for parliamentary reform. Russell remained as premier because the Conservatives were unable to form an administration. Nevertheless, the government coalition had by this time all but disintegrated. Russell and his cabinet were in an unenviable position (despite a budget surplus and an improving economic situation), and opposition to the continuation of income tax in 1851 meant that it was only renewed for one year. Thompson wrote that he would not be surprised to see a protectionist government in place before the next dissolution.[27]

After corn law repeal free traders turned to another conspicuous target, the navigation laws, which had long restricted the transportation of goods to British and colonial ships. The navigation laws were vulnerable because of the tax and tariff reforms of the 1840s, and the case against them was clearly made in a select committee of 1847. Repeal of the navigation laws was attractive to ministers because they expected it to win the support of free traders and Peelites, prove to middle-class voters that the government was committed to reform, and provoke minimal discontent within the Whig party. It would also weaken a bastion of protectionism, the shipping interests.[28] Ministers realised that their plan would provoke strong resistance, however, and they decided to begin with only a partial repeal.

Norman Gash has argued that repeal was 'largely symbolic', but it is difficult to accept this interpretation in view of the controversy of the time. The government would have felt no need to proceed carefully, indeed, had repeal not represented a significant departure. Sarah Palmer considers repeal 'a major change in Britain's commercial policy', and she demonstrates that the navigation laws offered more protection than has often been supposed. The commercial reforms of the 1820s had not affected the core principle of protection for shipping, and even in the late 1840s it was difficult to argue against the claim that the whole community benefited from the navigation laws.[29]

Early in 1848, seamen's groups organised petitions against the abandonment of the navigation laws, and the Conservative press reported that silk weavers, curriers, boot-makers, glove-makers and others were preparing to do the same. In April 1848 it seemed that ministerial resolve was giving way. There was more talk of modification than repeal, shipping interests made ready to block reform, and Thompson wondered if the government would be bullied into deferring even a mild deregulation.[30] On 15 May, however, he was encouraged by the remarks of Henry Labouchere, the president of the board of trade, who explained that while the coasting trade, fisheries, and manning of British vessels would remain untouched, the government wanted to remove restrictions on the purchase and employment of foreign-built ships and on the carrying of goods to and from foreign countries. Thompson responded:

> A country that has put down the monopoly of the landowners is not likely to tolerate the monopoly of the shipowners; and therefore the Navigation Laws may be considered as doomed. A truth once found out, is lost no more; and nothing can sweep the existing generation of the knowledge that all monopolies are to enable someone to sell dearer, and that the amount of any difference of price thus accomplished, falls on the community in the shape of a stupid loss, such as would arise from blunting the edge of razors that more barbers might be employed in shaving.[31]

Thompson was rather more sanguine than he had cause to be, for the government's proposals did not go as far as free traders wanted. Ministers had accommodated some of the concerns of shipowners and seamen. The role of the merchant marine in providing manpower and training for national defence had to be respected, it was decided, and colonial legislatures were to retain some authority over navigation. The government also included an element of reciprocity, so that Britain could refuse concessions to other powers if similar benefits were not offered by them. Government intentions were still not very clear, however, because ministers had not yet put together a formal measure to present to parliament. Protectionist agitation developed quickly, with large meetings in seaports and other towns. Many petitions were submitted against reform. Free traders found it difficult to mobilise opinion, and only nine petitions for repeal of the navigation laws were submitted in May and June 1848.[32]

Conservative resistance in the Commons was led by J. C. Herries, the MP for Stamford (and a former cabinet minister, 1827-30, 1834-5). The debate dragged on and Thompson urged reformers in the large commercial towns to make their views known.[33] On 17 July 1848 Russell announced that the subject would be deferred to the next session. Protectionists were jubilant while free traders regretted the delay and expressed doubts about the ministry's reforming disposition. The government's bill was finally published in August (its basic features were those outlined by Labouchere in May).[34]

As the new session approached, board of trade officials canvassed opinion abroad and protectionists were stirred by the Central Committee for Upholding the Navigation Laws (established by the Shipowners' Society in 1847). On 14 February 1849 Labouchere introduced the bill to amend the navigation laws. The only change to previous proposals was that the coasting trade was to be partially opened. Labouchere was sure that this would encourage other nations to make similar concessions to Britain, but Thompson did not see why the government should offer such an opportunity to the opponents of reform. By bringing in more elements of reciprocity, he thought, ministers jeopardised the whole project.[35]

Thompson told the Commons on 14 February that arguments from the Conservative side were completely unreasonable: 'some man's industry was to be put a stop to, in order to increase the produce of some other man's industry, with the *tertium quid* of something being taken from the consumer besides'. As for national defence, he denied that relaxing the navigation laws would be dangerous. British naval power depended on the nation's wealth, not the mercantile marine, and the way to increase wealth was to liberate trade.[36] But Conservative obstruction continued and the government's majority began to shrink. In March Labouchere announced alterations to the navigation bill, for it was clear that other nations would not admit British vessels to their coasting trades in return for the partial opening of Britain's coasting trade. Thompson lamented that free traders in the Commons had rarely replied to protectionists with vigour and that the opportunities presented by corn law repeal had not been seized.[37]

The Commons finally passed the navigation bill on 23 April 1849. In the Lords Stanley marshalled opposition peers and it survived its second reading by a margin of just ten votes on 9 May. On 21 May Stanley tried unsuccessfully to amend the measure, and the Lords passed it without a division on 13 June. Thompson had been worried that the Lords' decision would be affected by a new attack on the former leaders of the Anti-Corn Law League, especially in the *Morning Post*, which exploited Cobden's confession that corn law repeal had been less beneficial than expected. 'I cannot comprehend how he came to rush into such a manifest snare set for him', Thompson remarked, 'as giving the Protectionists leave to quote him as supporting them in their assertion of the public distress and poverty arising out of the abolition of the corn laws'.[38]

The repeal of the navigation laws was a costly victory for Russell's ministry. Instead of demonstrating Whig aptitude for reform, the contest promoted protectionist revival and drew together several pressure groups: the landed interest, City of London, provincial bankers and merchants, shipowners and shipbuilders, colonial lobbies, some manufacturers, and educational institutions in which protectionist doctrines held sway. On the government side in parliament, meanwhile, there had been no unanimity on navigation. Some radicals were still annoyed about the renewal of income tax in 1848, and they maintained that repeal of the navigation laws only partly made up for this. Most alarming for Thompson was the manner in which Conservative morale had risen, and the fact that protection was again a vital political cause, for the navigation struggle coincided with a sharp fall in wheat prices.[39]

In Thompson's opinion the most threatening sectional lobby of the time was the landed interest. The drop in wheat prices between 1849 and 1851 prompted ever louder demands for the restoration of the corn laws, and from May 1849 a new organisation was active, the National Association for the Protection of British Industry and Capital. This body pressed for a corn duty and banking reform, defended imperial preference and the navigation laws, and helped Conservative candidates at by-elections. Here was a broadening of protectionism, as agitation moved beyond the arguments and demands of the past. Within the Conservative party, moreover, Disraeli's ideas about giving up protection were still held in check by the opinions of Stanley and the rank and file. Nevertheless, Disraeli hoped to persuade his party that rather than try to reverse liberal policies, it would do better to obtain compensation for free trade, and relief for agriculture, through such means as tax reform.[40]

On 8 March 1849 Disraeli moved for a committee on agricultural grievances. He had in view a redistribution of the national burdens, and his speech won much praise. He spoke of agriculture and industry as complementary rather than antagonistic interests, and explained that to disregard 'territorial principles', or to ignore the problems of those who owned and farmed the land, would be to risk general economic decline. This speech signalled Disraeli's search for an alternative to protection (as well as his desire to impose some personal authority over Conservatives in the Commons). He wanted his party to abandon protection, but he was also determined to do something for agriculture. Free traders made poor speeches in reply, and Thompson's only comfort was that the Anti-Corn Law League had established certain 'truths' so that the liberal cause would not have to rely solely on ineffective speakers in the Commons. Disraeli's motion was defeated (15 March) by 280 to 189 votes. Thompson described Disraeli's concluding remarks as 'ludicrous ... beginning in a profession of demand for justice to an interest which for twenty years has been the plunderer of all the others, and ending by throwing off the mask and avowing the unalterable design of moving back to the old tyranny'. It was up to those who fully understood commercial questions to respond. In particular, free traders in parliament had to speak out more often, and no protectionist should go unanswered.[41]

Disraeli's motion had been lost by a margin of 91 votes. An earlier proposal for a committee on the state of the nation had been lost by 140 votes, mainly because the Commons viewed it as an attempt to revive protection. Therefore Disraeli's plan to assist agriculture without bringing back the corn laws had potential, while Thompson could only hope that the anti-protection majority would remain intact, and that Russell's government would not lose its nerve. In October 1849 Thompson expressed grave fears about the ministry's commitment to free trade after a conversation with Peter Borthwick, the former Conservative MP for Evesham. Borthwick, who was about to take over the *Morning Post*, claimed that Russell's cabinet had not ruled out a fixed duty on corn, and that some ministers wanted to protect home manufacturers who were most threatened by foreign competition. Such reverses, Thompson commented, were being 'wooed and courted' by free traders. The *Spectator* had recently revealed that leading radical MPs participated in only a third of Commons divisions (Thompson had not missed a single division). This typified the manner in which the free trade cause had sunk to its seemingly parlous position. Too many radical MPs had failed to do their duty.[42]

Borthwick's prognostications did not prove to be accurate, for the government decided against a corn duty. Russell was unwilling to grant landowners special treatment, and he told his colleagues that even a mild form of agricultural protection would increase popular unrest and deprive the government of Peelite support in parliament.[43] Yet this did not mean that free traders could relax, and Thompson never stopped preaching the need for vigilance. Indeed, when Disraeli introduced another motion on agricultural distress in February 1850 it was defeated by a margin of only 21 votes (273 to 252).[44] In February 1851 Disraeli introduced his third motion for the relief of agricultural distress. This was defeated by just 14 votes. Thompson hoped that the Anti-Corn Law League would be reactivated.[45]

To Bowring he declared that 'I will never again follow the lead of Hume and Cobden if I can help it, to the end of time', and he predicted dire consequences if the reformers' 'somnolence' continued: 'the protectionists have done all that ability and perseverance could do to support their cause, and what call themselves the Free Trade party have utterly rejected and thrown away every opportunity of maintaining and extending their principles'. Prominent radicals had insulted Thompson early in 1848 by trying to discourage him from addressing the Commons, but their squabbles and shortcomings had prompted him to speak out against their wishes. He was responsible for 'almost the only substantial attempts at the defence and illustration of Free Trade that have occurred. There may have been a flash speech or two made by the professed leaders, for the purpose of being talked of; but there was no systematic defence'. Although he trusted Wood and was willing to give the Whigs a fair trial, Thompson was annoyed because ministers had made little use of those radical MPs who were willing to assist them. He had expected to be included in several Commons committees, but the Whigs 'had no room for anybody but their enemies, whom they are more earnest not to vex than to conciliate friends'. With the Whigs disposed to make life difficult for themselves, and the free traders so feeble and incompetent in the Commons, Thompson confessed that he cared little about retaining his seat at the next election.[46]

Thompson was one of the most determined and conscientious free traders in the parliament of 1847 to 1852. But for him this period was rather disappointing. He believed that the Anti-Corn Law League should not have been dissolved, that it was primarily responsible for the repeal of the corn laws, that it could have used this victory as the basis for new campaigns, and that it would have helped to shape post-repeal politics by further educating the public, emboldening the Whig ministry, and successfully resisting the protectionists. To Thompson, therefore, the dissolution of the League was an avoidable mistake. Thereafter, Cobden, Bright and other League leaders were not active or resilient enough in advancing free trade. Indeed, radical leaders generally were too busy arguing among themselves and soliciting support for their own pet projects, and hence the radical bloc in the Commons was permanently disorganised and divided. Radicals had ignored the danger of a protectionist revival, and they should have tried to establish a better working relationship with Russell's government.

This was Thompson's analysis of the situation, and it was not unreasonable. In fact the only matters on which he might be faulted are his insistence that the League was primarily responsible for repeal, which is doubtful, and his assumption that it could have carried on, for this was probably not possible or expedient.[47] On other points Thompson's comments made sense. Cobden and Bright were still concerned about free trade, of course, but Thompson's activity was rather more focused, while their interests were broadening. Cobden's preoccupations were now international rather than domestic, and Bright gave primacy to parliamentary reform.[48] The problem was not that they were inactive, but that their priorities did not coincide with those of Thompson, and while he emerged as a single-minded spokesman for free trade, they attended to a wider range of issues. Thompson thought that they should have done more specifically to defend free trade, especially by replying to protectionist arguments in the Commons and carrying on the battle for hearts and minds.

Radical disunity brought fatal weaknesses, limited the constructive influence of radical MPs between 1847 and 1852, and led to isolation, decline, and defeats in later years. The League had been a force for unity, but the circumstances that made such a mobilisation possible were now passing away.[49] As for the Russell administration, its record shows plenty of honest endeavour in difficult circumstances, and although it has often been regarded as weak and ineffective, it did promote freer trade and thereby made a return to protection less likely. The Whigs were divided on many issues, however, and by itself a free trade policy could not guarantee cohesion.[50]

Was protectionism strong enough to pose a serious threat? Cobden thought not, and in 1852 he decided that there was no need to keep even the residual League machinery going in Manchester. Yet protection brought together a formidable alliance – not just landowners but also the City of London, colonial interests, shipowners, and many provincial bankers, merchants, and manufacturers. Free trade, it is clear, was not entirely dominant intellectually or practically in the mid-nineteenth century. British society was still in transition and liberal ideas and new economic sectors had to co-exist with older institutions and values. True, the Conservative party abandoned protection as a policy in 1852. But most of its members and supporters remained ideologically and emotionally attached to protection, and they were certain that state power had to be controlled by the landed interest rather than by manufacturing and commercial interests. Here was a conflict left unresolved by the repeal of the corn laws.

References

1. K. T. Hoppen, *The Mid-Victorian Generation* (Oxford, 1998), p. 127; A. Howe, *Free Trade and Liberal England, 1846-1946* (Oxford, 1997), p. 1.

2. A. Macintyre, 'Lord George Bentinck and the Protectionists: A Lost Cause?' *Transactions of the Royal Historical Society*, 5th series, xxxix (1989), 141-65; A. Gambles, 'Rethinking the Politics of Protection: Conservatism and the Corn Laws, 1830-52', *English Historical Review*, cxiii (1998), 928-52; R. Stewart, *The Politics of Protection* (Cambridge, 1971).

3. *Sheffield Iris*, 17 July 1845; A. Prentice, *History of the Anti-Corn Law League* (2 vols, London, 1853), ii. 441-2; T. P. Thompson to J. Bowring, 10 Aug. 1846, B[rynmor] J[ones] L[ibrary], University of Hull, Thompson Papers, DTH 4/11. See also N. McCord, *The Anti-Corn Law League* (London, 1968), pp. 203-7 on the League's dissolution. Thompson feared that leading Manchester reformers would retreat into quiescence and inactivity. He sent an article for publication in the *Manchester Examiner* at the end of 1846, but it was rejected because of its forceful emphasis on 'the tendency of present proceedings to drive the Free Traders into closer union with the popular party'. This union was exactly what Thompson wanted, and he complained that former Leaguers were far too cautious about such things. T. P. Thompson to H. B. Peacock, 22,24 Dec. 1846, J[ohn] R[ylands] L[ibrary], University of Manchester, English MS 1180/117-18.

4. N. Gash, *Aristocracy and People: Britain, 1815-65* (London, 1979), p. 245.

5. See correspondence in BJL, DTH 3/19,28,29, especially the letters of May 1847, and *Bradford Observer*, 27 May 1847. Divisions among Bradford liberals on education and other matters were discussed in *Leeds Mercury*, 15,29 May, 5,12,26 June 1847, but for detailed coverage see *Bradford Observer*, 27 May, 3,10,17,24 June, 1,8,15,22,29 July, 5 Aug. 1847. Thompson applied to Manchester and to the provincial reform press for help with his election campaign in Bradford, and his letters often referred to difficulties with Bradford's Dissenters. E.g. Thompson to Peacock, 25 Mar., 23 May, 4,10,12,30 June, 5,9,19,23,31 July 1847, JRL, Eng. MS 1180/125, 127, 129-38; Thompson to G. Wilson, 5,12,15,16 June, 9,13,14,19,21,22,31 July 1847, Manchester Central Library, Archives and Local Studies, George Wilson Papers, M20/12,13. See also J. A. Jowitt, 'Dissenters, Voluntaryism and Liberal Unity: The 1847 Election', in *Nineteenth Century Bradford Elections*, ed. J. A. Jowitt and R. K. S. Taylor (Leeds, 1979), pp. 7-23.

6. Gash, *Aristocracy and People*, pp. 244-5; G. Searle, *Entrepreneurial Politics in Mid-Victorian Britain* (Oxford, 1993), p. 51; A. Sykes, *The Rise and Fall of British Liberalism, 1776-1988* (London, 1997), p. 37; Prentice, *History of the League*, ii, 444; P. Adelman, *Victorian Radicalism: The Middle Class Experience* (London,

1984), pp. 73-4; M. Taylor, *The Decline of British Radicalism, 1847-60* (Oxford, 1995), p. 77.

7. Gash, *Aristocracy and People*, pp. 244-5; R. Blake, *The Conservative Party from Peel to Churchill* (London, 1979), pp. 67-72, 77-9, 282.

8. Sykes, *British Liberalism*, pp. 31-5; E. J. Evans, *The Forging of the Modern State* (London, 1996), pp. 340-2; Taylor, *Decline of Radicalism*, pp. 7-8; N. Gash, *Reaction and Reconstruction in English Politics, 1832-52* (Oxford, 1956), pp. 192-5, and idem, *Aristocracy and People*, pp. 244, 246-8; R. Blake, *Disraeli* (London, 1998), pp. 298-9; Hoppen, *Mid-Victorian Generation*, pp. 132, 139-41; N. C. Edsall, 'A Failed National Movement: The Parliamentary and Financial Reform Association, 1848-54', *Bulletin of the Institute of Historical Research*, xlix (1976), 108-31; T. Jenkins, *The Liberal Ascendancy, 1830-86* (London, 1994), pp. 55-62, 67.

9. R. Stewart, *Party and Politics, 1830-52* (Basingstoke, 1989), pp. 86, 89-92; Evans, *Forging of the Modern State*, p. 342; Blake, *Disraeli*, chs. 11, 13, and idem, *Conservative Party*, pp. 80-3; Gambles, 'Rethinking Protection', pp. 944, 951; Hoppen, *Mid-Victorian Generation*, pp. 134-6; Gash, *Reaction and Reconstruction*, pp. 153-5; I. Machin, *Disraeli* (London, 1995), pp. 64-73.

10. 'To the Secretary of the Bradford Reform Association', proofs, BJL, DTH 3/30 (part 1); *Sun*, 2 Feb. 1848.

11. 'To the Secretary of the Metropolitan Reform Association', new series of proofs, BJL, DTH 3/30 (part 2); *Sun*, 5 Feb. 1849.

12. See notes in BJL, DTH 5/37.

13. 'To the Secretary of the Bradford Reform Association', BJL, DTH 3/30; *Sun*, 9 Feb. 1848; *Hansard*, 3rd series, xcvi (1848), 7-79, 84-168. The opening of British markets and waning of imperial preference accorded with the logic of corn law repeal. Peel had already reduced the preferential duties on colonial sugar in 1844. Howe, *Free Trade*, pp. 17-18, 50-2.

14. 'To the Secretary of the Bradford Reform Association', BJL, DTH 3/30; *Sun*, 23 Feb., 19 June 1848. On the continuing strength of antislavery sentiment, see Taylor, *Decline of Radicalism*, pp. 179-83.

15. *Hansard*, xcix (1848), 1414-70; 'To the Secretary of the Bradford Reform Association', BJL, DTH 3/30; *Sun*, 21,26,28 June, 3,5 July 1848. Thompson's favoured solution was to allow the West Indians a moderate duty for a fixed term, on the clear understanding that foreign sugar would be treated equally thereafter.

16. *Hansard*, c (1848), 310-80; 'To the Secretary of the Bradford Reform Association', BJL, DTH 3/30; *Sun*, 10,12 July 1848.

17. 'To the Secretary of the Bradford Reform Association', BJL, DTH 3/30; *Sun*, 23 Aug. 1848; *Hansard*, ci (1848), 376-88.

18. *Hansard*, xcvi (1848), 425-54; 'To the Secretary of the Bradford Reform Association', BJL, DTH 3/30; *Sun*, 14 Feb. 1848.

19. Thompson to Bowring, 23 Feb. 1850, BJL, DTH 4/13.

20. 'To the Secretary of the Bradford Reform Association', BJL, DTH 3/31; *Sun*, 9 July 1851; *Hansard*, cxviii (1851), 351-6.

21. Gash, *Aristocracy and People*, p. 246, and idem, *Reaction and Reconstruction*, p. 195; Taylor, *Decline of Radicalism*, ch. 4; Searle, *Entrepreneurial Politics*, ch. 2; Howe, *Free Trade*, pp. 44-9; Hoppen, *Mid-Victorian Generation*, pp. 142-4; Jenkins, *Liberal Ascendancy*, pp. 57, 63-6.

22. *Hansard*, xcvii (1848), 162-231, 235-310, 363-454, 460-535, xcviii (1848), 809-16; 'To the Secretary of the Bradford Reform Association', BJL, DTH 3/30; *Sun*, 13,15 Mar., 10 May 1848.

23. *Hansard*, xcviii (1848), 431-46, ci (1848), 597-613, 721-6, 756-7; 'To the Secretary of the Bradford Reform Association', BJL, DTH 3/30; *Sun*, 19 Apr., 29 May, 30 Aug., 4 Sept. 1848; *Halifax Guardian*, 13 May 1848.

24. *Hansard*, cxvi (1851), 604-37.

25. 'To the Secretary of the Bradford Reform Association', BJL, DTH 3/31; *Sun*, 7 May 1851.

26. 'To the Secretary of the Bradford Reform Association', BJL, DTH 3/31; *Sun*, 26 May, 30 July 1851; *Hansard*, cxvi (1851), 1299-1308, cxviii (1851), 1716-22.

27. 'To the Secretary of the Bradford Reform Association', BJL, DTH 3/31; *Sun*, 9,18 June, 16 July 1851; *Hansard*, cxvii (1851), 511-33, 899-916, 1384-1415, cxviii (1851), 795-834.

28. Howe, *Free Trade*, pp. 56-9.

29. Gash, *Aristocracy and People*, p. 247; S. Palmer, *Politics, Shipping and the Repeal of the Navigation Laws* (Manchester, 1990), chs. 2-4; B. Gordon, *Economic Doctrine and Tory Liberalism, 1824-30* (London, 1979), pp. 103-5.

30. 'To the Secretary of the Bradford Reform Association', BJL, DTH 3/30; *Sun*, 14 Feb., 5 Apr. 1848.

31. *Hansard*, xcviii (1848), 988-1055; Palmer, *Navigation Laws*, pp. 126-8; 'To the Secretary of the Bradford Reform Association', BJL, DTH 3/30; *Sun*, 17 May 1848.

32. Palmer, *Navigation Laws*, pp. 126-31.

33. 'To the Secretary of the Bradford Reform Association', BJL, DTH 3/30; *Sun*, 31 May, 5,12 June 1848; *Hansard*, xcix (1848), 9-70, 179-324, 510-59, 573-673; Palmer, *Navigation Laws*, pp. 131-2.

34. Palmer, *Navigation Laws*, pp. 132-6; Howe, *Free Trade*, pp. 59-60; *Hansard*, xcix (1848), 792-5, c (1848), 512-34.

35. 'To the Secretary of the Metropolitan Reform Association', BJL, DTH 3/30; *Sun*, 19 Feb. 1849; Palmer, *Navigation Laws*, pp. 137-41, 143-7; *Hansard*, cii (1849), 680-741.

36. *Hansard*, cii (1849), 720-3; Thompson to Peacock, 15 Feb. 1849, JRL, Eng. MS 1180/151; Thompson to Bowring, 24 Feb. 1849, BJL, DTH 4/13; *Daily News*, 15 Feb. 1849.

37. *Hansard*, cii (1849), 760-1, ciii (1849), 464-534, 540-629, 1196-1256; Searle, *Entrepreneurial Politics*, pp. 45-50; 'To the Secretary of the Metropolitan Reform Association', BJL, DTH 3/30; *Sun*, 12,14,26 Mar. 1849; Palmer, *Navigation Laws*, pp. 147-53.

38. Thompson to Peacock, 5 June 1849, JRL, Eng. MS 1180/153.

39. *Hansard*, civ (1849), 622-706, cv (1849), 1-120, 687-758, cvi (1849), 11-49; Palmer, *Navigation Laws*, pp. 153-62; Blake, *Disraeli*, p. 289; Howe, *Free Trade*, pp. 60-1, and idem, 'Free Trade and the City of London, 1820-70', *History*, lxxvii (1992), 393-410; Macintyre, 'Bentinck and the Protectionists', pp. 142, 149, 154, 157, 163-4; Gambles, 'Rethinking Protectionism', pp. 931-5, 938-9, 943-5; Jenkins, *Liberal Ascendancy*, p. 57; Hoppen, *Mid-Victorian Generation*, p. 136.

40. Gambles, 'Rethinking Protectionism', p. 950; Stewart, *Party and Politics*, p. 91; Evans, *Forging of the Modern State*, p. 342; Hoppen, *Mid-Victorian Generation*, pp. 136-7; Machin, *Disraeli*, pp. 71-2.

41. 'To the Secretary of the Metropolitan Reform Association', BJL, DTH 3/30; *Sun*, 12,19 Mar. 1849; *Hansard*, ciii (1849), 424-62, 702-47, 758-864; Blake, *Disraeli*, p. 288.

42. Thompson to Bowring, 19 Oct. 1849, BJL, DTH 4/13; *Spectator*, 13 Oct. 1849.

43. Howe, *Free Trade*, p. 47; Gash, *Reaction and Reconstruction*, p. 196.

44. Blake, *Disraeli*, pp. 290-1, 295; Hoppen, *Mid-Victorian Generation*, p. 137; *Hansard*, cviii (1850), 1026-1112, 1179-1275.

45. 'To the Secretary of the Bradford Reform Association', BJL, DTH 3/31; *Sun*, 12 Feb. 1851; *Hansard*, cxiv (1851), 374-450, 509-607; Hoppen, *Mid-Victorian Generation*, p. 137.

46. Thompson to Bowring, 24 Feb., 24 Mar., 18 Apr., 19 June, 17 July, 19 Aug., 23 Sept. 1851, and to G. Pryme, 18 Sept. 1851, BJL, DTH 4/14, and Brotherton Library, University of Leeds, Thompson Papers, MS277/1/75. Thompson did offer himself for re-election in Bradford in 1852, losing his seat by only 6 votes. He regained the seat in 1857.

47. Sykes, *British Liberalism*, pp. 35-6; Gash, *Aristocracy and People*, p. 246; Adelman, *Victorian Radicalism*, pp. 23-7; Stewart, *Party and Politics*, p. 87; Howe, *Free Trade*, pp. 5-7, 18-37, 105-10; Searle, *Entrepreneurial Politics*, ch. 1; Hoppen, *Mid-Victorian Generation*, p. 128; McCord, *Anti-Corn Law League*, pp. 208-15. Later reformers may have followed the example not of the League but of the Anti-Slavery Society: Taylor, *Decline of Radicalism*, p. 9.

48. Howe, *Free Trade*, ch. 3; N. C. Edsall, *Richard Cobden: Independent Radical* (London, 1986), chs. 17-18; Taylor, *Decline of Radicalism*, ch. 6; A. Tyrrell, *Joseph Sturge and the Moral Radical Party in early Victorian Britain* (London, 1987), ch. 13; K. Robbins, *John Bright* (London, 1979), pp. 78-91.

49. Adelman, *Victorian Radicalism*, p. 27 and ch. 2; Taylor, *Decline of Radicalism*, pp. 154-5, 157; Jenkins, *Liberal Ascendancy*, p. 72; Robbins, *Bright*, ch. 7; D. Read, *Cobden and Bright: A Victorian Political Partnership* (London, 1967), part 3; Edsall, *Cobden*, chs. 14-18; M. J. Turner, 'Before the Manchester School: Economic Ideas in Early Nineteenth-Century Manchester', *History*, lxxix (1994), 216-41; A. Howe, *The Cotton Masters, 1830-60* (Oxford, 1984), pp. 209-15, 229-44; C. Schonhardt-Bailey, 'Lessons in Lobbying for Free Trade in Nineteenth-Century Britain: To Concentrate or Not', *American Political Science Review*, lxxxv (1991), 52.

50. Howe, *Free Trade*, pp. 38-44, 64-5; Jenkins, *Liberal Ascendancy*, p. 72.

Chapter 6

The Joint Stock Company in Politics*

In 1855, the Limited Liability Bill was being debated in the Commons. The Bill would restrict the liability of shareholders in joint stock companies to the value of their shares, rather than placing shareholders' entire fortunes at the disposal of creditors in the event of company failure. The prime minister, Palmerston, asserted that the measure was a simple 'question of free trade against monopoly.'[1] Historians have largely agreed with Palmerston, presenting the reform of company law as part of the early- and mid-Victorian drive towards free trade and retrenchment. But they have failed to explore the paradox that while this legislation was passed in the name of political economy and free trade, it contravened Adam Smith's writings on the subject, and was opposed by some of the most prominent free traders of the day. Both supporters and opponents of the Limited Liability Bill invoked the principles of free trade and non-interference. For the Liberal Viscount Goderich, limited liability was a reform 'consistent with the whole course of their recent commercial legislation'.[2] But for the radical Archibald Hastie, the move towards general limited liability was 'a march of retrogression' which threatened the nation's commercial eminence.[3] Notable free traders could be found on each side of the debate: while the supporters of limited liability included Nassau Senior, John Stuart Mill, Richard Cobden, and Robert Lowe, the opponents had among their number Thomas Tooke, J. R. McCulloch, Lord Overstone, and William Gladstone. The arguments of the winning side, endorsed by historians, have been well detailed; the opinions of the losers have been marginalised or belittled. This essay seeks to redress the balance by examining the free trade case against joint stock companies.

The history of the relationship between joint stock companies and the state first attracted sustained attention in the 1930s. Articles by H. A. Shannon were followed by monographs covering first the nineteenth century, by Bishop Hunt, then the eighteenth century, by Armand DuBois, and a survey of business organisation since the mid-nineteenth-century, by James B. Jefferys.[4] This work, particularly that of Shannon and Hunt, established an interpretation of the changes in the laws regulating joint stock companies through the nineteenth-century which has in many ways persisted until the present day. According to this interpretation, the so-called 'Bubble

Act', passed in response to the speculative boom of 1719-20, placed a block on economic development for over a century until it was wisely repealed during another boom in 1825. However, so this argument runs, due to conservatism and prejudice, legislators and lawyers were slow to appreciate the necessity of removing all impediments to joint stock enterprise, and the country had to wait until acts of 1844, 1855, and 1856 before restrictions on access to corporate advantages were completely removed. This interpretation is characterised by a belief in the inevitability of the change in the law, and by a tone of impatience with those who resisted it. Shannon gave no sense of the deep ideological conflict underlying debate in this period. Reform was inevitable, for without it, 'full economic development was impossible.'[5] The conservatism of the legal profession and of certain businessmen and the indifference of the legislature conspired to delay 'the correction of an unsuitable body of law'.[6] In Shannon's account, the unquestionable superiority of the reformers' arguments eventually secured the necessary changes. We are told, for example, that following Robert Lowe's speech in 1856 outlining his limited liability bill, 'There was no debate – there could hardly be any after his speech – and the Bill passed easily.'[7]

Hunt served up a similar account. He was dismissive of the nineteenth-century 'prejudice' against the company as a form of business organisation, and contended that 'Hoary ideas of partnership' tended 'to confuse thinking with regard to corporate enterprise.'[8] For Hunt, the history of the joint stock company in England 'during the one hundred and fifty years following the statute of 1720 is the story of an economic necessity forcing its way slowly and painfully to legal recognition against strong commercial prejudice in favour of "individual" enterprise, and in the face of determined attempts of both the legislature and the courts to deny it.'[9] Left wing historians produced conclusions indistinguishable from Hunt's. John Saville found no reason to question the identification of limited liability with free trade, holding that, 'With the acceptance of limited liability in 1855 a free-trade parliament had at last applied the principles of a laissez faire political economy to money and commercial dealings.' Hesitancy, he explained, had been due to 'the carryover of traditional ways of thinking and the confusions which resulted therefrom.'[10]

These early views have coloured the subsequent literature to a great extent. The interpretations of Hunt and Shannon and others are frequently recycled, sometimes without criticism. In 1979, P. S. Atiyah saw the reforms of 1855-6 as part of the rise of the principle of freedom of contract. He blamed the 'old-fashioned' views of senior legal authorities for the state's slowness to grant companies full rights of incorporation: Lord Chancellor Eldon's judgements were 'irresponsible', Chief Justice Best 'sided against history.' At one point, Atiyah, evidently impatient with such obstructionism, declares, 'Clearly, this could not go on in the new age.'[11] Later, he comments on the controversy over limited liability, that 'the outcome of the debate appears today to have had an air of inevitability about it.'[12] Henry Butler's account of the change in company law posits a straightforward struggle between the forces of 'liberalisation' and conservatism. Aside from conservatism, ignorance was the other principal obstacle to reform: 'the absence of a complete understanding of the important economic role of limited liability in the corporate firm may account for the tardiness of granting this final attribute of corporateness.'[13] Nevertheless, ultimately it was the case that 'the political atmosphere of the time probably made it impossible to legislate against the freedom of contract'.[14]

There are exceptions, however. Ron Harris has rejected earlier assumptions that the process of company law reform was 'linear and progressive', and has attempted to detail a more nuanced process.[15] Boyd Hilton has produced an insightful account of the way in which limited liability generated a real intellectual and religious division of opinion in mid-nineteenth century Britain. Hilton comments that both sides claimed that their views were consistent with free trade, and speculates briefly as to what each side meant by the term 'free trade'.[16] Despite these valuable contributions, however, there remains a need for a study of the profound disagreements opened up in free trade thought by the issue of joint stock companies. The following essay explores this schism, and tries to undermine the still common crude identification of the company law reforms of 1844-56 with free trade.[17]

Robert Lowe, one of the most outspoken supporters of the principle of limited liability in Victorian Britain, explained his views to the Commons when president of the board of trade in 1856. He argued that the government should never 'interfere with and abridge men's liberty'. The right to form limited companies was based on 'natural law'.[18] He was keen to invoke the principles of political economy in support of his position, yet, as Lowe's critics pointed out, Adam Smith had been unequivocally sceptical about the public benefits of joint stock companies. 'To establish a joint stock company', Smith wrote, 'for any undertaking, merely because such a company might be capable of managing it successfully; or to exempt a particular set of dealers from some of the general laws which take place with regard to all their neighbours...would certainly not be reasonable.' The establishment of such companies, he continued, could 'scarce ever fail to do more harm than good.'[19] Smith and his followers saw no reason for companies to be exempted from partnership law, which provided a fair and free system within which business could operate. It was not restrictive, and allowed firms of any size to conduct a business. John George, a barrister writing in 1825 to clarify the state of the law, pointed out that under the current law, 'every person may lawfully carry on any trade, or manual occupation for gaining his livelihood, in any place he chooses, and either alone, or in partnership with others, and with as many others, as he pleases.'[20]

When large companies sought special powers from the state, the livelihoods of existing businesses which traded without these special powers were threatened. As a result, the public interest was placed in jeopardy. If individual traders were, as so many feared they would be, driven out of the market, then the public would be left at the mercy of a few powerful monopolies. More joint stock companies therefore meant less competition. John George opposed the grant of powers of suing and being sued in the name of an agent to any company engaged in a domestic trade in competition with individuals, viewing the legal inconveniences faced by companies as a natural shield for individual enterprise. George stressed the unreasonableness of companies' demands on this score:

> The Joint Stock Company is, in substance, saying – 'We, by means of our great capital, shall be able to supply you with milk, or garden stuff, or fish, at a lower price than the ordinary milkman, market gardener, or fishmonger can afford them to you for. But from our very numbers we are exposed to some natural and necessary inconveniences in the bringing of actions, which we will thank you to remove, in order that we, who are a giant, may the more successfully oppose and drive out of the market the common tradesman, the little isolated dealer, who is working to support himself and his family by his individual exertions. We request you to aid and further us, the giant, in our designs against the pigmy, against this man who has it not in his power to compete with us.'[21]

Even more potent was the power of limited liability, which made it easier for companies to amass large capitals than small partnerships or individual traders. Edmund Phillips, a staunch opponent of all monopolies, from the corn laws to the Bank of England's charter, opposed limited liability on the grounds that it was a form of privileged trading which minimised risk while leaving the way open to huge profits. The competition which would ensue between companies and small traders was unfair, for the risks undergone by the two parties were unequal. If the small trader failed, 'he and his family are by the Bankruptcy laws stripped of every earthly thing which they possess, even to their very beds', but if the company failed, the members only had to pay what they had subscribed, money they could afford to lose.[22] He argued that limited liability had created 'a host of little monopolies, to swallow up the small and industrious traders, and to derange the whole course of business.' These companies would have the effect of 'making serfs of' small traders, and since the wellbeing of the nation depended upon the independence and prosperity of these traders, the result would be 'to transform a great country into a very little one.'[23] Thomas Tooke agreed, arguing that the law of partnership was the normal state, and limited liability the exception. He opposed moves to introduce the French system of *en commandite* partnerships, whereby the liability of non-directing partners was limited, on the grounds that such a system was an unwarranted interference in trade.

> There seems to prevail, among those who incline to the introduction of the *commandite* system, a vague notion that something like a right exists, on the part of individuals, to circumscribe their liability, as the condition of their embarking a certain sum in trade; and that it is only by the special interference of the law of partnership that they are prevented from exercising that right; that the law is an interference with what otherwise would be the free, and probably, therefore, the best direction of capital in trade; and that the permission to invest in *commandite* is consequently only the removal of an impolitic restriction.[24]

Tooke attempted to refute this argument, holding that 'the *commandite* is a privilege and has not the shadow of foundation as a natural right', because the universal rule of commerce was that the individual was fully liable for engagements entered into by himself, or jointly with others. It was 'only by the interposition of a special law' that he could be shielded from this rule, and such an imposition 'must be considered as conferring a privilege.'[25]

Parliamentary debates in the 1820s and 1830s reveal a keen awareness across the political spectrum of the monopolistic implications of creating large companies in fields hitherto occupied by private traders. The Equitable Loan Company Bill in 1824 was opposed by various politicians who thought such a company would unfairly threaten the livelihood of London's pawnbrokers, and by implication, the interests of the consumer. William Whitbread 'looked with great jealousy at the combination of gentlemen to destroy the trade of individuals.'[26] John Cam Hobhouse, the radical, opposed the Bill 'for the sake of all tradesmen; for, if this bill were carried, there was no reason why joint-stock companies of butchers or bakers should not be established. The real object of the promoters of the bill was private profit, and by that profit the public would be losers.'[27] When, in the following session, the Bill reached the Lords, Lauderdale stated that he 'could not concur in the assertion, that joint stock companies encouraged competition. So far from it that he thought the direct effect of them was to destroy all competition and to bring the most ruinous consequences upon trade.'[28] The Metropolitan Fish Company Bill of 1825 was opposed on similar lines. John Grant, the Whig lawyer, 'thought that the House could not do any thing more injurious to the regular supply of the market, than to give a chimerical company advantages which were not possessed by the regular fishermen.'[29] His fellow Whig John Calcraft argued that the 'effect of this and every similar company was, to take the bread out of the mouths of industrious individuals…The public would derive no benefit from these companies, as they already procured fish at as cheap a rate as the nature of the commerce would allow.'[30]

In 1833, the St. George's Steam Packet Company's Bill was opposed by many Members who thought the state ought not to create monopolistic corporations by granting special powers to some businesses and denying them to others. For the radical Fergus O'Connor, the Bill represented a reversal of the government's commendable battle against corporations. Existing steam packet monopolies kept the freight charges of Irish produce artificially high. The House should not add to these monopolies, especially now, 'just at the time when the House was doing away with other corporations. This Bill did, in fact, go to establish a corporation on the high seas.'[31] His fellow radical John Jervis, subsequently attorney-general, thought it was the duty of the House to 'protect the public, and take care the public should have as cheap and expeditious a conveyance from one part of the country to another as possible.'[32] The company in question was an 'unnatural coalition' of shipowners who had joined together as shareholders in order to obtain special privileges from the House, in order to ruin other Companies and to deny the public cheap and safe transport.³³ The Whig Earl of Ormelie agreed, arguing that the Bill was '*pro tanto* a monopoly; for the provision for suing and being sued was a privilege beyond the common law.' He continued that the 'object and the practice of the Company had been to throw out every competitor, and the parties now came to parliament to enable them to perpetuate the system.'³⁴

These, and many similar debates, reveal the association commonly made between joint stock companies and monopoly. Joint stock companies were widely seen as a form of exclusive dealing which if carried on extensively would be harmful to the public interest. The *Times* vividly articulated this orthodoxy, arguing that 'private trade and enterprise are the life and support of a country, its strength and riches; and joint-stock companies are but occasional remedies, powerful and efficacious in certain disorders and contingencies, but destructive, debilitating, and disorganising, when used as food, and applied habitually.'³⁵

In some trades, Smith had conceded, joint stock companies were unobjectionable. These were enterprises that could be reduced to a routine, those that required a large capital, and those which were of undoubted public utility. Among these he counted banks, insurance companies, inland navigations, and water companies. Eighty years on, J. R. McCulloch was of the same opinion, merely extending the list to include railways, docks, and gas companies.³⁶ In all other fields, joint stock companies were unnecessary and harmful. This stance was inspired not solely by fears of the unfair competition which would ensue between companies and individuals, but by the conviction that joint stock concerns could never be nearly so well managed as small partnerships or private firms. Smith had written that the directors of companies

> being the managers rather of other people's money than of their own, it cannot well be expected, that they should watch over it with the same anxious vigilance with which the partners in a private copartnery frequently watch over their own. Like the stewards of a rich man, they are apt to consider attention to small matters as not for their master's honour, and very easily give themselves a dispensation from having it. Negligence and profusion, therefore, must always prevail, more or less, in the management of the affairs of such a company.³⁷

His views continued to influence political economists long into the nineteenth century. Tooke held that 'according to all recorded observation, public companies are rarely, if ever, so carefully, economically and skilfully conducted as private establishments.'³⁸ George Larpent, a member of the Political Economy Club, thought that limited companies would reduce incentives to industry by making it safe for capitalists to unite in large partnerships in ordinary trades, leaving the actual management to paid subalterns of inferior talents. This would 'deteriorate the talents and character of the mercantile and manufacturing classes.' There would be no compensating gain to these classes from the ranks of the paid managers, for they would have no incentive to work hard, as no amount of saving from a salary would enable such a manager to become a capitalist himself.³⁹ McCulloch thought that in small partnerships, each partner was fully aware of his interests and responsibilities, and 'exerts himself to obviate extravagance or mismanagement in the conduct of the business, and to make it a source of profit.' This attentiveness did not characterise great associations in which individual members felt that their efforts were likely to have little influence or effect, and carelessness shaded into recklessness and foolhardiness when the business was carried on with limited liability and therefore limited risk.[40] For the *Times* the operations of large companies 'can no more be conducted with the economy of private concerns than can those of a Government.'[41]

Why, asked the proponents of joint stock companies, should limited liability be dreaded if companies were inherently inferior to individual enterprise? What had partnerships to fear from organisations hampered by inefficient and extravagant management? The answer typically given was that joint stock companies, especially those with limited liability, could profoundly derange trade. The greater the number of companies trading with limited responsibility, the greater the opportunities for irresponsible speculation. That the prospect of unlimited gain should be balanced by the possibility of unlimited loss was of more than moral interest: if risk were lessened, and responsibility curtailed, the normal working of the rules of demand and supply would be undermined, to the detriment of the community. Trades which were currently conducted to the healthy profit of individual businessmen would be invaded by companies, established by speculators jealous of these profits, who hoped they would be able to earn similar returns, and knew that their losses should they fail would be restricted. The prospect of unlimited gain with limited risk was sufficient to tempt capital into channels already naturally full. Boards would be constituted, subscriptions opened, works constructed, all in expectation of, rather than in response to, demand. Such companies would eventually fail, but only after they had glutted the market, causing severe damage to existing traders, as 'the farce of supply before demand [was] turned into a tragedy'.[42]

The boom and bust of the so-called 'railway mania' of the mid-1840s led contemporaries to diametrically opposed conclusions. Some argued that it was not limited liability *per se* that caused the railway mania, but its incomplete concession. As limited liability was only freely available in the field of railway enterprise, capital was dangerously over-concentrated in this one area. If limited liability were made available in all trades, capital would be more healthily distributed across the economy.[43] Others argued that to make limited liability more generally available would only encourage the extension of the wanton speculation of the mania to the rest of the economy. Huge damage would be done by drawing capital away from legitimate trade. Honest, patient labour would be abandoned in favour of speculation made safe by statute.[44]

Supporters of limited liability claimed that unlimited liability was obstructive and restrictive. Richard Cobden complained that at present, 'capital was dammed up';[45] according to William Ewart, 'capital was constantly struggling to break the bonds which beset it'.[46] Limited liability would allow capital to flow freely throughout the economy. Others used similar imagery to opposite effect. 'All that this nation requires is plain, straightforward dealing, at the fountains of its commerce; then all its streams will flow freely and profitably, without any extraneous and un-English protection.'[47] Many free traders believed that no artificial stimulants were required to boost commercial activity. All sound enterprises which promised fair profits would find capital: if a firm had difficulty in attracting backing, this was for good reason. Similarly, all valuable inventions would find private capital to develop them: there was no need to limit responsibility in order to encourage investment in them.[48] In the 1830s, Tooke wrote that enterprise was 'on the full stretch in every accessible branch of industry', and 'an abundance, I should almost say an exuberance, of capital presents itself as being ready to embark in any enterprise that holds out a specious prospect of gain'.[49] Twenty years later, McCulloch was making the same point. More could be said for limited liability if people were reluctant to engage in ordinary partnerships, thought McCulloch. But this was not the case. 'Why relieve them of their natural responsibility', he asked, 'to make them embrace pursuits in which they are ready and anxious to engage without any extraordinary stimulus?'[50] Limited liability would not encourage trade, for trade did not need encouragement. Rather it would derange trade by encouraging over-speculation. The nation's commercial and industrial supremacy was built on the notion of personal responsibility. The adoption of a contrary system might 'mark the era of our decline'.[51]

Supporters of joint stock enterprise often resorted to freedom of contract arguments to justify the general adoption of limited liability. If an individual was willing to lend to a company on terms of limited liability, why should the state forbid it? If the public were willing to deal with these companies, why should the state interfere? But these superficially plausible arguments hid the fact that these freedoms already existed: individual contracts based on limited liability could be drawn up if all parties concerned agreed on the limitation, but it was another thing entirely to argue that the state should automatically enforce limited liability in all contracts. The Scottish judge John Marshall argued that partners in a concern should only be absolved from their obligations by an explicit and unequivocal agreement from the creditors of the business. They should not be freed by a general act of parliament: without an agreement with the creditors, unlimited liability ought to be presumed. A system of general limited liability would not require a partner to prove or even to allege that there had been an agreement between him and the creditor that the former's liability was limited.[52] It was far safer and fairer to insist that limited liability be written into every individual contract.

Freedom of contract arguments also overlooked the fact that, given the realities of the complex web of commercial transactions which characterised nineteenth-century trade, there were such things as unintentional creditors. William Hawes, a merchant, disagreed with those who argued that anyone giving credit to a company did so at his peril and therefore deserved any misfortune which arose from the transaction. 'Such writers know little of the working of commercial operations in this country; they forget, or are ignorant of, how much involuntary credit is given; how Bills pass from hand to hand'.[53] He went on to explain that bills drawn by a limited company on another limited company might be remitted to a trader with unlimited liability. In this way, the fortunes of such traders would become dependent on the vicissitudes of the joint stock economy.

Supporters of limited liability argued that the public did not have to deal with limited liability companies if they did not want to. Even after limited liability was made general, there would still be choice. William Thomson, an Edinburgh shipbroker who backed limited liability, stated, 'I am quite satisfied joint stock companies never will successfully compete with private enterprise and management in any well-known business, and within the range of ordinary capital.'[54] But others were not so sure. Not only would private partnerships struggle to compete with limited companies, they would also be tempted to convert to this form of organisation. Edward Cox, editor of the *Law Times*, thought the principle of limited liability immoral, but urged private traders to avail themselves of it in order to avoid being ruined by unfair competition.[55] In such a scenario, public choice would become non-existent as consumers were forced to deal with limited companies.

Supporters of limited liability believed that the principle posed no threat to the public because limited companies were self-regulating. They claimed that, provided adequate information on companies was made available to the public, rotten or fraudulent concerns would fail, because no one would invest in them.[56] Others claimed that such hopes were unrealistic. McCulloch argued that publication of accounts was no safeguard, for it was easy to 'dress up a return, to make a rickety or bankrupt concern appear to be flourishing and wealthy'.[57] Hawes was dismissive of the argument that people should be free to deal with others on any terms they liked, provided 'the terms are known', because they gave a false picture of the state of the company. The terms referred to were the details of the subscribers to the company, and the amount subscribed by each one. But this did not provide the full picture. To make the terms fully known, the liabilities of the company had to be publicised as well:

> every speculation which may risk more than the invested and registered capital, must be at once published – every untoward loss declared, otherwise the notices of the names of the partners and the capital advanced, proposed by the advocates of this system, to be posted over the doors, counters, and desks, would be but a delusion and a snare for the ignorant and unwary, and specially dangerous and delusive, because countenanced by Act of Parliament.[58]

Cox agreed. Ascertaining the amount of capital a company traded with revealed nothing to a potential creditor: just because a company began business with a certain capital, there was no guarantee it would still be in possession of it at the time the inquiry was made. Lists of shareholders were of little use, and none whatsoever if the shares were fully paid up, for they bore no additional liability.[59]

Furthermore, even if extensive information was made available, many doubted that the public could ever be efficient regulators. Companies paraded illustrious lists of names to show what support they had, and this often blinded the public to the realities of the business before them. J. Hooper Hartnoll, proprietor and editor of the *Post Magazine*, complained that people were frequently 'entrapped by the array of *Majors, Captains, Esquires, and MP's* which figure in the prospectuses of many rotten companies'.[60] *Punch* was of the opinion that the public would be flawed regulators, for they were all too easily caught up in the excitement of speculation and in such a mood were easily made the dupes of roguish company promoters. One cartoon, from November 1845, depicts John Bull stepping on a train-shaped skate marked 'SPEC' and losing his balance: he skitters down the road, shares and scrip falling out of his pockets, to his ruin.[61]

Paradoxically, while enemies of general limited liability opposed it in the name of free trade and unrestricted competition, they were forced into the position of supporting a significant role for the state in determining economic development, since it was the state that had to decide every exception made to the principle of unlimited liability. Charles Poulett Thomson, Whig president of the board of trade in the 1830s and staunch free trader, was keen to ensure that only concerns which could not raise capital under partnership law should gain corporate privileges. He was firmly of the view that the board was the best authority for determining which companies required these privileges. A board of trade minute of 1834 reveals Thomson's philosophy: it was necessary to take care that special powers were not conferred 'indiscriminately', and that 'facilities should not be afforded to Joint Stock Partnerships which may interfere with private enterprise carried on under those laws, unless the circumstances and objects of such Joint Stock Companies are of a nature fully to justify such interference, upon the ground of general public advantage.'[62] The board's subsequent minutes reveal that Thomson put his principles into practice, as indeed did his Conservative counterpart, Alexander Baring, during Peel's brief ministry of 1834-5.[63] The board's reluctance to permit companies with any form of special privileges to compete with private traders indicates how supporters of non-interference were nonetheless keen to afford a prominent role to government discretion.

Although Thomson had considered the board's powers an important protection for the public, Gladstone, president of the board under Peel from 1843, thought they were a nuisance. He confided in the House 'that when he was sitting in the board of trade with others about him, attending, to the best of his ability, to his duties, there was nothing gave the board so much uneasiness and annoyance as the exercise of the discretionary powers already vested in them as to the management of commercial matters.'[64] The result was the Joint Stock Companies Act of 1844, which extended to companies many of the privileges of incorporation on registration, such as a separate legal persona, and the power of suing and being sued in the courts. While this was intended as much to protect the public, by making companies more answerable for their actions in law, as to encourage corporate enterprise, a key impetus behind the measure was the desire to put an end to the board's troublesome function of dispensing corporate privileges. However, while Gladstone wanted to improve access to corporate privileges, he did not want to concede general limited liability. Companies registering under the Act were not granted this privilege. Subsequent presidents of the board of trade shared Gladstone's reservations on this score, notably Henry Labouchere,[65] and Edward Cardwell. The latter, who served in Aberdeen's coalition government, argued that to create great numbers of limited companies would be to subvert fundamental economic and moral rules. The law made 'every one who shares in the profit of a trading concern responsible for the loss, to the whole extent of his fortune; a principle which is laid down in the law books as founded on natural justice, and for which every possible authority can be cited, from Lord Mansfield to this day.'[66] Cardwell asked, 'In the case of insolvency, where somebody must lose, who should bear the loss but those who have enjoyed the chances of gain?'[67]

But as the numbers of high risk or capital-intensive projects grew, the state was called upon to reach decisions on an ever-increasing number of schemes. Parliament passed 135 acts granting limited liability in the ten years between 1844 and 1853. In the same period, the board of trade granted 65 charters conferring limited liability, and refused 50.[68] With such a level of activity, the position of those who supported unlimited liability, but who were willing to make exceptions for certain businesses, was easily characterised as unhealthily paternalistic and unnecessarily interventionist. The *Morning Herald* argued that the potential for corruption in the state's role was too great:

> The Board of Trade have the power of granting charters of limited liability; but it is obvious that the power of opening or closing vast sources of wealth and industry should not be placed in the hands of any department of the Government, to be used at its discretion – to be moved by intrigue, jobbing, or favouritism – a privilege to be conferred or withheld according to some arbitrary rule.[69]

The *Westminster Review* held that 'Government has neither the mission nor the power to guide its subjects to good, or to drive them from bad investments.'[70] Edwin Field, a company solicitor, thought it unfair that a secret inquisition such as the board should have such power over parties associating for trade, and condemned what he called 'the Paternal Theory of Commercial Legislation'.[71]

Even Cardwell, who, as we have seen, was in favour of unlimited liability, complained in parliament of 'the invidious power vested in him' of granting charters.[72] In a cabinet memorandum of January 1853, he confessed, 'I heartily wish that the law was self-acting, and that the power of interposition did not belong to the Board of Trade.'[73] To confer the powers entirely on parliament was equally unsatisfactory: the potential for corruption in parliamentary committees on private bills, a bugbear of radicals and others since the 1820s, was dramatically underlined by the railway mania of the 1840s, and continued to be discussed into the 1850s.[74] In this context, supporters of limited liability found it easier than their opponents to couch their arguments in laissez faire terms. With a system of automatic registration, the role of both parliament and board of trade was eliminated altogether, and the spectre of corrupt legislators and improper approaches to the executive disappeared.

The fall of Aberdeen's government and the arrival of Palmerston prompted the introduction of bills to widen the availability of limited liability to joint stock companies and partnerships. This brought the conflict between free traders out into the open. Palmerston stated his surprise 'that Gentlemen who have been the strenuous and successful advocates of the principles of free trade should now turn round and try to defeat these Bills, which are based upon those very principles'.[75] Conversely, the Manchester merchant Edmund Potter was startled that a paper such as the *Economist*, 'hitherto professedly the organ of free trade opinions', should advocate general limited liability,[76] while Lord Overstone complained that politicians were endeavouring 'through the most flimsy sophistry' to associate limited liability with free trade, 'matters which have the same relation to each other which Darkness has to light.'[77] Supporters of limited liability made sense of the situation by imputing sinister motives to their opponents, who were 'large capitalists' like Overstone, bent on defending their monopoly of capital. Some went as far as to make limited liability a class issue. The *Morning Chronicle* painted all opponents to general limited liability as self-interested 'mouthpieces of the capitalist class'.[78] *Lloyd's Weekly Newspaper* highlighted the resistance of George Muntz, a Birmingham iron master and radical free trader, to general limited liability. Muntz admired individual enterprise, but objected to companies, because he did not want to have to compete with them.

> Pass the Limited Liabilities Bill, and companies made up of ten pound individuals must, at least, rise to the gigantic height of Muntz; even if they do not somewhat dwarf him. Mr. Muntz is now the brass Colossus of Birmingham: with limited liabilities made the law, Mr. Muntz is no bigger than Mr. Company.[79]

Even Palmerston, hardly a keen democrat, joined in portraying the struggle for limited liability as a contest 'between the few and the many'.[80] McCulloch, on the other hand, thought that to argue that supporters of unlimited liability were advocating monopoly was absurd. Under the law as it stood, entrepreneurs could engage in any business they liked, but they had to abide by the results of their actions, accepting profits, or paying debts as appropriate. These were 'the dictates of plain common sense', argued McCulloch, and had 'as much in common with monopoly as they have with the theory of the tides'.[81]

But the Limited Liability Bill was passed on the tide of unpopularity of the 'large capitalists'.[82] Cobden told the House that these men, hitherto the champions of economical reform, opposed limited liability because they were blinded to their real interests, and to the public interest, by their closeness to the subject. He compared them to the agriculturalists who had opposed the repeal of the corn laws, and the shipowners who had opposed the repeal of the navigation acts, and who now basked in unprecedented prosperity. The case was the same with the capitalists: they were 'afraid that a law of limited liability would injure capital.' But their opinion meant nothing, because 'he did not think that any class could be trusted to legislate in favour of its own interest'. In reality, nothing could be 'more suicidal on the part of capitalists than to oppose' limited liability, for it would open up unimaginable new fields for their capital.[83] Other, less sympathetic critics than Cobden accused the large capitalists of base hypocrisy: the Conservative *Morning Herald* crowed that they had 'evinced great public spirit once upon a time; they could afford to be free-traders at the expense of others; but when the application of the principle comes home to themselves they are its bitter opponents'.[84] Opponents of the reform found themselves outnumbered and outmanoeuvred in parliament, and general limited liability for joint stock companies was enshrined in law in acts of 1855, 1856, 1858, and 1862.

The subject of joint stock companies caused a serious division in free trade thought, a fact which was obscured by much contemporary rhetoric and political strategy, and which has not been fully appreciated by historians too keen to accept the arguments of the winning side uncritically. Men like Tooke, McCulloch, and Potter opposed limited liability using the language of non-interference and natural justice. This was more than a debating technique. In supporting unlimited liability, they believed they were upholding some of the basic principles of free trade and individualism. Yet their reliance on the state to determine which enterprises were worthy and which unworthy of special privileges fatally undermined their position. This function of the state, employed more frequently than ever before in the 1840s and 1850s, came to be seen in an increasingly negative light. At the same time, an alternative model based, so its proponents argued, on freedom of contract, non-interference, and regulation by the public rather than the state, gained the support of growing numbers of economists, lawyers, businessmen, and politicians. As a result, unlimited liability, upheld for so long in the name of free trade, was abandoned, in the name of free trade.

References

*I would like to thank Hugh Cunningham and Emily Payne for comments on earlier drafts of this essay. My research has been funded by an AHRB Postgraduate Studentship held at the University of Kent, and an Economic History Society Postdoctoral Fellowship held at the Institute of Historical Research.

1. *Hansard*, third series, cxxxix (26 July 1855), 1390. All references are to the third series, unless stated.

2. *Hansard*, cxxxiv (27 June 1854), 760.

3. Ibid., cxxxix (29 June 1855), 357.

4. H. A. Shannon, 'The Coming of General Limited Liability', *Economic History*, ii (1931), 267-91, and idem, 'The First Five Thousand Limited Companies and their Duration', *Economic History*, iii (1932), 396-424; C. Hunt, *The Development of the Business Corporation in England, 1800-1867* (New York, 1936); A. Dubois, *The English Business Company after the Bubble Act, 1720-1800* (Massachusetts, 1938); J. B. Jefferys, 'Trends in Business Organisation in Great Britain Since 1856' (University of London, PhD thesis, 1938).

5. Shannon, 'General Limited Liability', p. 274.

6. Ibid., p. 271.

7. Ibid., p. 289.

8. Hunt, *Development of the Business Corporation*, pp. 129-31.

9. Ibid., p. 13

10. J. Saville, 'Sleeping Partnership and Limited Liability, 1850-1856', *Economic History Review*, viii (1956), 418-33 at 431.

11. P. S. Atiyah, *The Rise and Fall of Freedom of Contract* (Oxford, 1979), p. 564.

12. Ibid., p. 566.

13. H. N. Butler, 'General Incorporation in Nineteenth-Century England: Interaction of Common Law and Legislative Processes', *International Review of Law and Economics*, vi (1986), 169-87 at 181.

14. Ibid., p. 182.

15. R. Harris, 'Industrialisation Without Free Incorporation: The Legal Framework of Business Organisation in England, 1720-1844' (Columbia University, PhD thesis, 1994), p. 9. See also idem, *Industrialising English Law: Entrepreneurship and Business Organisation, 1720-1844* (Cambridge, 2000). But the limitations of Harris's approach are concisely exposed in P. Ireland, 'History, Critical Legal Studies and the Mysterious Disappearance of Capitalism', *The Modern Law Review*, lxv (2002), 120-40.

16. B. Hilton, *The Age of Atonement: The Influence of Evangelicalism on Social and Economic Thought*, 1785-1865 (Oxford, 1988), pp. 255-67.

17. For a fuller exploration of nineteenth-century views on joint stock enterprise, see J. Taylor, '"Wealth Makes Worship": Attitudes to Joint Stock Enterprise in British Law, Politics, and Culture, c.1800–c.1870' (University of Kent, PhD thesis, 2002).

18. *Hansard*, cxl (1 Feb. 1856), 138.

19. A. Smith, *An Inquiry into the Nature and Causes of the Wealth of Nations* [1776] (Oxford, 1976), pp. 757-8.

20. J. George, *A View of the Existing Law Affecting Unincorporated Joint Stock Companies* (London, 1825), p. 5.

21. Ibid., p. 73.

22. E. Phillips, *Bank of England Charter, Currency, Limited Liability Companies, and Free Trade* (London, 1856), p. 36.

23. Ibid., p. 35.

24. *Report on the Law of Partnership*, P[arliamentary] P[apers], 1837 (530) XLIV, 399, p. 34.

25. Ibid.

26. *Hansard*, second series, xi (1 June 1824), 960.

27. Ibid.

28. Ibid., xiii (14 June 1825), 1135.

29. Ibid., xii (9 Mar. 1825), 966.

30. Ibid., (15 Mar. 1825), 1021.

31. Ibid., third series, xviii (19 June 1833) 995.

32. Ibid.

33. Ibid., 997.

34. Ibid.

35. *Times*, 9 Nov. 1840.

36. J. R. McCulloch, *Considerations on Partnerships With Limited Liability* (London, 1856), p. 4.

37. Smith, *Wealth of Nations*, p. 741.

38. *Report on the Law of Partnership*, PP, 1837, p. 33.

39. Ibid., p. 40.

40. McCulloch, *Considerations on Partnerships*, pp. 5-6.

41. *Times*, 9 Nov. 1840.

42. E. Potter, *Practical Opinions Against Partnership with Limited Liability, in a Letter to a Friend* (London, 1855), pp. 22-7.

43. Lord Hobart, *Remarks on the Law of Partnership Liability* (London, 1853).

44. E. W. Cox, *The Joint Stock Companies Act 1856, For the Regulation of Companies With or Without Limited Liability* (London, 1856), p. ix.

45. *Hansard*, cixx (17 Feb. 1852), 683.

46. Ibid., 684.

47. Phillips, *Bank of England Charter*, p. 35.

48. Potter, *Practical Opinions*, p. 53.

49. *Report on the Law of Partnership*, PP, 1837, p. 33.

50. McCulloch, *Considerations on Partnerships*, p. 12.

51. Ibid., p. 26.

52. *Royal Commission on the Assimilation of Mercantile Laws in the UK and Amendments in the Law of Partnership, as Regards the Question of Limited or Unlimited Responsibility*, PP, 1854 (1791) XXVII.445, p. 13.

53. W. Hawes, *Observations on Unlimited and Limited Liability; and Suggestions for the Improvements of the Law of Partnership* (London, 1854), p. 13.

54. *Royal Commission on Mercantile Laws*, PP, 1854, p. 76.

55. E. W. Cox, *The New Law and Practice of Joint Stock Companies, With and Without Limited Liability* (London, 1857), pp. xvii-xxi.

56. See for example the arguments of Edward Bouverie, *Hansard*, cxxxix (29 June 1855), 325.

57. McCulloch, *Observations on Partnerships*, p. 9.

58. Hawes, *Observations on Unlimited and Limited Liability*, p. 29.

59. Cox, *The Joint Stock Companies Act 1856*, p. ix.

60. J. H. Hartnoll, *A Letter to the Right Hon. E. Cardwell, M.P., President of the Board of Trade, on the Inoperative Character of the Joint Stock Companies Registration Act, as a Means of Preventing the Formation of Bubble Assurance Companies, or of Regulating the Action of those Honourably and Legitimately Instituted*, second edition (London, 1853), p. 10.

61. *Punch*, ix (1845), 202.

62. *Copy of the Minute of the Lords of the Committee of Privy Council for Trade, dated 4 November 1834, on Granting Letters Patent*, PP, 1837 (337) XXXIX.287, p. 1.

63. Public Record Office, BT 5/42, fos. 260-2 (4 Nov. 1834); BT 5/42, fo. 316 (20 Jan. 1835); BT 5/42, fo. 357 (20 Feb. 1835); BT 5/44, fos. 236-7 (10 Mar. 1837); BT 5/44, fos. 295-6 (18 Apr. 1837).

64. *Hansard*, lxxvi (3 July 1844), 276.

65. Ibid., cxix (17 Feb. 1852), 674.

66. E. Cardwell, 'Limited Liability', confidential memorandum dated 14 Jan. 1853, British Library, Gladstone Papers, Add.MS 44,570/169-73.

67. Ibid.

68. These figures exclude applications for supplemental charters. *Returns of All Applications to the Board of Trade for Grants of Charters With Limited Liability*, PP, 1854 (299) LXV.611.

69. *Morning Herald*, 10 July 1855.

70. Anon., 'Partnerships with Limited Liability', *Westminster Review*, lx (Oct. 1853), 375-416 at 398.

71. E. W. Field, *Observations of a Solicitor on the Right of the Public to Form Limited Liability Partnerships, and On the Theory, Practice, and Cost of Commercial Charters* (London, 1854), pp. iii, 84.

72. *Hansard*, cxxxiv (27 June 1854), 772.

73. Cardwell, 'Limited Liability', p. 9.

74. [A. Pulling], 'Private Bill Legislation', *Edinburgh Review*, cl (Jan. 1855), 151-91.

75. *Hansard*, cxxxix (26 July 1855), 1389.

76. Potter, *Practical Opinions*, preface, p. 5.

77. Overstone to Lord Granville, 21 Mar. 1856, in *Correspondence of Lord Overstone*, ed. D. P. O'Brien (3 vols, Cambridge, 1971), ii. 643.

78. *Morning Chronicle*, 11 Aug. 1855.

79. *Lloyd's Weekly Newspaper*, 5 Aug. 1855.

80. *Hansard*, cxxxix (26 July 1855), 1389.

81. McCulloch, *Observations on Partnerships*, p. 27.

82. The bill which would have extended limited liability to partnerships failed.

83. *Hansard*, cxxxiv (27 June 1854), 784.

84. *Morning Herald*, 30 July 1855.

Chapter 7

After Chartism: Metropolitan Perspectives on the Chartist Movement in Decline, 1848-1860

In his influential 'Rethinking Chartism', Gareth Stedman Jones questioned the emphasis on the 'local and occupational peculiarities' of the Chartist movement. He appealed instead for national perspectives that provided an overall picture of the agitation.[1] In recent years the local dimension to Chartism and post-Chartist reformism has apparently been superseded. James Vernon, Patrick Joyce, and Eugenio Biagini have constructed a national picture from the micro-level studies produced in the 1960s and 1970s.[2] In such work Chartism and its successor movements are interpreted as a national movement, and Chartist activity itself integrated into a broader consideration of radical culture and Liberal political mobilisation. Despite their ambitions to weave a national narrative of reform politics, much of this work remains rooted in the local case study with a strong bias towards the small mill towns of the North-West and the West Riding. This draws on an ideal-type of Liberalism. Following the tradition established by nineteenth-century Liberal standard-bearers like Henry Jephson, Joyce and Vernon recreate an idealised picture of provincial Liberalism as represented by and for the consumption of contemporaries.[3] Following the view of nineteenth-century Liberals themselves, it shows Liberal culture as an untroubled unity, drawing on a shared political culture with radicalism, and celebrating an untroubled Gladstonian Age of Equipoise.

This view is rather different from the periodic alarms of government and the moral panics of some Victorian commentators in the city that really mattered to contemporaries: the national and imperial capital of London. Recently a new metropolitan analysis has problematised London as a site of conflict over places of public meeting, gender, town planning, local government and the relief of poverty.[4] From an early stage London was seen as outside the norms of political, social and moral behaviour. A tension is therefore apparent between those historians who see the ascendancy of Liberal reformism at mid-century as uncontested, and those who detect a fault-line in the relationship between Liberalism and the radical constituency over reform, accentuated by the stresses of policing and weak local government in the metropolis.

This essay reappraises the less well-known metropolitan examples of popular reform politics in the years following the demise of the Chartist movement. Embracing a London-centred emphasis, it examines the continuing vitality of late Chartism and popular reformism in the capital as a corrective to a historiography that draws too derivatively on a regional perspective. It argues that current debates about continuity in radicalism may be modified by an analysis that considers the persistence of a vibrant radical identity existing outside Liberalism and expressed through club life, concern for the preservation of open spaces, and a culture of riotous assembly. In this it is informed by recent cultural readings of London.[5] Here the city acts as a lens, highlighting the divisions between the regions and the capital, and seeking to explain the apparent vitality of radicalism in the metropolis in terms of its proximity to central government, and the absence of those religious and cultural factors that favoured the formation of a popular Liberal consensus in the provinces. Even before the crisis of the 1880s, the vision of London as a hellish labyrinth was already widely established. In the 1860s London was less a site of enchantment than a place of corruption and social danger. For contemporaries radicalism in London was in part social threat, but was also emblematic of London's dissolving, crumbling polity itself.

In addition this essay seeks to remedy the deficiencies in the historiography of party forms. Historians of Chartism have sought to account for the demise of the movement by stressing changes within the workplace and new cultural forms of protest within the wider community. Much of this scholarship fails to relate radical activity to the framework of electoral and constituency politics. At the same time, despite the boom in 'continuity' studies, the historians of party have seen the 1850s as relatively unimportant in comparison to the great changes occurring in the aftermath of the 1867 Reform Act. Many of the recent generalisations about the formation of a popular Liberal milieu have been rooted in a reading of the politics of the 1860s that simply transposes better-known models onto the pre-1860 period.[6] In many ways the 1850s has become a no-man's-land falling between historiographical approaches in which the popular politics of the decade presents a lost dimension. The element that is conspicuously missing from work on this period is assessment of the relationship between surviving radical forms, particularly at grass-roots level, and emergent party structures. This has meant that there have been relatively few attempts to recapture the role of existing political groups and parties in either militating against, or, on occasion, encouraging, continuing traditions of mass participatory political action.

The traditional view of metropolitan politics is that the capital was difficult to mobilise, proved highly resistant to organisational innovation, and seldom provided the base for a national leadership whose absence amongst bickering factions hindered the Chartist movement in its closing stages. Francis Place's much quoted remarks about the difficulties of stimulating a response in London show the capital as a vacuum, impeding, rather than encouraging, the cause of reform.[7] Yet Place's comments grew out of his work as an agent for the Anti-Corn Law League, and may say more about the failure of the ACLL to establish itself in London than about the weaknesses of reformism in the capital more generally. As D. J. Rowe and others have noted, Chartism's growth as a movement was undoubtedly retarded by the sheer size of London and the attendant difficulties of organising a movement in such a huge area and amongst such a vast diversity of artisan trades and economic 'out' groups.[8] Nevertheless, historians have overlooked the degree to which Chartism surmounted these difficulties, both in 1842, and, building on that success, in 1848.[9] Indeed, outside the West Riding of Yorkshire the one area of significant Chartist revival in 1848 was London. More recent interpretations have argued for the debilitating impact of central government's policing methods on Chartist fortunes in 1848-9.[10] Whilst this may be true of the regions, in London Chartist organisation survived the backlash intact and established an infrastructure of radical organisation for its successor agitations.

In the 1840s Chartists in London confounded Place's gloomy prognosis and provided a strong organisational base for the movement. The triumph of Chartism in London during these years was largely an organisational one. After 1844 the National Charter Association was increasingly dominated by metropolitan delegates who monopolised key positions. This tendency became even more pronounced between 1848 and 1852. Whilst boding ill for the national administration of the movement and contributing to the breakdown of national perspectives within Chartism after 1850, this development preserved the agitational core of metropolitan radicalism intact.[11] Moreover, the movement's strong links with the metropolitan trades enabled it to create enduring branches rooted in individual trade associations that set up bridging groups between Chartist organisation and radical trades like the bootmakers, woodworkers, and portworkers. With their roots deep in the artisanal politics of the capital, organisations like the National Association of United Trades and the National Organisation of United Trades established a joint framework for collective action that consolidated the personnel in both camps.[12] An overemphasis on the clandestine revolutionary element grafted onto Chartism by its connection with Irish Confederate Clubs has also led historians to underestimate the organisational benefits conferred by mutual Irish and Chartist strategic planning during these years.[13] In London such benefits were considerable. Irish Confederate Clubs augmented the activities of the National Charter Association by providing a second, more convivial tier of organisation, through groups like the Ernest Jones Brigade and the Robert Emmet Club. The continuing vitality and strength of radicalism in the capital was dictated by Chartism's vigour in 1848. In some districts the movement was strong enough to flout government restrictions entirely and meet in defiance of police guards and spies following the arrest of leading conspirators in the summer.[14] The metropolitan radical scene had traditionally been characterised by a resilient counterculture of public houses and debating societies that preserved a nucleus of key personnel and leaders during periods of government repression.[15] This factor was as true of Chartism in

London in the period 1848-50 as it had been of the radicalism of the early 1820s. In the late 1840s in particular, the metropolitan focus of the NCA meant that Metropolitan Chartism retained a localised leadership structure and was able to sustain itself in the capital as it failed to do elsewhere. During this period it proved self-renewing: George Odger, William Newton, Peter Henriette, Charles Bradlaugh and George Howell (who were all to play a major part in the radical politics of the 1860s and 1870s) were amongst those radicalised in the early 1850s at a time when Chartism in the regions was fading. In marked contrast, in Manchester the movement collapsed after the arrest of 29 local leaders left local organisation in disarray.[16]

A number of factors made London fertile ground for radical activism in the 1850s and 1860s when the movement was in abeyance elsewhere. Existing franchise provision in particular played an especially important role in laying down the foundations for a durable movement of radical protest. London already had a small pool of working-class voters before 1832. In Southwark and Westminster occupational franchises had created a group of traditionally radical electors supportive of opponents of 'Old Corruption' like John Wilkes and Francis Burdett. In theory the high price of property in the capital meant that any franchise measure tethered exclusively to the value of property favoured the extension of the vote. Most metropolitan houses were rated at £10 and above in the 1840s.[17] However, it was London's heterogeneous shopkeeping and small tradesman element that profited the most from the 1832 Reform Act. Elsewhere the working-class vote was shrinking. In the larger boroughs like Lambeth and Tower Hamlets working-class voters did exist, but anomalies in the metropolitan franchise kept their numbers small.[18] Under the terms of the 1832 Reform Act, lodgers, defined as those who rented rooms from a non-resident landlord, were not entitled to the vote. As contemporaries made clear, lodging was the norm for working-class households in the poorer parts of London.[19] Most working-class families lived not in London's £10 houses, but in individual rented rooms. Compounding provided a further barrier to the extension of the metropolitan franchise. Compounding occurred where vestries claimed rates on property from the landlord, not the tenant. Compound householders were eligible for the franchise, but could register for the vote only when they applied to pay their own rate, a process that had to be repeated as many as six times a year when the rates were due. This acted as a deterrent to compounders who applied for voter status. In 1849 Sir William Clay estimated that as many as 16,000 householders were disenfranchised by compounding in Tower Hamlets alone.[20] Finally, the twelve months residence clause in the 1832 Reform Act disadvantaged a shifting, itinerant labour force dependent on casualised or seasonal work patterns. Here movement and mobility, part of the traditional rhythms of London employment, served artificially to depress the numbers of working-class voters.[21] Where movement occurred within a borough, electors faced the problem of re-registering their vote, but lost it altogether for the full twelve-month period if they moved outside the borough boundaries. Metropolitan radicals condemned the injustices of a voting system in which 'the exercise of the right to vote in the making of the laws we are bound to obey should depend on the state of a rent book', and noted the detrimental effect of itinerancy on enfranchisement in the capital where 'there were whole parishes in which not a single lodger had taken the trouble to have his name placed on the register'.[22]

These factors not only kept the metropolitan electorate small in areas in which it was already tiny, but also ensured that the franchise remained a contentious issue in the London boroughs. In contrast to Manchester or Leeds, where enfranchisement rates were rising steadily in the 1850s as property increased in value, in London they were in decline.[23] Moreover, the fact that all property in London was already rated at £10 or above meant that simply lowering the property threshold at which householders became eligible for the vote would not solve London's enfranchisement problems. In 1860 a £6 franchise proposal in John Bright's reform bill of that year was opposed by metropolitan reformers on these grounds and was acknowledged by Gladstone in the mid-1860s to have been entirely inadequate to meet London's needs: 'The bill of 1860 was, it might almost be said, of no use at all in London. Such was the scale of rents in the metropolis that a descent from £10 to £6 was of no importance whatever'.[24] London was uniquely the one area of the country where the number of voters per head of population was in decline. The limitations of the working-class franchise in London encouraged metropolitan reformers to favour radical solutions to the reform question. The only answer to the peculiarities of the metropolitan franchise was manhood suffrage or some variation on it. For this reason the Chartist platform remained a logical and acceptable one in London, with a continuing legitimacy that it lacked outside London. In the regions as the number of plebeian voters increased, so the franchise was ceasing to be an issue.[25]

The other important element in the metropolitan equation was religion (or the absence of it). Despite the fact that the headquarters of all the major overseas missionary societies were located in the capital, contemporary stereotypes of 'Godless London' were confirmed by the 1851 religious census. Church attendance was limited and intermittent. In larger boroughs like Lambeth and Tower Hamlets, attendance rates were barely 30 per cent.[26] The major religious denominations were weak in London. Nonconformity in particular was almost non-existent in the inner London boroughs; in 1851 aggregate attendances for the Dissenting sects were smaller than anywhere else in the country.[27] Anglicanism did retain a presence, but by the 1850s, as Henry Pelling has pointed out, the Church of England had all but abandoned its pastoral mission in the East End. Pew rents and absentee pastors had alienated much of its following, leading to a retreat to the suburbs and the wealthier quarters of Westminster and the City.[28] Not until the 1880s did the experience of missionary work amongst the poor and dispossessed provide a model for a regenerated salvationism under William Booth that saw the East End as a place of opportunity rather than defeat.[29] Catholicism was also marginal. It put down deep roots only amongst the settled Irish and Italian communities of Clerkenwell and Holborn.

The weakness of organised religion in the capital meant that political factions tended not to be defined in religious terms. In the regions, the strength of religious adherence and the popularity of Anglican-inspired Protestantism meant that religious affiliation increasingly dictated the nature of political allegiance. Militant Nonconformity, however, was much less pronounced in London than elsewhere. Nor is there much evidence of the kind of politics traditionally associated with it. In contrast to Lancashire and Yorkshire, there was little common identity of interest between London's radical MPs and the Nonconformist sects. Of the capital's sixteen MPs, only three actively identified with the Dissenting interest. Without the anti-tithe and burial agitation of Manchester and Leeds linked to the Whig anti-ritualism of the 1850s, metropolitan Liberalism lacked the religious dimension that nurtured a generation of activists in the provinces.[30] Nor is there much evidence of a reactive popular Conservatism buoyed up by the Orange interest and fuelled by anti-Irish feeling. In the absence of any cross-London local authority there was no outlet for sectarian tensions. School boards were not established until 1870, and the London County Council was resolutely non-sectarian, abolishing all religious discussion from its meetings. Party conflict was therefore quite alien to London in the 1850s. Ultimately, limited religious adherence in the capital meant that political allegiances were not defined in religious terms, either for Liberalism or for Toryism, a factor that hampered the growth of formal party structures during this period.

The key electoral and religious elements that contributed to party formation in the regions were lacking in London. The capital provided an example of a 'partyless' political culture. In part this was due to the collapse of metropolitan Toryism. The Tories never recovered from their schism over the corn laws and were at their weakest in the years between 1852 and 1860. Only the city of London constituency was regularly contested by the Conservatives between 1847 and 1865. In 1857 they brought forward no candidates at all, and in 1859 only one solitary metropolitan Conservative stood for Marylebone.[31] Witnesses testifying before the 1860 Parliamentary Committee on Reform concluded that Conservative voters were effectively disenfranchised in the London boroughs.[32] Not until the Jingo agitation of 1877-8 were metropolitan Conservatives able to regain the political ground they had lost in the previous two decades.[33]

In the absence of a strong Tory opposition, London politics were characterised by a fragmented Liberal/radicalism. In the larger boroughs a multiplicity of Liberals could contest elections without the danger of a seat falling to the Tories. In Tower Hamlets in 1852, all five candidates for the borough's two seats were Liberals. In 1857 Finsbury was contested by four Liberals with no Tory opposition. Even so, London was distinguished by a remarkably low level of electoral contests in comparison to the regions. Neither Westminster nor Marylebone were contested in 1857, and in 1859 there were no elections at all in four of London's seven central boroughs: Westminster, the city, Tower Hamlets and Lambeth.[34] Frequently 'gentlemen's agreements' were the order of the day, resolving unnecessary conflict within the Liberal elite.

Without religious cleavages, the dynamics of London elections tended to be driven by friction between Liberal splinter groups. More often than not these were the result of personal differences. In the absence of party strife, the apparatus of electioneering failed to evolve as it did in the provinces. Outside the city of London constituency, where there was a Tory opposition, party apparatus was unknown. The highly sophisticated methods of canvassing, registration and candidate selection pioneered by the ACLL in Manchester were seldom employed in London until the 1880s. In these circumstances the sheer size of predominantly working-class boroughs like Lambeth and Tower Hamlets prohibited the development of effective electoral machinery. Most metropolitan Liberals dispensed with electoral management strategies altogether. In 1857, Thomas Slingsby Duncombe contested Finsbury with only a single paid secretary and a messenger in a campaign that cost him a mere £412.[35]

Politics in London remained recognisably eighteenth-century in nature well into the nineteenth. Without the discipline brought by party, London's Liberal MPs retained a strongly individualistic character. Most were wedded to an older radical tradition and continued to operate in a style reminiscent of popular demagogues like Wilkes or Burdett. The radical MPs for Finsbury, Thomas Wakley and T. S. Duncombe, were survivors of the early nineteenth-century generation of radicals. Indeed, Wakley had been a personal friend of Henry Hunt.[36] As in the previous century, radicalism amongst London's MPs tended to be measured in terms of their distance from the court, the throne, and the coffers of government patronage. This was the basis of the old 'Independent' position. Even the outward trappings of 'Independency' persisted. In 1857, when the reformer W. A. Wilkinson contested Lambeth, he did so under the 'blue and buff' colours of the old Wilkite banner.[37] Into the 1870s and 1880s metropolitan Liberal MPs were noted for their idiosyncratic approach to party loyalties. W. A. Torrens, MP for Finsbury between 1865 and 1885, became the role model for the mid-Victorian 'private member', promoting numerous private member's bills, refusing cabinet office, and flouting the wishes of his constituency party.[38]

In these circumstances electoral arrangements in London were haphazard. Most political activity was rooted in the public house, as it had been in the eighteenth century. During elections pubs were pressed into service as centres for canvassing, placarding, and public meetings. Within each borough rival networks of pubs also served to delineate the territory of contending parliamentary candidates. The central role of the public house in London's political life retarded the bond that developed between Liberalism and the temperance movement in the regions. In the north of England, Liberalism cohered around the organisational framework of Liberalism, Nonconformity and temperance. In London it was almost unknown for Liberals to stand on a temperance platform. Whereas in the provinces the drink interest had become identified with popular Toryism by the 1860s, in London most brewers were politically non-aligned, distributing their favours equally between contending factions, whether Tory versus Liberal, or Liberal versus Liberal. When the temperance campaigner Harper Twelvetrees contested Marylebone in 1852, he faced the combined power of the brewing interest and came bottom of the poll with only one vote.[39] As the metropolitan political agent W. A James explained in 1860: 'in consequence of his determining upon high principles not to engage public houses, but to hold committee rooms at private houses… no public houses were taken by him, and the consequence was that the whole of the publicans voted in a body against him'.[40]

When metropolitan MPs campaigned, they did so in the style of eighteenth-century electioneering. The public meeting in London retained a central importance as the space at which they were beholden to the electorate. It was a place, first and foremost of unmediated contact, but also of popular theatre and accountability. Its attendant processions, hustings, effigy-burnings and even violence continued to matter in London as probably nowhere else in the country. Without party to support them, London's MPs were excessively vulnerable to currents of opinion within the electorate. The absence of cushioning electoral machinery exposed them to the vagaries of non-electors, to the whims of militant radicals, and, most important of all, to the caprices of the crowd. For crowd politicians the public meeting was a place where the sacred compact between the elected, the voter and non-electors was cemented. Here the collectivity of the people's will was on display. The absence of political machinery meant that the majority of working-class electors were never integrated into the political system and they constituted an uncontrolled, ungovernable element within metropolitan politics. Parliamentary candidates vied with one another to acquire the mantle of the radical representative by appeasing militant supporters at the forum of the public meeting.

Metropolitan radicals were expert at working these crowd situations. The Chartists in particular were instrumental in establishing a hustings presence that exerted considerable pressure on MPs. The fact that the Chartists were one of the few well-organised political groupings in the metropolis placed them in a good position to cause large-scale disruption at public meetings. Equally, access to the popular platform gave them a much higher public profile than their provincial counterparts. In contrast to Manchester, where ticketing and indoor meetings enabled Anti-Corn Law Leaguers to keep disruption at public meetings to a minimum, the momentum of London politics still turned on issues of popular accountability debated openly before the people.[41] Moreover, metropolitan radicals were adept at orchestrating opposition to the popular and programmatic Liberal movements of London. Agitations like the Parliamentary and Financial Reform Association, the National and Constitutional Association, and the Administrative Reform Association, founded in emulation of the Anti-Corn Law League in Manchester, rapidly succumbed to Chartist opposition. In 1852 Chartists invaded the national conference of the Parliamentary and Financial

Reform Association and delayed proceedings for seven hours. At the inaugural meeting of the National and Constitutional Association in 1855, resolutions supporting the programme of the body were overturned by amendments in favour of the Charter.[42] Without a policy of 'packing' and ticket-only assemblies, London's Liberals exposed themselves to harassment and attack by a well-organised Chartist rump. The pressure exerted by this style of crowd politics pushed most metropolitan MPs in a radical direction. William Newton of Tower Hamlets and Duncombe and Wakley of Finsbury were all heavily dependent on Chartist popular support; in 1859 all of London's sixteen MPs were elected on a reform programme of varying shades of militancy. In the 1860s a spur to Charles Dilke's radicalism in Chelsea was provided by his vociferous plebeian following in the Eleusis Club that united the radical reformers of Chelsea. Even Gladstone noted the 'somewhat advanced Liberalism' of London's MPs in a speech in 1866.[43]

The realignment of forces which resulted in the erosion of Chartism in the 1850s was in large measure a political process. In those areas where Chartism lost the political argument it declined rapidly after 1848. In the provinces the collapse of Chartism enabled middle-class radicals to draw on many of the issues that had sustained the radical movement during the 1840s. In the process they created a broad radical coalition that provided the basis for Liberal successes into the 1860s and 1870s. In a converse of the situation existing in the regions after 1848, the middle-class reform movement in London faltered and allowed the political initiative to remain with the Chartists. The model of an emergent grass roots Liberalism that flourished in the regions had only the shallowest of roots in a metropolitan setting. There a broad popular Liberalism was slow to emerge, allowing older radical forms to retard the development of party. Liberalism was as a result weak in the metropolis, and London remained the home of a truculent radicalism grounded in surviving Chartist associations and memories, whose zeal was not tempered as it was by Liberalism in the regions.

This survival was in part the consequence of pressures on London's social and geographical space. The expense involved in hiring large opulent halls for political meetings could only seldom be met by poverty-stricken radical organisations. Instead, reformers tended to be forced back on public houses and London's areas of open ground. The classic London meeting was usually held on a brown-field site or a redundant area of wasteland or common. The widow of one elderly radical veteran recalled:

> some years ago, open-air discussion meetings, consisting chiefly of workmen, were held in certain parts of London on Sunday mornings. The railway arches near the Euston Road, and the open space at the north end of Chelsea Bridge were favourite spots for these gatherings. Groups were formed around lecturers of many shades of belief: Secularists, Methodists, Humanitarians, Unitarians, Vegetarians and Teetotallers were all represented.[44]

The open ground of the capital became sacred space where the people met to agitate and dispute. Places like Primrose Hill, Bishop Bonner's Fields, Clerkenwell Green, Copenhagen Fields and Peckham Rye were sites steeped in the collective traditions of metropolitan radicalism. There were the spaces where atheists, blasphemers, and 'radical spouters' tested the tolerance of the state and achieved notoriety in blasphemy and libel cases.[45] Beatrice Webb recalled attending meetings at Victoria Park in the East End in the 1880s where 'the thickest crowd surrounded the banner of the social democrat'.[46] Even invasions of the West End were justified by a radical reading of London's geography and history. When rioters surged down the Strand in 1886 they saw themselves as the spiritual heirs to Wat Tyler's 1381 peasant rebels, responsible for the plunder of Savoy Palace, the London residence of the 'tax-exacter' John of Gaunt. Tyler was an iconic figure for metropolitan radicals. London Chartist branches were named after him in 1848, and he featured prominently on reform banners into the 1860s.[47]

As the metropolitan open spaces were enclosed or built over, so radicals mounted campaigns to preserve the people's land from occupation by 'commons' eaters'. In the 1870s this campaign preserved Wimbledon Common and Hampstead Heath for the people of London, although the methods used to defend them resulted in brushes with the law and the police.[48] Those who were imprisoned for their part in these disturbances were celebrated as 'people's martyrs'. The spatial geography and social space of London in the 1850s favoured Chartist survival in a way that was unique to the metropolis. Conflict over the open ground where radicalism had put down deep roots tended to the combustible. The absence of metropolitan local government interposed between Londoners and Whitehall accentuated the distance between government and the governed in London. In addition, control of policing by the home office transformed every conflict over open space into a dispute with central government itself. At a time when the regional centres were largely quiescent, London gained a reputation for ungovernability over public space. When the 'mobocracy' colonised London's ceremonial centres like Trafalgar Square, the Mall and the Strand, it threatened to overwhelm the imperial symbolism of the capital itself.[49] Moreover, the heightened tensions surrounding such meetings created periodic flashpoints in which radicals adopted an aggressive and confrontational stance inimical to the pluralistic outlook of reform Liberals in the regions.

Chartism also managed to perpetuate itself through the network of clubs and debating societies that formed a staple element of the radical culture of the capital from the Regency period onwards.[50] Iain McCalman has emphasised the centrality of metropolitan club-life to the transmission of radical ideology, and in maintaining the coherence of the reform movement in the periods following the contraction of the popular platform. This pattern repeated itself in the 1850s. Pubs were important in this process, and Chartist branches continued to meet there. Radical ideas, however, found their strongest expression through London's long-established debating club circuit. In the regions such clubs were all but extinct; in London they continued to thrive. The debating clubs, whose roots were in the Restoration period, provided an easy blend of conviviality and informal political debate. Coger's Club near St. Bride's Church could trace its origins back to 1755. The Green Dragon in Fleet Street was founded in the 1650s.[51] Most had strong links with the city's radical tradition. Coger's counted John Wilkes and Henry Hunt amongst its former members. In Fleet Street the veteran Chartist and campaigner against the 'taxes on knowledge' William Carpenter was the proprietor of the Temple Forum. The debating clubs kept together a body of ideas and a clientele who provided a point of contact with earlier movements for a new generation of radicals emerging in the 1850s. The role of the clubs as centres of debate created an accessible lecture circuit where former Chartists like Thomas Cooper and Bronterre O'Brien found employment as lecturers. George Howell recalled of his experiences in the clubs: 'Some of the leading Chartists of 1848 I did not know, they had either died, left the movement, or migrated elsewhere before I came to London. But for years I heard all they had to say and was conversant with their writings'.[52] A network of coffeehouses provided a further outlet for political debate. They not only stocked newspapers and even books, but were also free from the pressures exerted by landlords, brewers, and magistrates. Howell was instrumental in the formation of one such club at Mills' Coffee House, christened the Milton Club after his literary hero, John Milton:

> Mills was an old Chartist as had been several of those who inaugurated the club – Bartlett, Avery and several others kept it going for nearly two years. I venture to say that the friendly discussions at that club once a week were equal, if not superior, to the more set debates at the old established discussion halls.[53]

The persistence of an infrastructure of radical activity in London prevented the dispersal and diffusion of energies that characterised Chartism in the regions. Outside London the 1850s were a critical period in the evolution of movements dedicated to limited economic aims, rather than to the overall transformation of society. Strategies like co-operation and temperance, which prospered particularly in Lancashire and the West Riding of Yorkshire, promoted the benefits of an accord with Liberalism for minimal social rewards. As John Walton has noted, co-ops, building societies and temperance groups in Lancashire held out the prospect of profitable sinecures for radicals in their declining years.[54] In London, where Chartism retained a significant agitational presence, this development was much less marked. Recent historiography has noted the absence of a strong co-operative tradition in the capital, and the failure of the Christian Socialist initiatives in retail co-operation that were so successful in the regions.[55] By the end of the 1850s there was still no cross-London clearing-house system for commodities on the model of the CWS in Manchester. Metropolitan co-ops faced immense problems in overcoming the barriers to retail provision posed by the sheer size of London and the immense diversity of its trading base. For this reason the lifespan of individual co-operative associations in London was short. In 1861 the commitment of London's co-operators was questioned within the movement, whilst Percy Redfern, the historian of the movement, was dismissive of metropolitan co-operation, writing of it as 'a galaxy of distinguished men (who) provided a force rich in colonels and generals, but (were) desperately short of common soldiers'.[56]

Similarly, Brian Harrison has described London as the 'bugbear' of the temperance movement.[57] The temperance campaign in London never succeeded in overcoming the central role of the public house in London's commercial, recreational and political life. Despite mid-century attempts to contest the grip of public house culture on plebeian life in London, it remained central.[58] Election committees campaigned from pubs, workmen were paid there, and trades unionists used them as ports of call, and as centres for discussion, organisation and strike action. The sheer size of London meant that protest could only be orchestrated effectively through committees meeting in local pubs. Chartism used this method of mobilisation in the 1830s, and, despite Ernest Jones' attempt to wean Chartist branches away from the public house, it persisted into the 1850s and 1860s.[59] London Chartists remained more dependent on public house culture than their regional counterparts. In the 1840s regional Chartism had stabilised around a network of permanent club and meeting-house facilities; in London, however, high property prices precluded the construction of purpose-built premises for public meetings. As with trade societies, local Chartist branches continued to identify themselves with a particular pub long after the practice had died out elsewhere. Some of London's most prominent Chartists were publicans, amongst them the engineers' leader William Newton and veteran reformer William Morgan, whose pub the 'Bull's Head' in Crown Street, Soho, provided a venue for unrepentant Chartists until the 1870s.[60]

London remained the heartland of Chartism in its declining stages. Chartism's ability to act as a vehicle for popular discontents gave it a coherence and vitality in the capital that made it resistant to erosion by the movements that had arisen out of the disintegration of Chartism in the provinces. Loyalty to its memory and a continuing perception of the movement as an effective agent of change inhibited the development of a popular Liberal consensus in London throughout the period when a fused Cobdenite Liberalism was in the ascendant in the provincial urban centres. Chartism survived in London through its continuing command of the political agenda. Dorothy Thompson has suggested that by the 1840s Chartism had lost the argument over free trade. Chartists predicted the baleful effects of corn law repeal, and of the unrestrained competition provided by free trade policies. Absence of protection, they asserted, would lead to the production of cheaper goods for sale in international markets, high food prices, and a depression of domestic wage levels.[61] In the north after 1850 Chartist economic arguments were fallacious. The self-evident prosperity of manufacturing industry in Lancashire and Yorkshire, especially in the good trade year of 1853, made the issue a difficult one to exploit for electoral gain. In such areas Cobdenite radicals were extremely successful in mobilising popular support against Lord Derby's attempts to reintroduce a sliding scale on corn. Their manipulation of this issue reopened the wider debate on protectionism, and resulted in the resurrection of the Anti-Corn Law League in 1852 to defend the benefits of freedom of trade.[62] In

London, however, Chartists were more effective in highlighting the disadvantages of free trade policies for the casualised labourers and outworkers in declining industries.

Most of the industries that suffered disproportionately from the absence of protectionist policies were concentrated in London. Chartist radicalism retained the initiative amongst groups of outworkers including the slop-workers and the sweated trades who were the human casualties of free trade.[63] From the 1830s the emblem of these out-groups became the debased Spitalfields silk weaver who the Chartists elevated into an icon of dispossession and internal exile at the hands of cheap imports and a cowardly government afraid to preserve domestic industries from undercutting by a revived Bonapartist France.[64] A Silk Weavers' Protection Society established in 1852 became a major propagandist vehicle in London against free trade doctrines. Henry Mayhew's articles in the *Morning Star* also exposed the suffering among sections of the clothing, the boot and shoe, silk-weaving and dockside trades. At appearances on Chartist platforms he pointed to the undercutting of prices by foreign manufacturers, the resultant widespread casualisation in London, and employers' wage reductions to bring pay in line with falling bread prices. At meetings with tailors, coal heavers and carpenters he was highly critical of the free trade platform of Cobden and Bright.[65] All this was seriously to undermine the position of the restored Anti-Corn Law League in London in the short term, and to discredit free trade nostrums in London into the 1860s.

London was the heartland of post-Chartist radicalism. A febrile crowd politics, unmediated through Liberalism, became the hallmark of radical continuities in London. In 1855 Chartists were still conspicuous in the Sunday Trading Bill riots and in co-ordinating opposition to high grain prices during the Crimean War.[66] Nowhere else in Britain was the public sphere, and uncontested access to it, of such sensitivity as in London. Above all, metropolitan politics were slow to change. As late as the 1880s metropolitan Liberals were still dragged in a radical direction by the dynamics of ungovernable crowd politics and a strong grass-roots radicalism. Some historians have seen an element of populism in metropolitan crowd action that could drift in either a radical or a Tory direction, helping to account for the strength of Toryism in London from the 1890s.[67] The Liberal Party certainly felt that London could not be mastered, even by the New Liberalism. Charles Masterman, amongst others, rooted his notion of a neurotic urban mass prone to fickle urges and periodic spasms of unrest in the 'City Type' created by rootless metropolitan living.[68]

In conclusion, this essay has problematised the issue of London in recent literature concerning radical continuity in mid-nineteenth century Britain. It has provided fresh evidence on the strength and vitality of metropolitan Chartism in the period of the movement's decline. Through scrutiny of the local context of London Chartism, it reappraises the value of a metropolitan approach, and prioritises a reading that emphasises the importance of a structural understanding of London. It is informed by a comparative methodology, highlighting differences and similarities with overlapping movements of political protest in the regions. By moving beyond Liberalism's own conception of itself, this essay has argued for a closer analysis of the links between party forms, the political platform and the role of the franchise in curtailing or encouraging militancy over the franchise. In so doing it seeks to modify the historiography of late Chartism, and questions recent assumptions about the continuities between popular radicalism and Liberalism in the period between 1848 and 1860.

References

1. G. S. Jones, *Languages of Class: Studies in English Working-Class History, 1832-1982* (Cambridge, 1983), p. 99.

2. E. Biagini, *Liberty, Retrenchment and Reform: Popular Liberalism in the Age of Gladstone, 1860-1880* (Cambridge, 1992); P. Joyce, *Visions of the People: Industrial England and the Question of Class* (Cambridge, 1991); P. Joyce, *Democratic Subjects: The Self and the Social in Nineteenth Century England* (Cambridge, 1994); J. Vernon, *Politics and the People: A Study in English Political Culture*, c.1815-1867 (Cambridge, 1993).

3. H. Jephson, *The Platform: Its Rise and Progress* (2 vols, London, 1892), ii, chs. 1-3.

4. S. Inwood, *A History of London* (London, 1998), chs.19-20; S. Pennybacker, *A Vision for London, 1889-1914: Labour, Everyday Life and the LCC Experiment* (London, 1995); J. Walkowitz, *City of Dreadful Delight: Narratives of Sexual Danger in Late Victorian London* (1992), ch. 1.

5. K. Beckson, *London in the 1890s: A Cultural History* (London, 1992), ch. 1; J. Schneer, *London 1900: The Imperial Metropolis* (New Haven, 1999), chs. 7, 10.

6. See the introduction in *Currents of Radicalism: Popular Radicalism, Organised Labour and Party Politics in Britain, 1850-1914*, ed. E. Biagini and A. Reid (Cambridge, 1991).

7. N. McCord, *The Anti-Corn Law League, 1838-1846* (London, 1958), pp. 75-7.

8. D. J. Rowe, 'The Failure of London Chartism', *Historical Journal*, xi (1968), 472-87; D. Large, 'London in the Year of Revolutions', in *London in the Age of Reform*, ed. J. Stevenson (London, 1977), pp. 177-211.

9. D. Goodway, *London Chartism, 1838-1848* (Cambridge, 1982), p. 13.

10. J. Saville, *1848: The British State and the Chartist Movement* (Cambridge, 1987), ch. 1.

11. A. Taylor, 'Modes of Political Expression and Working-Class Radicalism: The London and Manchester Examples' (University of Manchester, PhD thesis, 1992), ch. 1.

12. J. Belchem, 'Chartism and the Trades, 1848-1850', *English Historical Review*, xcviii (1983), 558-87.

13. Goodway, *London Chartism*, p. 13.

14. *Northern Star*, 26 Aug. 1848.

15. I. McCalman, *Radical Underworld: Prophets, Revolutionaries and Pornographers in London, 1795-1840* (Cambridge, 1988), chs. 6-7.

16. I. Prothero, *Radical Artisans in England and France, 1830-1870* (Cambridge, 1997), ch. 11.

17. Taylor, 'Modes of Political Expression', ch. 2.

18. H. J. Hanham, *Dod's Electoral Facts, 1832-1852* (Brighton, 1972), pp. 316-17.

19. T. Wright, *Some Customs and Habits of the Working Classes* (London, 1867), pp. 262-76.

20. M. B. Baer, 'The Politics of London, 1852-1868: Parties, Voters and Representation', (University of Iowa, PhD thesis, 1976), p. 368.

21. R. Samuel, 'Comers and Goers', in *The Victorian City: Images and Realities*, ed. H. J. Dyos and M. Wolff (2 vols, London, 1973), ii, 123-60.

22. See discussions at the Manhood Suffrage League, and the Patriotic Club, Clerkenwell, reported in *National Reformer*, 10 Jan. 1875, 9 Apr. 1876.

23. V. A. C. Gatrell, 'The Commercial Middle Class in Manchester, c.1820-1857' (University of Cambridge, PhD thesis, 1971), pp. 114-55.

24. *Hansard*, 3rd series, clxxii (1866), 35.

25. D. Fraser, *Urban Politics in Victorian England: The Structure of Politics in Victorian Cities* (Leicester, 1976), chs. 8, 10.

26. K. S. Inglis, 'Patterns of Religious Worship in 1851', *Journal of Ecclesiastical History*, ii (1960), 80.

27. H. McLeod, *Class and Religion in the Late Victorian City* (London, 1974), pp. 104-6.

28. H. Pelling, *Social Geography of British Elections, 1885-1910* (London, 1967), pp. 54-8; J. S. Reid, '"Ritualism Rampant in East London": Anglo-Catholicism and the Urban Poor', *Victorian Studies*, xxxi (1988), 375-403.

29. V. Bailey, 'In Darkest England and the Way Out: The Salvation Army, Social Reform and the Labour Movement, 1890-1910', *International Review of Social History*, xxix (1984), 133-171.

30. Fraser, *Urban Politics in Victorian England*, ch. 12.

31. Taylor, 'Modes of Political Expression', ch. 2.

32. *Report from the Select Committee of the House of Lords, Appointed to Inquire what would be the Probable Increase of the number of Electors in the Counties and Boroughs of England from a Reduction of the Franchise* (16 July, 1860), p. 355.

33. H. Cunningham, 'Jingoism in 1877-78', *Victorian Studies*, xiv (1971), 429-453.

34. Taylor, 'Modes of Political Expression', ch. 2.

35. G. Hill, *The Electoral History of the Borough of Lambeth* (London, 1879), pp. 178, 185.

36. S. S. Sprigge, *The Life and Times of Thomas Wakley* (London, 1897), pp. 310-16.

37. Hill, *Electoral History of the Borough of Lambeth*, pp. 106-13.

38. On Torrens see J. Parry, *The Rise and Fall of Liberal Government in Victorian Britain* (New Haven, 1993), p. 230.

39. B. Harrison, *Dictionary of British Temperance Biography* (Coventry, 1973), pp. 131-2.

40. *Report from the Select Committee of the House of Lords*, p. 357.

41. For the contrasts between the popular politics of London and Manchester, see A. Taylor, '"The Best Way to Get What He Wanted": Ernest Jones and the Boundaries of Liberalism in the Manchester Election of 1868', *Parliamentary History*, xvi (1997), 185-204.

42. K. Marx and F. Engels, *Collected Works* (49 vols, London, 1975-), xiv, 100; *Leader*, 6 Mar. 1852.

43. *Hansard*, clxxii, 35.

44. B. T. Hall, *Our Sixty Years: The Story of the Working-Men's Club and Institute Union* (London, 1922), pp. 319-20.

45. H. B. Bonner, *Penalties Upon Opinion* (London, 1934), pp. 118-19.

46. B. Webb, *My Apprenticeship* (2 vols, London, 1938), ii. 348.

47. Goodway, *London Chartism*, p. 13; *Commonwealth*, 12 Jan. 1867.

48. A. Taylor, '"Commons-Stealers", "Land-Grabbers" and "Jerry-Builders": Space, Popular Radicalism and the Politics of Public Access in London, 1848-1880', *International Review of Social History*, xl (1995), 383-407.

49. R. Mace, *Trafalgar Square: Emblem of Empire* (London, 1976), chs. 6-7; D. C. Richter, *Riotous Victorians* (Athens, Ohio, 1981), pp. 133-62.

50. I. McCalman, 'Ultra-Radicalism and Convivial Debating Clubs in London, 1795-1838', *English Historical Review*, cii (1987), 309-33.

51. C. M. Davies, *Heterodox London, or Phases of Free Thought in the Metropolis* (2 vols, London, 1875), ii, 264-6; W.E. Adams, *Memoirs of a Social Atom* (2 vols, London, 1903), ii, 314-17.

52. G. Howell, 'Autobiography of a Toiler' (3 vols, manuscript, n.d.), Howell Collection, Bishopsgate Institute, ii, 44.

53. Ibid., B, section 5, p. 58.

54. J. K. Walton, *Lancashire: A Social History, 1558-1939* (Manchester, 1987), pp. 244-5.

55. M. Purvis, 'The Development of Co-operative Retailing in England and Wales, 1851-1901: A Geographical Study', *Journal of Historical Geography*, iii (1990), 314-331.

56. *Co-operator*, 1 Apr. 1861; P. Redfern, *The New History of the C.W.S.* (London, 1938), p. 31.

57. B. Harrison, 'The Sunday Trading Riots of 1855', *Historical Journal*, viii (1965), 129-30.

58. H. Solly, *These Eighty Years*, (2 vols, London,1893), i, 379-99.

59. B. Harrison, 'Pubs', in Dyos and Wolff, *The Victorian City*, i, 162-80.

60. On the career of William Morgan, see S. Shipley, *Club Life and Socialism in Mid-Victorian London* (Oxford, 1971), pp. 51-3.

61. D. Thompson, *The Chartists: Popular Politics in the Industrial Revolution* (Aldershot, 1984), p. 333.

62. A. Howe, *The Cotton Masters, 1830-1860* (Oxford, 1987), pp. 216-27.

63. Taylor, 'Modes of Political Expression', ch. 3.

64. M. Steinberg, '"The Great End of All Government": Working-People's Construction of Citizenship Claims in Early Nineteenth-Century England, and the Question of Class', *International Review of Social History*, xl (1999), 19-50.

65. Taylor, 'Modes of Political Expression', ch. 3.

66. Harrison, 'Sunday Trading Riots', pp. 129-30.

67. G. S. Jones, *Outcast London: A Study in the Relationship Between Classes in Victorian Society* (Oxford, 1971), ch. 9.

68. C. Masterman, *The Condition of England* (London, 1911), pp. 101-2.

Chapter 8

The Acceptable Face of Carpet Baggery? W. H. Willans and Frome's Reformers

Protestant Dissenters were to be found in the House of Commons throughout the eighteenth century and they were not unknown in the Lords. They were to be found in increasingly representative numbers in the Commons in the nineteenth century, although the Lords remained another matter. But representative of what? Should the historian value them more for their significance or their interest? 'Power' is not a word to be applied to them, but is 'influence' much better? Any influence is probably best gauged at individual level – that of the MP who happened to be a Dissenter or who acknowledged some Dissenting connections or, which is not quite the same thing, of the Dissenter who happened to be an MP. That last category implies a closer degree of commitment, although none quite does justice to the man whose political career had been precipitated by his Dissent and continued to be informed by it however much it was moulded by his general political allegiance and kept afloat by the electoral and material good fortune without which even the most motivated political career was bound to sink. The question remains: representative of what? Why was their influence not greater than it was?

The reasons seem obvious. Dissenters had to breach the interlocking powers of long-established political connection and all the accompanying connections which linked the commanding heights of land, the armed forces, the national churches, the older professions, and commerce too, and which were fused by a particular education and an assured income. They had to breach that power, not let it take them over, yet success could not be achieved without a life-long commitment and the money to pay for it. Few were likely to meet those conditions before the last quarter of the nineteenth-century.

If this much seems obvious, how adequate is the obvious? Dissent was a political stance in which ingrained inferiority was in tension with spiritual superiority. Since spiritual is not necessarily to be separated from mental or intellectual superiority, that made for a marvellously suggestive state of being. It meant that true Dissenters were permanently in crisis, forever on the brink of decision. It countered the negative tendency inherent in Dissent with something positive. It predicated a reforming temper. Could there have been a more representatively Victorian state of mind?

Yet the most they achieved at Westminster was Bright and Chamberlain. That was no mean achievement, although for all their significance Bright and Chamberlain must surely remain politically as well as religiously eccentric. Was the reason for that a matter of luck? An untimely death? A failed election? A bankruptcy? The simple fact that the conviction of one generation cannot be assumed in the next? Or is the reason electoral – the fact that the political Dissenters' most representative point of influence lay in that brief period when the franchise, although significantly enlarged, nonetheless just as significantly stopped short of full manhood suffrage: that is to say, between 1868 and 1885?

Or have we tended to look at Dissenting MPs in the wrong way, trying to understand them as individuals who failed rather than as individuals who take on a different significance when woven into their cousinhoods, their ecclesiology, their brand of radicalism, their points of recreational, educational, intellectual, or commercial contact, networking them as Lewis Namier might have done, refusing to pigeon-hole them, taking them less for granted, yet recognising that they were as significant in their own settings as England's county families or Ireland's Protestant ascendancy, and as pervasive?

This essay will focus upon a man whose political career stopped short of Westminster thanks to an election which he should not have lost. His immediate contexts – chapel, family, business – are metropolitan, which means that they are nationwide. They are markedly representative. The constituency which he wooed and failed to win allows for a suggestive focus. An electoral wooing makes for rhetoric of purest essence, and it provides this story with its language and when story is shaped into history, the shaping encompasses inevitable yet unexpected twists.

On the face of it the story of W. H. Willans at Frome in 1874 provides a blatant case of opportunistic carpet-baggery which the electorate rejected. On examination the blatancy vanishes, the opportunism is as much the local party's as the candidate's, the carpet-baggery becomes acceptable, even honourable, and the note of reform is sustained.

Frome, though never a foregone conclusion, was Liberal more often than not.[1] It was a single member constituency with an electorate of just under fourteen hundred in 1874. The constituency's hub was a cloth manufacturing town but the hinterland was agricultural and it was a prime candidate for the next redrawing of boundaries. In 1885, when that had happened, the constituency with a greatly enlarged electorate included miners as well as Bath's outer suburbs. It was thus a constituency in which Dissenters had a significant role and in which they were pivotal to the Liberal cause.

For the traditionally minded Frome was the territory of two aristocratic families, the Thynnes and the Boyles, represented by the Marquess of Bath and the Earl of Cork respectively. Lord Bath's Longleat was a Tory house and its influence was actively and consistently Tory throughout the century. Lord Cork's Marston was a Whig house but its influence was steadily declining in the 1870s. Boyles had stood for Frome in 1835, 1837, and 1857, and sat for Frome from 1847 to 1857. Thynnes had stood for Frome from 1859 to 1865, and would again stand for Frome in 1885, 1892, and 1896, and sit for Frome from 1886 to 1892 and 1895 to 1896. It will be noted that there was something of a watershed in the 1850s. This was marked by the election in 1857 of Donald Nicoll, a youngish London businessman in the cloth trade.[2] He lasted barely two years at Frome but that *frisson* of 1857 was confirmed by the *bouleversement* of 1868 when the Radical Thomas Hughes of *Tom Brown* fame, 'a fine fellow, but not a great speaker' (his supporters discovered that he 'shone far more in replies to hecklers than in exposition of a policy') was elected.[3]

Hughes was an Anglican barrister but Frome's Dissenters regarded his victory as theirs, for Frome and its broader hinterland sweeping up from Somerset, round Wiltshire, to Gloucestershire, was prime Dissenting territory. Frome, Taunton, Shepton Mallet, Yeovil, Warminster, Trowbridge, Calne, Tetbury, Stroud, had Dissented since the seventeenth-century. Bath and Bristol had powerful Dissenting communities. All the denominations were to be found in them and most sections of society. For electoral purposes the Liberal key lay with the usual suspects: the tradesmen, the mental art men, but with a distinctive veneer of long established clothiers and manufacturers, alongside those frequently forgotten players on the Dissenting board, the gentlemen farmers into whom the clothiers often turned. Frome itself had two strong Baptist and two strong Congregational churches. The minister of one of these, Alfred Rowland of Zion, was particularly well placed. He was young, active, on a social and intellectual level with the grandees of his flock, and already marked out for wide denominational influence.[4]

Frome's Liberals should have had all to play for in 1874, thanks not least to the cutting edge of Alfred Rowland's Zion. Unfortunately they were caught on the hop. Alfred Rowland's autobiography provides the clue from their point of view: 'Thomas Hughes ... would have continued to hold the seat but for his unwisdom in giving public lectures in the district on the advantages of an Established Church. As ninety per cent of his supporters were Nonconformists, this made a second candidature for him impracticable'.[5] The reference to Hughes's bravely misdirected lectures brings in the large dog which failed to bark in Frome's 1874 election. Since 1852 the vicar of Frome Selwood had been W. J. E. Bennett, one of Anglicanism's most celebrated ritualists.[6] In Evangelical eyes his errors were compounded by the fact that in earlier years he had been a promising Low Churchman, but in the 1840s his practices at St Paul's Knightsbridge and latterly St Barnabas Pimlico had caused uproar. Emotions regularly reached boiling point in Frome, a previously Low Church parish to which he was appointed by the Dowager Marchioness of Bath. He restored the church in the

1860s – a decade which saw able new ministers at the four leading Dissenting chapels – so emphatically that no casual visitor could fail to place its churchmanship; as recently as June 1872 protracted heresy charges had been resolved in his favour. Perhaps by 1874 the now elderly Father Bennett had become a ruefully admired local fixture, but the memories were fresh, the notoriety was inescapable, and the influence of Tory Longleat and the anomalies of an established yet apparently uncontrollable Church were as pervasive and inextricable as ever. All were grist to Liberal and Dissenting mills but they made for difficult grinding, especially at election time.

Perhaps this is why, so Rowland recalled, Hughes threw up Frome for Marylebone, which he then also threw up for nothing at all. Liberal Frome, meanwhile, pinned its hopes on Thomas Milner Gibson, a famous old warhorse who had once been President of the Board of Trade.[7] He had been out of Westminster since 1868, but he dithered before declining. There was to be no renaissance of the Manchester School in Frome. The locals must by now have been desperate but they did in fact have a name. A London businessman, prompted by Donald Nicoll, had recently visited them, apparently out of the blue, had proposed himself as a possible candidate and then, learning that Milner Gibson was still in the frame, had written to suggest that they might wish to consider him on some future occasion. It came much sooner than he expected.[8]

The election was to be held on 6 February 1874. Parliament was dissolved on Monday, 26 January and news of the impending dissolution became public the previous Saturday morning. On the Sunday afternoon Frome's Liberal last hope received a telegram followed by a visit. On the Monday afternoon he arrived in the town. That evening he addressed, and sufficiently impressed, the leading local Liberals, and his adoption meeting followed on Tuesday in a packed Assembly Room. This is how he presented himself:

> He must apologise to them for having, at a moment's notice, when called upon by a telegram on a Sunday afternoon, while singing hymns with his children, responded to their invitation. Mr. Dunn came down upon him on Sunday evening very much like Mr. Gladstone's manifesto came down upon the country on Saturday. A telegram on a Sunday afternoon intimating that a gentleman from a Liberal borough like Frome would call upon him at half-past-eight, was enough to discompose a Christian and frighten a young man (laughter). When he told them that he met with opposition from wife and children – the strongest opposition a man could encounter; when he asserted that every consideration of family was urged against his severing of family ties and giving himself to parliamentary life; and that he decided to sever, to some extent, those ties, he asked them to remember the responsibility they (not he) had incurred. He had come to Frome in a great emergency (cheers).

It was well put. This bashful candidate was an accomplished, or at least an easy speaker who had recognised his audience. Sunday? Hymns? Children? Family? Call? Response? Who was he?

William Henry Willans was a forty-one-year-old woolbroker.[9] That is probably enough to explain how he had come to know Donald Nicoll. He had been a successful businessman for some years but 1874 saw a flowering of his interests. In addition to his own firm, Willans and Overbury, of which he became senior partner, he had recently become a director of Pawson and Leafs and he was about to become a director of the National Provident Institution, of which Samuel Smiles had ceased to be secretary barely two years before. Willans would become chairman of both. He would also become treasurer, chairman, and a vice-president of the London Chamber of Commerce and a member of the British Commissions for the International Exhibitions held in Antwerp, Brussels, Paris, and Glasgow between 1894 and 1901. He was thus a businessman to watch with wide interests, horizons, and houses to match.

He had lived in Islington since the late 1850s, marrying into Highbury Crescent and settling on Highbury Hill, although by 1879 he would have moved down to Kensington, taking a fine detached house in Holland Park and building High Clyffe, Seaton, on the South Devon coast, perfectly situated for sun and sea though the house itself should never have been allowed to leave Kensington.

As for his education, that had been in Yorkshire and Germany: Huddersfield College and a commercial finishing in Hamburg. He was at pains to stress the practical and social implications of this to his prospective constituents. He explained how, when he was sixteen or seventeen, he had been sent by his father to a cloth factory so that he would learn at first hand all the processes involved in producing broad cloth from the sorting board onwards. This had given him a tolerably long experience of working men while his duties as a Sunday and Ragged School teacher had taken him into their homes. He had no fears about their readiness for citizenship.

There was more to this than a male equivalent of Lady Bountiful. Willans's involvement with the Islington YMCA linked him to that significant and already significantly international movement while the German side of his business explains how he became a prime mover in one of Victorian England's most imaginative children's charities.

In the early 1860s Willans encountered the Rauhe Haus, the home for destitute boys established thirty years earlier in Hamburg, on the family system (this house was intended to be a *home*), by Dr. Wichern.[10] Willans's concern for giving a good, even natural, upbringing to very young boys who were not normally eligible for an orphanage, coincided with that of Robert Hanbury, the brewer and Liberal MP, who was also honorary secretary of the Reformatory and Refuge Union.[11] Hanbury's name was an instant passport to the Evangelical world of Lords Shaftesbury, Ebury, and Kinnaird. Willans, as will be seen, had his own connections. All of them, as it happens, were steady supporters of the YMCA.

On Friday, 2 October 1863 Willans was one of five men meeting in the Islington Shoe Black Society's Refuge.[12] That was effectively the first committee meeting of what became known as the Farningham and Swanley Homes for Little Boys. It was announced that Robert Hanbury was willing to be its president and that another four men were happy to join them. We might note the names of the Wesleyan glover Francis Lycett and the shipowner John Glover.[13] We might also note among the first subscribers a Miss Nicoll and, second only to Willans in his generosity, E. J. Sargood. Sargood is a name with powerful Australian reverberations.[14] Was Miss Nicoll a sister of Donald Nicoll? Four years and two moves later the homes were up and running in North Kent. The Princess of Wales laid their foundation stone (it was her first such duty in this country) and the Prince of Wales spoke. Lord Shaftesbury opened them. They were eventually to comprise ten 'cottages', each housing a 'family' of thirty boys, with a house mother and father. They were emphatically not an orphanage, a refuge, a school, or an asylum, and they were not the Workhouse. They pioneered in England the system that Dr. Barnardo took up a few years later.

They were, however, firmly in the mainstream of evangelical philanthropy. They were for Little Boys under the age of ten 'who are either homeless or destitute, or in danger of falling into crime'. These were fed, clothed, educated, 'above all ... taught the Word of God, and pointed to the Saviour', and trained to be industrious in tailoring, shoemaking, knitting, carpentry, printing, bakery, gardening, painting; and over the next twenty years members of the Royal Family, the House of Lords and the bench of bishops had presided at the Homes' high days along with industrialists, bankers, philanthropists, and generals. The list also included leading Nonconformist ministers and laymen. Henry Allon of Islington, Willans's minister for twenty years, was one; so was Alfred Rowland, now of Hornsey but formerly of Frome.[15] If the philanthropy itself were radical, the methods to sustain it were well-tried. They were carefully non-political and interdenominational. Moderation was inbuilt.

Willans was thus commercially and philanthropically networked with a firm metropolitan base. He was also, as several clues may have indicated, geographically and denominationally networked. The politics followed. His father, William Willans senior (1800-1863), was a Huddersfield woolbroker who had stood for Huddersfield in 1852 and been soundly beaten. The older Willans was prominent in West Riding politics and commerce, a prototype of urban England's movers and moulders. His elder sons, John Wrigley (1831-1910) and William Henry, took the woolbroking to London and his youngest son, James Edward (1842-1926), maintained the business in Huddersfield. Wrigley, however, returned north, first to join his carpet manufacturing brother-in-law, Sir Thomas Firth, in Brighouse and Heckmondwyke and then to join his newspaper-owning and publishing father-in-law, Sir Edward Baines, in Leeds.

That left a fourth son, Thomas Benjamin (1836-1897), who became a manufacturer in Rochdale and had proved a dashing mayor in the year before his adopted town's magnificent town hall was opened. When one adds the civic and commercial clout of their sisters' husbands and their wives' fathers and brothers the useful intensity of such webs of connection becomes apparent. The north is clearly foundational to this but the metropolis consolidates it and there are useful staging posts elsewhere.[16] Could Frome be fitted into this?

W. H. Willans was disarmingly frank: 'He was a stranger in a strange place. Twenty years ago he came here to try to sell some wool. He was a manufacturer of long standing. Since that time until about a month ago he had not been in the town'. Yet, if one looked at the furthest limits of Frome's commercial reach, was that quite true? Take the Overburys of Willans and Overbury. They too were Londoners, Highbury people like Willans but already well established when he settled there. Their roots, however, lay in Tetbury.[17] Tetbury is not Frome but like Frome it is in south-west England's clothing county. Is that why Willans had been trying to sell wool there in the 1850s? And it may not be entirely coincidental that Wrigley Willans would find his second wife in Fairford, in the same county.

What is certainly not coincidental is the common Nonconformity of the Overburys, the Willanses, and their immediate connections. For the Willans family the Dissent was firmly Congregational. Willans's father and each of his brothers and sisters were active Congregationalists. Willans himself was an office holder at Henry Allon's Union Chapel, Islington, which was on the verge of a mammoth rebuilding to which Willans would give £500, and his wife came from a Union family. When they moved to Holland Park they would transfer their membership to the immensely solid Congregational church in Allen Street, Kensington.[18] He was also a denominational figure. He addressed the Congregational Union in 1873 on 'Attendance at Public Worship', favouring shorter sermons and a stronger liturgical sense, and from the early 1860s he had worked actively for a purpose-built denominational London headquarters. By 1874 Congregationalism's Memorial Hall was within sight of completion on Farringdon Street, in the City.[19] Such things might not impress a truly democratic electorate and they would certainly depress any electorate with an inbuilt Tory majority because they carried so much emotive political baggage, but in a place like Frome they could help. Willans was no more and no less an outsider than his Liberal predecessors Hughes, Sir Henry Rawlinson (the explorer and proconsul), and Donald Nicoll.[20] He was as yet quite unknown as a public figure but there were innumerable points of contact and recognition.

It is possible that one of these contributed to his selection. By 1874 his minister, Henry Allon, was nationally respected in Dissenting circles and increasingly recognised as a useful man to know in Liberal circles. Successful Nonconformist ministers had wide contacts and were good judges of character. Allon had an unlikely, primarily literary, friendship with the Oxford mediaevalist E. A. Freeman, who had failed as clearly in Mid-Somerset in 1868 as old William Willans had in Huddersfield in 1852. Did either Allon or Freeman play any part in nudging William Henry Willans in the direction of Frome?[21] Perhaps not, but once he was in Frome Willans could not be other than the chapel candidate, the best man for the Liberal Party at prayer. While the Tories relied confidently on the influence of Longleat, Whig Marston stood ostentatiously aside. No Boyles graced Willans's platforms, but the Baptist and Congregational ministers and their deacons certainly did.

The evidence for this is provided by the *Somerset and Wilts Journal*, a clearly Radical newspaper whose highly intelligent coverage of the 1874 election bent over backwards to tone down the sectarian issues which all locals knew were there and which all their leaders were determined to present as 'sectarian' only when twisted into such by their opponents. Not once, for example, was Father Bennett mentioned. When, however, it is realised that the *Journal's* printers and publishers were the rapidly expanding firms of Butler and Tanner and that the Butlers and the Tanners were Zion families, the clues fall thick and fast. The man behind the firm's expansion was Joseph Tanner (d. 1896), his minister's 'chief friend in Frome ... possessed of great shrewdness and business ability'.[22] One of his sons was J. R. Tanner, the future naval and constitutional historian, for this was the successful mental art man's world where boarding school and Cambridge, perhaps Oxford, now beckoned as matters of course.[23]

The *Journal* set the scene for a short but sharp electoral battle with meticulously detached partisanship. It prefaced the fight itself with three informative set pieces on Queen Victoria's parliaments, 'The Two Policies', and 'The Two Candidates'. These set the tone for the campaign's rhetoric.

The recent dissolution was the Queen's ninth. She had seen eight parliaments and twelve administrations. Of her eight prime ministers, five were dead and one was in retirement. That left Gladstone and Disraeli to hold the field. And their policies? These were deftly if predictably presented as Reaction, which was Tory, and Reform, which was Liberal. The Tories were reactionary warmongers; the Liberals were steadily and credibly effective reformers whose work over the best part of forty years had transformed society. That was a radical achievement. The presentation was deft because if the Liberals were the national party of government, with a proven record of consistent delivery, never deviating from their traditional watchword, and loyal to a noble leader, their cumulatively successful policy had been that of the Manchester School, though that phrase was nowhere used. Radicalism in 1874 was mainstream. Or so the *Journal* presented it. Yet if the Tory leader and his local candidate

> could have had their way, the Irish Church and the Irish Land Laws would be untouched to this hour; the power of spiteful landlords and employers to punish honest men for their votes would be still uncurbed by the Ballot; the parson's control over national education would be unchallenged and unassailed; the

monstrous abuse of Purchase in the Army would be still sanctioned; the public services would be slumbering on, undisturbed by fear of reductions or economies; and not a few taxes on the poor man's necessaries and luxuries of life would be still undiminished for the benefit of some phantom protectionist producer or importer ...[In forty years that] energy at home, which Mr. Disraeli deprecates, has given us free trade, open corporations, civil marriages, freedom from church rates, open universities, a popular press, cheaper law, and extended electoral rights, together with a hundred minor reforms, every one of which has safely 'harassed' some class or body of men that was deeply interested in retaining each several abuse. It is no secret that a 'True Blue' laments all these things as results of a mischievously misdirected 'energy' and sighs for the good old days of Addington and Perceval and Liverpool, when every cry for domestic reform was successfully smothered in the well-sustained excitement of energy abroad.

Tories, in short, were restless, dangerous agitators and their leader's 'epigrammatic manifesto has brought us clearly back by its implied contrast to the time-honoured watchword of the united Liberal party. Let the Electors of Frome not fail to raise it anew, and to return Mr. Willans in triumph to the ever electrical cry, PEACE, RETRENCHMENT AND REFORM!'

And the two candidates? The Tory was Henry Charles Lopes, genial when it came to drinks and treats, who claimed to be a local man. Liberals were not convinced. Though the head of his family was a Devon landowner and MP, and he himself had been a Cornish MP since 1868 and would be elevated to the peerage shortly before his death, in Liberal Frome eyes Lopes was a career lawyer whose views were undeviatingly reactionary, however 'Liberal' their gloss, and whose heart was set firmly on a judgeship. For those with long political memories, past Peterloo to the days of Pitt and Addington, the name was synonymous with blatant electoral corruption.[24] For the *Journal* it was enough to call Lopes an old-fashioned Tory

> who will oppose any measure for giving the franchise to working men in the counties, who will oppose Trades' Unions, who will oppose such a modification of the Education Act as would deprive the 'priests' of the sole control of our village schools, who (as a lawyer) will oppose the cheapening of the legal processes in the transfer of landed or house property by which it may be made more attainable by working men of provident habits, who will support the Game Laws, the law of Entail, and every vestige of privilege to the upper classes.

Thus did the *Journal* prepare the ground for Willans:

> a gentleman engaged in mercantile pursuits, and therefore one who has acquired business habits, who has no personal ends to serve in entering parliament, who does not aspire to become Solicitor-General, Attorney-General, or Lord Chancellor, a gentleman who by his antecedents and his associates has manifested his deep sympathy with working men, and has shown himself to be possessed of a mental grasp which will well qualify him to deal with those great questions which are now

coming to the front in the legislation of our country. The duty of the electors is therefore clear.

The *Journal's* care in emphasising the role of workingmen in the first general election since the Ballot Act is noteworthy. Willans was faced with a balancing act. His core supporters were Frome's Dissenters and especially its Congregationalists. His prime attraction lay in his reputation for combining sensible yet imaginative philanthropy with broad-horizoned yet sound business acumen. He had nonetheless to remember that Frome, like all other constituencies, had its Liberal drinkers, even drinksellers, and its Liberal Churchmen. Their votes were critical. Ninety either way could swing it. He had to cover issues of national leadership, foreign policy, reform, economics, disestablishment, local option, education, and Ireland without either compromising his own Radicalism (which the *Journal* broadly identified as that of Messrs Mundella and Samuel Morley)[25] or frightening off Liberal waverers at a point when waverers were still more likely to have votes than Radicals.

On the whole he succeeded. His speeches were natural, fluent, sometimes punchy. His generalisations sounded authoritative. His supporters rallied round. The dissolution had caught Frome by surprise but the Tories already had their hopeful and he issued his address on the very day that the Liberals' possible hopeful arrived. Willans boldly published his address before he had been formally adopted, canvassing had already begun and 'the walls of the several inns and hostelries have been covered with red or blue bills' (in Frome the Tories were blue; in many other constituencies blue was still the traditional Whig colour). At his adoption meeting the tone was clear. Any still Liberal county families were represented by William Strachey of The Elms, but the chair was taken by Philip le Gros, 'a man of culture and considerable wealth', who was one of Alfred Rowland's deacons at Zion.[26] Other Zionists on the platform included two Tanners, a Butler, and William Brett Harvey, whom Rowland recalled as 'one of the best deacons I ever had'. He was a chemist and stationer, 'the prime mover in temperance work and musical societies of various kinds'.[27] It goes without saying that Rowland himself was one of the three parsons on the platform.[28]

It was a well-orchestrated adoption meeting. Willans presented himself; then he presented the late parliament's record:

> It was summoned to disestablish the Irish Church; to re-arrange, alter, and amend the laws connected with the land tenure in Ireland ... also to undertake the work of providing for national education and university reform. The abolition of purchase in the army was promised. The most gigantic scheme of reform in the judicature ever introduced had also been passed. As if all the rest were not enough the government had introduced and carried a measure for voting by ballot (cheers).

Better yet: the national debt had been reduced by £20 million, taxes by £12.5 million, £9 million had been spent on buying the country's telegraphs, the *Alabama* indemnity had been paid, and still there was a £5 million surplus. All that could confidently be set against what should be the next parliament's record. First must come local taxation, and he carefully quoted Gladstone's characteristic determination 'to strengthen the invaluable traditions and to improve the organs of local government, to keep central control within the limits of sound policy ... to avoid the danger which would arise, if parliament were gradually to lay upon labour a portion of the burdens hitherto borne by property'. Next would come the abolition of income tax, which he mysteriously described as a war tax originally introduced by Peel, followed by the abolition of such 'articles of popular consumption' as sugar ('His friend, John Bright, had a very strong preference for a free breakfast table').[29] That left the 'assimilation of the borough and county franchise' and, though here he floundered, some improvements to Forster's Education Act. For the rest he ranged generally over the 'laws respecting the transfer, the descent and the occupation of land; the Game Laws; the laws respecting the sale of spirituous liquors; the laws affecting the relations between employer and employed; the laws of rating and of local government'. On none was he precise. It was enough to have mentioned them. He could afford to end (to 'loud and long continued applause') on a note of high cliché:

> The glory and honour of a seat in parliament he coveted more than anything else in the world, although it would involve a great amount of self sacrifice. It behoved them to be up and doing, with a long pull, a strong pull, and a pull altogether; otherwise they might find themselves in a position which the Liberals of Frome had never been in before when united. He, for one, would not believe that possible.

That show of local unity was confirmed when Trotman, a Liberal drinkseller, proposed Willans's adoption and Snelling, a Liberal workingman, seconded him, and the wider horizons were hinted at by the speech of 'Mr. Glover of London' who, by his own account, had come down not indeed as a Frome elector but as an Englishman who wished to serve two friends. One was Willans, who 'was not capable of being anything else but a Liberal', and the other was 'the one man in England, to whom all Englishmen and the great mass of mankind, were under great obligation ... Human nature was under obligation to Mr. Gladstone. Had they not since he had held the reins of power, had a new and sweeter breath and a loftier tone in politics?' But that did not prevent Glover from also having his say on income tax, that 'great enemy to economy', that 'most horrible and iniquitous tax ever levied, which had demoralised the people who had paid it'.

Mr. Glover was John Glover. Like Willans he lived well in Highbury. Like Willans he was a Union Chapel man. They had been friends at least since 1863 and Glover would be one of Willans's executors. On Census Day 1881, by which time the Willanses had moved down to Holland Park and the Glovers up to Highgate, Willans's two daughters were staying with the Glovers. Glover, however, was in shipping, not wool. He was the senior partner and the driving force in Glover Brothers of Bishopsgate. 1874 was as significant a year for his business as it was for Willans's, for the arrival of a third Glover brother into the firm considerably enlarged it. He was to become Chairman of the Mercantile Steamship Company, a Lloyd's Underwriter, a committee member and eventually Chairman of Lloyd's Registry of Shipping. If Willans was to be a power in the Chamber of Commerce, Glover was to be a power in the Chamber of Shipping.[30]

Glover was a Tynesider. His father was to South Shields what Willans's father was to Huddersfield, although he never stood for parliament, and his brothers were as usefully networked as Willans's.[31] Robert and Septimus had joined him in London, William carried on the family auctioneering business in Shields, while Thomas and Terrot ran its docks. That left Richard, who was already an influential and soon would be a nationally known Baptist minister in Bristol.[32] Clearly Liberal England was full of Glovers and Willanses broking their way through the nation's commerce and politics as well as its Baptist, Congregational, and Presbyterian chapels.

The contest, or at least the *Journal*'s picture of it, continued as it had begun. Its mid-point peak was a 'Monster Liberal Public Meeting' in the Mechanics' Institute. The same names filled the platform – Doggerell and Hiskett, Trotman and Flatman, Sage and Snelling, the Trade and the tradesmen and the workingmen. Mr. Strachey, however, was not there, though Mr. le Gros again took the chair and three of Frome's ministers were still to the fore.[33] Willans rehearsed what he had already said in his adoption speech, presenting himself as a model of Radical moderation. He praised the Liberal record. He welcomed a future in which 'the highest positions in church and State would be within the reach of the poorest'. Religious instruction in schools? He could not bring himself to exclude the Book of books from the schools of his country and he saw no reason why it should be either forced into or excluded from any rate-supported school. Disestablishment? He did not like the principle of an established church but he recognised that England's Church had gathered round it 'a large share of the heart's affections of the people (cheers)' and the time was not ripe for it to go: 'they ought to be careful before they laid hands ruthlessly upon an institution which had done, and was doing, great good (hear, hear)'. His stance, indeed, was pure Gladstone:

> Let it alone, and if the voice of the country should at some future time be spoken out as unmistakably as in the case of the Irish Church, he would be ready when the time came to join with others in doing away with its State connection altogether (cheers).

And he turned with relief to the ballot, whose workings Frome's Mr. Dunn was regularly explaining to worried voters. At times he was almost preternaturally cautious. Take Drink, and the Permissive Bill. That bill appealed to his most vocal supporters. In general the temperance lobby was prepared to accept a candidate's public neutrality on the issue. Willans, however, would only guarantee his neutrality in private; he needed to maintain Mr. Trotman's support and Trotman had, after all, found Willans a candidate to be proud of. 'There was a true honest ring about all his words'. Nonetheless the temperance atmosphere pervaded his meetings. Three of the Monster Meeting's speakers dwelt on the evils of drink, its impact on the working man, and its encouragement by their Tory opponents, though it fell to one of the three ministers, the Baptist, T. G. Rooke, to turn the attack directly on the local landed interest:

> Mr. Disraeli complained that Mr. Gladstone's legislation had been harassing, probably it had to such as Lord Bath and other landlords who now found they were unable to put on the screw any longer (applause). If Mr. Willans was sent to parliament the Conservatives would be harassed still more (applause). The game laws, one of the grandest instruments of torture in the hands of the Conservative party, were also to be got rid of (applause).

It was Glover from London whose speech summed up what the Liberals hoped was the tone of their election. He was the ninth, even the tenth, to speak, still 'if some of their opponents could stay up till twelve the previous night drinking, probably those present would not object to stay five minutes longer'. The thrust of his message was loyalty to Gladstone, 'a man whose name was already big in history', and his exemplification in Willans, whom opponents dismissed as a 'stop gap'.[34] Glover's technique was sound. He 'had no hesitation in saying that Mr. Willans would be a "stop gap"'. And he played the Dick Whittington card:

> It was true Mr. Willans was not an Admiral nor a General; indeed he was not even a QC, but he was a man of business (applause). He was an honourable merchant of London, an eminent member of one of the London Churches, had been a teacher in a Ragged and a Sunday School; the superintendent of a large Sunday School; and was now treasurer of a large London charity, which fed and clothed three hundred little boys (applause).

In its wider coverage the *Journal* cast its eye over 'Elections in Other Constituencies'. Discerning readers could pick out the shadings of Radical and Dissenting significance. Some were hopeless causes but in each a chapel connection might be identified and set in the industrial or commercial context, sometimes the agricultural context, which had disrupted, then formed and reformed its community. And then it homed in on Gladstone's speech to an immense crowd in Blackheath, one of his set occasions, its power enhanced by the dense fog and steady drizzle that enveloped and penetrated his auditory.

If the *Journal* had had its way the ringing memory of the election, incidentally picking up one of its insistent motifs, would have been the song contributed by 'A Working Man':

> Liberal men be up and doing, work together, heart and hand,
> If ye be but swift and willing, Gladstone still must rule the land.
> Let our watchword, 'Vote for Willans', echo in each Liberal heart,
> In the hall of Old St Stephen's, he will bear a manly part.

Chorus

Work, boys, work but not with tramping,
Idle bluster dies away,
'Tis the steady persevering, and the honest, earnest working
That will gain for us the well-won day.

Though 'a stranger', yet we know him, true of heart and clear of head,
And, we working men will show him, we can follow when thus led;
Let our watchword, 'Vote for Willans', coupled with the stirring cry;
Frome expects her Liberal men will nobly gain the Victory.

Chorus

Work, boys, work ...

'Tis not Tory opposition, Tory boasting, Tory pride,
Tory drinking, paid for smoking, that will turn our votes aside;
Lopes says that he is certain, of a vast majority,
But that, in by gone times, has proved to mean a large minority.

Chorus

Work, boys, work ...

The uncertain rhythm of that last line proved prophetic. The lasting memory, however, was probably that recalled fifty years later by Zion's Alfred Rowland: drink and rural oppression.

> The church and the publicans were openly leagued for mutual support, feeling ran very high, and drink was poured out lavishly; in fact, free beer was on draught for months afterwards for those who had voted on the right side. We organised a band of sixty 'watchers', who on the night before the poll literally dragged out half-intoxicated voters from public houses, and saw them safely home. A jobbing gardener, who often worked for me, whose chief fault was his love for whisky, was an ardent Liberal when sober, but on polling day he disappeared. News came that he had been discovered hopelessly drunk shut up in a gamekeeper's lodge on the Longleat estate, five miles away. As we were within three hours of the close of the poll (three o'clock), a member of my congregation drove over to the cottage and brought him back triumphantly in his dog-cart, hidden under the seat. The unfortunate man was put under the pump, drenched with soda-water, and safely polled a few minutes before time.[35]

Anyway, Willans lost. He polled only fourteen votes fewer than Tom Hughes in 1868, but the Tory vote had risen by a hundred and sixty-six.[36]

And what happened? Lopes got his judgeship and at the by-election that followed in 1876 the Liberals were returned: the figures of 1876 neatly reversed those of 1874. The new MP, H. B. Samuelson, was a carpet-bagging career Liberal, young, rich, and mainstream but with occasional Radical tendencies, a Londoner whose wealth was founded on Liverpool commerce. He was a budding dynast, but he was no Dissenter.[37] As for Willans, the nearest he got to Westminster was Middlesex County Council, of which he became an Alderman. His friend Glover also got no nearer to Westminster than Middlesex County Council, although he fought the 1885 election in Scarborough where, for all the obvious differences and notwithstanding the passage of time, the elements and the rhetoric were much as they had been in Frome and the result was the same.[38]

And the twists in the story? Willans remained a loyal Gladstonian but at some point in the 1880s he switched less perhaps his religious allegiance than his religious attendance. He joined the congregation of St Peter's, Vere Street, which saw itself as conserving the true Broad Church Anglicanism of F. D. Maurice and of which Tom Hughes was a notable adherent. Yet even that change may have been less obvious than it seems and after Willans's death his widow and their unmarried daughter returned to an admittedly eccentric nearby set of Congregational pews.[39] Glover remained a Congregationalist but within months of 1885 the man who had seemed Gladstonian through and through had become an active Liberal Unionist, as had his brothers. That probably explains his knighthood in 1900. Glover outlived Willans. Both had changed, but their forays into Westminster politics had already been justified by the career of a bright nephew of Willans's, educated by him when a fatherless boy, who certainly moved among the highest in the land and whose descendants still live not far from Frome. He was H. H. Asquith. But what should one make of the fact that the octogenarian Alfred Rowland, recalling his formative first pastorate in Frome, its personalities and its electors, should when apparently writing of the 1874 election not have mentioned the name of its Liberal candidate nor, indeed, the connection with Asquith? Men like Rowland were usually alert to such things. Perhaps there was less body to Willans than this essay has suggested. Even so, such men play their part in the consolidation of political beliefs.[40]

References

1. For the best Dissenting eye-view of the constituency in the 1860s and 1870s see A. Rowland, *An Independent Parson* (London, 1923), pp. 54-67; for electoral details see *McCalmont's Parliamentary Poll Book: British Election Results, 1832-1918*, ed. J. Vincent and M. Stenton (Brighton, 1971), pp. 115-16, 218; for the position from 1884 see H. Pelling, *Social Geography of British Elections, 1883-1910* (London, 1967), p. 153.

2. For Nicoll (b. 1820) see M. Stenton, *Who's Who of British Members of Parliament, 1832-85* (Hassocks, 1976), p. 284.

3. Rowland, *Independent Parson*, p. 65. For Hughes (1823-96) see Stenton, *Members of Parliament*, p. 204, and *D[ictionary of] N[ational] B[iography]* (22 vols., London, 1908-9), xxii, 879-82.

4. For Rowland (1840-1925) see *Congregational Year Book* (London, 1926), pp. 180-1.

5. Rowland, *Independent Parson*, p. 65.

6. For Bennett (1804-86) see *DNB*, xxii, 169-71.

7. For Gibson (1807-1884) see Stenton, *Members of Parliament*, p. 154, and *DNB*, vii, 1164-5.

8. The following account and all quotations unless otherwise noted come from *Somerset and Wilts Journal*, and *Supplement to the Somerset and Wilts Journal*, 31 Jan. 1874. I am greatly indebted to David Bromwich (Somerset Studies Librarian) for alerting me to this.

9. For Willans (1833-1904) see *Who Was Who, 1897-1916* (London, 1920), p. 764.

10. K. Heasman, *Evangelicals in Action* (London, 1962), pp. 98, 184-5; *The HLB Old Boys' Journal*, Jan. 1905, p.2.

11. For Hanbury (1823-67) see Stenton, *Members of Parliament*, p. 177.

12. This section is based on a copy of the first minutes of the Farningham and Swanley Homes, *The HLB Old Boys' Journal*, Jan. 1905; *Congregational Year Book* (1870), p.8; and an eight-page advertisement inserted at the end of *Congregational Year Book* (1886). I am greatly indebted for much information to Mr. R. Faulkner, Mr. Felix Hull (late Kent County Archives), Mr. L. Skinner and Mr. H.O. Tester.

13. For (Sir) Francis Lycett (1803-80) see *A Dictionary of Methodism in Britain and Ireland*, ed. J. A. Vickers (Peterborough, 2000). For (Sir) John Glover (1829-1920) see below n.30.

14. For F. J. Sargood's son, Sir Frederick Thomas Sargood (1834-1903), of Melbourne, see *Who Was Who, 1897-1916*, p. 628.

15. For Henry Allon (1818-92), see *DNB*, xxii, 41-2. Rowland ministered at Park Chapel, Crouch End (1875-1911), where the membership topped 1000 by 1900.

16. These connections (and their particular bearing on the formation of H. H. Asquith) are explored in C. Binfield, 'Asquith: The Formation of a Prime Minister', *Journal of the United Reformed Church Society*, ii (1991), 204-42; and idem, *A Congregational Formation: An Edwardian Prime Minister's Victorian Education*, The Congregational Lecture 1996 (London, 1996).

17. The clue seems to lie in Mill Hill, the north London Dissenting school. Three Overburys, all Tetbury clothiers, had sons there in 1819; one had a house in Highbury, as did a Mill Hill Overbury parent in the next generation: E. Hampden-Cook, *The Register of Mill Hill School, 1807-1926* (London, 1926), pp. 21, 24, 25, 104.

18. This information is taken from the records of Union Chapel, Islington, and Kensington United Reformed Church, in the possession of those churches when I consulted them.

19. *Congregational Year Book* (1874), pp. 54-61; C. Binfield, 'Memory Enstructured: The Case of Memorial Hall', in *Memory and Memorials, 1789-1914: Literary and Cultural Perspectives*, ed. M. Campbell, J. Labbe, S. Shuttleworth (London, 2000), pp. 160-74, 223-6, esp. pp. 170-1.

20. For Rawlinson (1810-95), MP Frome 1865-8, see Stenton, *Members of Parliament*, p. 324, and *DNB*, xvi, 771-4.

21. For the Allon-Freeman friendship, and Allon's political connections, see A. Peel, *Letters to a Victorian Editor* (London, 1929), pp. 75-166. For Edward Augustus Freeman (1823-92) see *DNB*, xxii, 672-6.

22. Rowland, *Independent Parson*, p. 61.

23. Four Tanner brothers proceeded to Mill Hill and Cambridge; one (E.R Tanner, solicitor in Bristol) remained an active Congregationalist but L.R. Tanner (1865-1921), 'an ideal employer, gentleman and friend', who took over the firm, became chairman of the Unionist Association, and was buried at Holy Trinity,

Frome: Hampden-Cook, *Mill Hill School*, pp. 148, 155, 170, 177. For J. R. Tanner (1860-1931) see *Dictionary of National Biography, 1931-40*, ed. L. G. W. Legg (London, 1949), pp. 846-7.

24. For H. C. Lopes, 1st Baron Ludlow (1828-99) and his elder brother, Sir Massey Lopes (1818-1908) see Stenton, *Members of Parliament*, p. 243 and *DNB*, xxii, 982-3; for Sir Manasseh Masseh Lopes (1st Bt, 1755-1831), imprisoned for bribery 1819-20, see R. G. Thorne, *The House of Commons, 1790-1820* (5 vols, London, 1986), iv, 455-7, and *DNB*, xii, 132.

25. For Morley (1809-86), the Congregational manufacturer and backbencher par excellence, see Stenton, *Members of Parliament*, p.278 and *DNB*, xiii, 979-81. For Mundella (1825-97), Anglican manufacturer and up-and-coming Radical, see M. Stenton and S. Lees, *Who's Who of British Members of Parliament, 1886-1918* (Hassocks, 1978), p. 261 and *DNB*, xxii, 1081-4.

26. For Strachey (b. 1821), late of the Colonial Office, and uncle of Lytton Strachey, see *Walford's County Families of The United Kingdom* (London, 1898), p. 986. For le Gros (d. 1881) see Rowland, *Independent Parson*, p. 61; like Tanner, he sent his four sons to Mill Hill School: Hampden-Cook, *Mill Hill School*, pp. 144, 159, 173, 189.

27. Rowland, *Independent Parson*, p. 61.

28. The other two confirm the status of Frome's Dissent. T.G. Rooke (d. 1892), solicitor's son and expert in Oriental languages, had been intended for the Bar but became a Baptist minister, at Sheppard's Barton, Frome 1863-1876, and President of Rawdon, the Baptist theological college near Bradford, thereafter. He had promoted Frome's Working Men's Liberal Association in 1868: *Baptist Hand Book* (London, 1892), pp. 130-1. John Milnes (1839-1914), minister at the older Congregational church, Rook Lane, 1867-1879, was less of a public figure. He was a London graduate, the son of a Bradford cotton spinner, educated at Mill Hill, to which in turn he (like Alfred Rowland) sent his sons: *Congregational Year Book* (1915), pp. 165-6; Hampden-Cook, *Mill Hill School*, pp. 101, 172, 205, 343, 356. I am indebted to Mrs Susan Mills, Librarian, Angus Library, Regent's Park College, Oxford, for much information about Frome's Baptists.

29. Was this with his chairman, Philip le Gros in mind? The eldest of the le Gros boys became a London sugar merchant.

30. For Sir John Glover (1829-1920) see *Who Was Who, 1916-28*, p. 413; *Glover Brothers, 1853-1953* (London, 1953); 'A Knighthood for a Shieldsman: Sir John Glover', *Shields Gazette*, 23 May 1900; *Shields Gazette*, 6 Apr. 1914.

31. For Alderman Terrot Glover (1802-85) see *Shields Daily Gazette*, 24 Feb. 1885, and *Glover Brothers*.

32. For Richard Glover (1837-1919) see D. T. Roberts, 'Mission Home and Overseas: Richard Glover of Bristol', *Baptist Quarterly*, xxxv (1993), 108-20.

33. Rook and Rowland, although Milnes, the Congregationalist, was absent, and in his place was William Burton (d. 1917), minister at Badcox Lane Baptist Church 1861-93: 'No figure was better known than his, tall, upright, striding with his black cane across the Market Place at 4 pm for his daily hour at the Literary Institute ... There were times too, specially about 1874-5 and 1883-4, when large numbers were added to the Church under his clear and gracious evangelism': A. H. Coombs, *A History of Badcox Lane Baptist Church, Frome* (Frome, c.1924), pp. 27-9.

34. Glover's Gladstonianism was reflected in his ships and his family: his first vessel was the 'W. E. Gladstone' and his youngest son (a surgeon who became Mayor of Hampstead in 1936) was Lewis Gladstone Glover (b. 1868).

35. Rowland, *Independent Parson*, p.66.

36. H. C. Lopes – 642; W. H. Willans – 557.

37. H. B. Samuelson – 661; Sir James Fergusson – 568. For Sir H. B. Samuelson (1845-1937), MP Frome 1876-85, see Stenton and Lees, *British Members of Parliament, 1886-1918*, p. 318.

38. Sir George Sitwell – 2188; J. Glover – 2048. See also Pelling, *Social Geography of British Elections*, pp. 312-13.

39. Cutting, 1 Oct. 1904 in Obituary Cuttings, 1893-1916, Huddersfield Library; *The H.L.B Old Boys' Journal*, Jan. 1905, p. 3; the Congregational Church to which the Willans ladies returned was the King's Weigh House, near Grosvenor Square, whose minister, W. E. Orchard, became a Roman Catholic priest.

40. To give an example of such links: Alfred Rowland's closest ministerial friend was Charles Edward Baines Reed (1845-84), Cambridge graduate and a cousin of Mrs Wrigley Willans. From 1871 to 1874 he had been minister of Common Close Congregational Church, in the heart of Lord Bath's domain but outside the Frome constituency. In 1874, when he returned to London, W. H. Willans joined the Board of the National Provident Institution, where a fellow director was Reed's father Sir Charles Reed (1819-81), City merchant and Liberal politician, MP Hackney 1868-74. For Sir Charles Reed see Stenton, *Members of Parliament*, p. 325 and *DNB*, xvi,832-4; see also N. Toulson, *The Squirrel and*

the Clock: National Provident Institution, 1835-1985 (London, 1985). I am grateful to Mr. Toulson and Lord Remnant for information about the NPI and the Willans connection with it.

Chapter 9

Re-thinking Popular Conservatism in Liverpool: Democracy and Reform in the Later Nineteenth Century

Liverpool's place within British political historiography has typically been one of exceptionalism.[1] Given Liverpool's relatively recent reputation as a hotbed of extreme Labour militancy, coupled with Bleasdalesque representations of the proverbial 'Bolshy Scouser', it can be something of a surprise to those unacquainted with the city's political heritage to find that it is, in fact, one of abiding popular Conservatism. The Liverpool Labour Party won its first parliamentary seat in 1923, and as late as 1939 only three of Liverpool's eleven parliamentary divisions had Labour MPs, with five constituencies still having never returned a Labour candidate to parliament.[2] The extent of the Labour Party's failure in Liverpool is more notable still in municipal politics. By 1914, the Labour Party occupied only seven of a possible 140 seats on the city council, and it was only in 1955 that Labour achieved its first municipal majority in the city. Thus, in terms of aggregate electoral support for the Labour Party in Britain's major cities down to 1960, Liverpool can boast penultimate position.[3]

Largely a consequence of the prevailing focus upon organised Labour and trade unionism among historians of British popular politics, Liverpool has long been held up as an aberrant case, where popular sectarian identities were all powerful. During the 1960s and 1970s, Labour historians tended to interpret the apparent absence of a strong historical tradition of exclusively 'class' based political affiliation in Liverpool as a sort of Marxian false consciousness.[4] Within this narrative, popular Conservatism is synonymous with political deviance and thus symptomatic of the perversity of working-class Liverpudlians on the whole. Since Liverpool did not fit the 'dialectical materialist' mould, the city was presented as the exception that proved the rule. Religion became the new dialectic as historians juxtaposed the Protestantism of Liverpool's indigenous population with the staunch Catholicism of the geographically segregated and culturally insulated Irish migrant community, to discover an intriguing working-class dichotomy. Cleavages along the lines of religion, nationalism and ethnicity had apparently fomented the political identities of 'Orange' and 'Green' in

Liverpool, where the Conservative Party, always opportunistic, was quick to exploit organic popular allegiance to the Established Church and British constitution. The Liverpool Irish, meanwhile, simply continued the valiant struggle for a united Ireland through their representative T. P. O'Connor and his thriving Irish Nationalist Party.[5] Thus, according to this rather one dimensional, sectarian account of Liverpool's political history, militant denominationalism in the city had retarded the natural development of a unified working-class consciousness and, consequently, the forward march of Labour.[6] The simultaneous publication of a number of pseudo-sociological surveys, which claimed to demonstrate that contemporary working-class support for the Conservative Party in Britain was indicative of psychological deference and social aspiration, lent a modish legitimacy to this interpretation.[7] Consequently, in Liverpool, where the Conservative Party maintained an almost uninterrupted parliamentary and municipal hegemony down to the Second World War, a rather objectionable picture of the city's working-class electorate emerged.

Through the 1980s, the trend for grand historical narratives and pseudo-sociological surveys gave way to a new approach to the study of popular politics. Moving beyond theories of a labour aristocracy and internal stratification, and revising traditional notions of the British working class as a relatively homogeneous group, historians began to explore the link between community, popular culture and political affiliation. Inherent within this approach was the problematisation of that hitherto automatic link between apparently objective economic interests and electoral behaviour. In the Liverpool context, the work of John Belchem, Joan Smith, Andy Shallice, John Bohstedt and Sam Davies made a significant contribution to this new departure, emphasising both the diversity of social identities and the informal and social dimension of popular political mobilisation.[8] Whilst accepting the centrality of the link between religious and nationalist identities and practical politics in Liverpool, their work has nevertheless continued to explore not only the formal organisation of political parties in Liverpool, but also the way in which patterns of employment, spatial segregation and associational culture reinforced and sustained a sectional and sectarian style of politics in the city. This has resulted in a far more positive reading of Liverpool's political history in which the value of more functional denominational and ethnic organisations of mutuality and self help, such as friendly societies, tontines, co-operatives and burial societies, are given due recognition. Furthermore, because it was the Irish community and the Catholic Church in particular that formed the vanguard of welfare provision and charitable effort in Liverpool during the later decades of the nineteenth century, their work has simultaneously pioneered the recent explosion of revisionist texts which have begun a timely reinterpretation of the historiography surrounding Irish migrants in nineteenth-century Britain.[9]

More recently, however, post-modernist and post-structuralist theory has challenged the very notion of social class as a unifying or even a defining abstract. Although post-modernist theory remains a highly contested sphere, historians are now more likely to stress the 'fluidity of social identities, whilst examining the ways in which political organisations deployed rhetoric, narrative and other discursive practices to construct identities, to create constituencies of support and to forge alliances amongst heterogeneous social groups'.[10] Simply put, it is no longer acceptable for historians to view political parties as the passive beneficiaries of pre-existing structural divisions in society. Within popular political historiography the 'linguistic turn', as pioneered by Gareth Stedman Jones, rejected the social determinism of earlier historians in favour of a language centred approach to political analysis.[11] Subsequently criticised for failing to engage adequately with heated contemporary controversies about post-structuralism and social history, and for working from a hazy theoretical premise, Stedman Jones' commonsense approach nevertheless recognised that

> in nearly all writings on Chartism, except that of Chartists themselves, it had been the movement's class character, social composition or more simply the hunger and distress of which it was thought to be the manifestation, rather than its platform or programme which had formed the focal point of enquiry.[12]

Stedman Jones held that in order to isolate the more salient features of popular political mobilisation, one should begin with a close reading of what the participants actually said and wrote. At the same time, Stedman Jones' portrayal of social class as a 'discursive rather than as an ontological reality' posed the first credible challenge within popular political historiography to what had become an almost Marxist-liberal orthodoxy.[13]

It is with the new emphasis upon political discourse and programme that this essay is concerned. British historiographical preoccupation with social and economic divisions are far less apparent in the Liverpool context, where the Conservative Party's political hegemony has been explained, almost exclusively, as a direct consequence of pre-existing religious affiliations and popular sectarian identities amongst the electorate. Whilst religious sectarianism and the street violence associated with it was an undeniable, if unsavoury facet of social identity in Liverpool, the overstated link between Church and party has nevertheless resulted in a rather one-dimensional, reductionist reading of Liverpool's political history.[14] Just as scholarly development has forced the problematisation of the link between social class and electoral behaviour elsewhere, likewise the link between religion and political affiliation in nineteenth-century Liverpool is in need of revision. A close reading of the language, ideology and programme of popular Conservatism in late nineteenth-century Liverpool provides a timely corrective to the 'Orange' orthodoxy whilst placing Liverpool at the helm of democratic and social reform.

It is surprisingly difficult to locate any explicit appeal to sectarian identities within the formal public discourse of Liverpool Conservatism during the late nineteenth century. With few exceptions, it is safe to say that where electoral appeals to religious sentiment did occur, they were generally of minor significance, restricted to specific historical junctures, and invariably coaxed from reluctant Tory candidates who were prevailed upon by extreme Protestant organisations or individual Protestant demagogues. For the period down to the First World War, the dominant Tory electoral cry in Liverpool was that of Democratic Conservatism.[15]

The term 'Tory Democrat' was coined during the 1882 Liverpool by-election, in which the Conservative leader, Arthur Forwood, challenged the Liberal Samuel Smith. The phrase was used by the *London Standard* to describe the 'unprincipled programme' outlined in Forwood's electoral address. To an audience of 6,000 he pledged his commitment to universal household suffrage, a redistribution of parliamentary seats, temperance reforms and an extended Employers Liability Act. Though Forwood declared a commitment to the continued union of Church and State, he nevertheless continued to assert that the Conservative Party did not 'claim for the Church of England a superior position in this country to that of other denominations, for I think we are all engaged in good work, and we are all on an equal footing as regards that'.[16] Nationally, the Tory press noted a 'dangerous' collective agenda 'professedly conceived in the interest of the working classes.... a direct appeal to the mob as against the upper ten', whilst Liberal journals remarked upon 'the hugger mugger creed of a political quack'.[17]

Tory Democracy has been the subject of considerable scholarly debate. It is typically associated with the aristocratic Lord Randolph Churchill, who, in an article published in the *Fortnightly Review* some six months after Forwood's electoral defeat, contrived his own association with the creed by declaring that Forwood had used the expression in 1882 'without knowing what he was talking about'.[18] Further complicated by the lack of a cohesive agenda, Tory Democracy is best interpreted as an elastic ideology, open to reinterpretation and redefinition in accordance with the shifting political climate. Thus, for Churchill Tory Democracy was 'principally opportunism', whilst for W. S. Blunt, Tory MP for Camberwell in 1885, Tory Democracy encompassed a fundamental commitment to Irish Home Rule.[19] According to Forwood, the phrase simply translated as the 'representation of all, irrespective of trade or class distinction'.[20] Forwood's own definition, as set out in an article published in the *Contemporary Review* in 1883, centred upon making politics more representative, not merely through the framing of policy with a mind upon the perceived interests of an increasingly urban working-class electorate, but also through radical electoral reform.[21]

Forwood's conversion to the democratic cause was no doubt part of that wider mood of trepidation with which the majority of Conservatives anticipated the inevitable encroachment of democracy.[22] Reform had created an electorate dominated by men without property, who were protected by the secret ballot and who could not be 'bought' following restrictions on electoral spending and corrupt practices after 1883. As the traditional party of property and aristocracy, Conservatives had nightmares about an inexorable march toward socialism and searched for new direction. Patrician insecurities concerning the inevitability of an accompanying decline of Conservatism, however, were not shared by an emerging breed of provincial politician. These men recognised that their purchase upon the popular urban vote could be consolidated through the inauguration of 'caucus' style political machines, the fusion of municipal and parliamentary politics, and the identification of party with social aspects of working-class culture.[23] Joseph Chamberlain epitomised this new approach, and Forwood was determined that Liverpool should follow his lead. In 1883 Forwood wrote:

> My official duties have brought me into constant and close connection with Conservatives of every class and position, and I have no hesitation in stating that if, as a party, Conservatism is simply to be the brake on the wheel of legislation, having no enlightened or progressive policy of its own, it will soon cease, and deservedly so, to exercise any political power in the city of Liverpool. Birmingham has taken the lead in the country, of the party aiming at revolutionary changes; in a like manner the Conservatives of Liverpool aspire to head that phalanx of men who, whilst sound upon constitutional principles, are yet alive to the necessity for such progress as the growing intelligence of the age demands...[The Tories] will only have themselves to blame if revolutionary or socialistic ideas extend.[24]

So the creed of the Tory Democrat was one of social reconciliation, and in Forwood's opinion a collective Conservative programme of progressive municipal policy furnished the best vehicle through which provincial Tories could capture the electoral allegiance of the urban working classes. Forwood held that municipal policy affected working men and women more immediately, and, blurring the boundary between municipal action and parliamentary policy, the Liverpool Conservative Party campaigned on a platform of social reform. Forwood's *forte* was municipal housing.

Liverpool's contemporary reputation as a pioneer in the sphere of Victorian housing reform and corporation housing arose from its corresponding notoriety as custodian of the worst slums outside the metropolis to 1914. The origins, growth and abhorrent sanitary condition of Liverpool's overcrowded court and cellar dwellings throughout the nineteenth and early twentieth centuries has been comprehensively documented in numerous local studies, whilst the city features prominently in the broader national historiography of urban growth, social amelioration and working-class housing.[25] Nevertheless, the Conservative Party's position as the leading local proponent of municipal housing in Liverpool, particularly under the direction of Archibald Salvidge after 1900, has been understated, receiving consideration only within what is essentially a social and economic historical narrative.[26] Consequently, it is more often the Irish Nationalists in Liverpool who are credited with the political vanguardism which prompted Liverpool's radical social programme of slum clearance and rehousing for the city's indigent poor.[27]

By 1863, mortality rates in Liverpool had reached a staggering 33 per thousand. This figure, despite having dropped to 23.8 per thousand by 1894, was still the highest of any city in the county, including London, Birmingham, Glasgow and Manchester. Overcrowding in the city's slums was similarly the worst in England by 1894, when the population per acre reached 97.3, compared with 58.2 in London and 40.3 in Manchester. The Conservative Party first seized upon the idea of turning Liverpool's housing problem into a political concern in November 1883, when Forwood, the party chairman, published a paper in which he envisaged an expenditure of £1.5 million on municipal housing for the city.[28] Forwood claimed that the Conservative Party hoped to negotiate the removal of no less than 12,000 of Liverpool's insanitary slum dwellings and simultaneously to provide two new tenements for every three homes removed, with affordable rentals on the basis of one shilling per room, per week. He calculated that this would cost Liverpool's ratepayers in the region of £14,538 per annum, or 'a little over a penny in the pound on the rates'.[29] By contemporary standards this was a relatively negligible sum, but at a time when 'character' was thought to direct economic status, and amidst the vestiges of Malthusianism and *laissez-faire* theories of self-help, the concept of subsidised housing for Liverpool's residuum verged upon political militancy. Forwood's radicalism was certainly symptomatic of that wider public furore which followed publication of Andrew Mearns' sensational Congregationalist tract, *The Bitter Cry of Outcast London* (1883), in which he catalogued the wretched and immoral lives led by the inhabitants of Britain's industrial slums.[30] Yet the Liverpool Conservative Party's far reaching influence, both upon the Royal Commission of 1884 and on subsequent social policy, has largely been ignored.[31]

It was a fundamental emphasis upon affordability, the central theme of Forwood's paper, that set it apart from the reports of acclaimed contemporary commentators such as Lord Salisbury and Joseph Chamberlain.[32] Forwood aired his radicalism curtly, insisting that the only point of controversy should be upon whom the onus of responsibility for housing the country's urban poor ought to fall, 'the State or the individual?'[33] While Lord Salisbury was circumspect and Chamberlain tame, Forwood introduced a marked class inflection to the debate with his insistence that local authorities should shoulder the responsibility, as this would prove to be the most expedient way in which the country's urban elite could safeguard its social position and wealth: 'For if the majority see that the minority of their fellow countrymen thus use their riches and their position, they will loose that bitterness which neglect and callousness engender, class distinctions will be forgotten, and the great democracy will acquiesce in that healthful influence'.[34]

Predictably hindered by less progressive thinkers locally, it was not until 1915 that Forwood's scheme was eventually realised and Liverpool's Conservative city council achieved the goal of building some 2,230 individual tenements and houses and re-housing around 11,500 former slum dwellers. In 1901, the Conservative council ruled that henceforth, corporation property would be restricted to those dispossessed by slum clearance, a move which helped to explode the myth of a 'deserving' and 'undeserving' poor. At the ceremonial opening of the new labourers' dwellings in

Bevington Street in June 1912, the city council celebrated the improving nature of quality housing for the poor:

> It is extremely gratifying to notice the improvements in the habits and cleanliness of these people as indicated by the appearance of their dwellings. A walk around these improved districts during the day or night will indicate the atmosphere of quietness and comparative comfort which prevails... although in many cases they are the 'poorest of the poor' there appears to be an endeavour to make an effort to improve the internal arrangement of the dwelling. It is also interesting to note that there is a higher moral tone; self-respect is more in evidence, and a keener love of home prevails. The condition of the children who formerly resided in courts shews a very marked improvement; they are better cared for, suitably clothed and are being trained and reared in an environment which is bound to be productive of much moral and physical good.[35]

Sectarian and, remarkably, even gender considerations do not appear to have played any part in the selection process for tenants and there is no indication whatsoever of partiality on the part of the Conservative Party in the leasing of property to the city's 'Protestant boys'.[36] Moreover, by 1891 Liverpool Corporation's entire housing stock was sited within the boundaries of the city's Irish 'enclave', Scotland division, and yet the census returns for that year do not reveal an overwhelmingly Irish born tenantry. The Liverpool census returns for 1891 show that of the 124 tenements at St. Martin's Cottages, only 42, or less than 34 per cent, had a 'head of household' of Irish birth. Similarly, at the council's Juvenal Dwellings only 21 of the 101 tenements were tenanted by families with an Irish-born head of household.[37] Indeed, analysis of the data confirms that corporation tenants were a diverse group and, in keeping with the city's cosmopolitan character, tenants were not overwhelmingly from any one country or region. This is particularly noteworthy given the way in which historians have likened Conservatism and municipal politics in Liverpool to American machine or 'boss' politics. Such analogies are loaded with innuendo, implying profiteering, criminality and jobbery on the part of Liverpool's Tory councillors.[38] In relation to the allocation of council housing, however, where one would expect to see at least some indication of a partisan distribution of municipal 'spoils', there is no compelling evidence of improper practice. Indeed, if the 'Tammany Hall' model can be considered comparable to the political dynamics of any one party in Liverpool, it would be more usefully applied to a reading of Irish Nationalism.

Far from leading the way toward municipal housing for the working classes, Liverpool's popular Nationalist 'boss', T. P. O'Connor, was primarily concerned that a Tory scheme of slum clearance should not adulterate the unique Irish electoral preponderance of the Scotland and Vauxhall wards of the city, where the Irish congregated close to the waterfront casual labour markets in an area with the worst housing conditions in the city and consistently higher mortality rates and overcrowding than elsewhere. Irish Nationalist Party strength emanated from the electoral discipline of a large and localised Irish community. With a popular tradition of strategic voting and ready-made electioneering mechanisms in the Catholic Church and Irish pub, Irish Nationalists were able to maximise their influence, both locally and in national politics. Typically portrayed as the working man's friend, T. P. O'Connor dictated the Nationalist position on housing at a special meeting of the North West branch of the Irish Nationalist League, in February 1887, at which he urged 'the ratepayers of Scotland Ward [to] enter a determined protest against the attempts of the Corporation to annihilate the Irish power in the constituency under the pretext of improving the sanitation of the district.'[39] This allusion to conspiracy was typical of the somewhat paranoid rhetoric of Irish Nationalism in Liverpool. As a political lever the language was calculated to incite collective indignation in a community that was highly sensitive to any suggestion of victimisation. At the same time, O'Connor's directive highlights the way in which an Irish Nationalist political agenda in Liverpool was often incompatible with the practical economic needs of the local, albeit 'Irish' community. For O'Connor the ideologue, the political ethic was paramount, transcending social responsibility, and it was his belief that municipal policy on slum clearance was primarily 'a party question in that it meant the maintenance or destruction of Nationalist superiority in the constituency'.[40] Irish Nationalists held firm to this position over the subsequent decade, and, through a tactical alliance with Liberals on the council, they were able to ensure that all corporation housing was built within the boundaries of the Scotland and Vauxhall wards of the city down to 1891, and that as late as 1916, more than 59 per cent of the municipal housing stock was sited within the Scotland division.[41]

Thus the rhetoric of Tory Democracy centred upon the Conservative Party's commitment to making politics more representative, not merely through the framing of practical policy with a mind upon the perceived interests of an urban working-class electorate, but also through radical electoral reform.[42] Arthur Forwood's 'firm reliance upon and belief in the Conservative instincts of the people' had made him a leading advocate of extending the county franchise to agricultural labourers, albeit conditional upon its introduction in conjunction with a redistribution of parliamentary seats. Forwood argued that the sub-division of urban constituencies would result in a fairer system of proportionate representation. He was nevertheless keen to reassure the urban middle classes that a 'tyranny of the majority' would not necessarily follow parliamentary redistribution because he had noted that 'in large towns where people of position and property usually congregate, the well-to-do people would have a separate district and thus secure representation of their interests'.[43] According to the calculations of the Conservative Party in Liverpool, redistribution would see the city divided into twelve single member constituencies, of which 'eight would fall to us, two to Home Rulers and two to Liberals, ensuring a perfect system of representation of all interests'.[44] At the same time, Liverpool Tories were in favour of extending polling hours. They anticipated that this would effectively enfranchise the considerable section of the working classes whose homes were so distant from their place of work as to have made it impossible for them to register their vote without sacrificing a day's pay.[45] Indeed, as early as 1883 the Liverpool Conservative Party was genuinely committed to maximising the working-class vote in the city, and, consequently, highly critical of a clause in the Parliamentary Elections Act that prohibited the use of hired conveyances (because it was not accompanied by an extension in the hours of polling). One opponent had 'endeavoured to meet this difficulty by promoting the introduction of a clause permitting electors to select the polling station they found most convenient. He was, however, successfully opposed by her Majesty's Ministers'.[46]

Simultaneously alive to the need for large numbers of unpaid canvassers as a consequence of this new legislation, the Council of the Constitutional Association made 'a special appeal to Conservatives to join in large numbers the various ward and district committees, and to impress upon these bodies that they have important and responsible duties to perform'.[47] Thus from 1883, Liverpool's Tory elite was keen to make the formal party organisation in Liverpool more inclusive and more representative. At the same time, the rhetoric of Tory Democracy could be tailored to engage an influential middle-class audience, to which redistribution was presented as a the only means by which it could secure just and proportionate representation of its interests at Westminster. Furthermore, Forwood complained that geographical electoral inequities, or the preference shown to rural above urban constituencies in the distribution of parliamentary seats, was mirrored 'in the composition of ministries [where] an overpowering weight is given to land, property and status, to the exclusion of bankers, manufacturers and traders, the backbone of the country'.[48] Thus, the quintessence of Tory Democracy was the rhetoric of representation. This is not to say that for aristocratic democrats such as Lord Randolph Churchill, Tory Democracy was anything more than a novel rhetorical tool with which to mobilise the masses. However, for parochial democrats like Forwood, who lacked the aristocratic credentials that had hitherto been necessary for parliamentary candidature, it meant challenging the parameters of popular political agency.

Historians have often struggled to define this most 'bizarre feature of Democratic Conservatism; the way in which the democratic flag could be made to wave rhetorically over both the middle and the working classes'.[49] In the Liverpool context, Tory Democracy was simply sold as a struggle against political exclusion.

Another consequence of sectarian interpretations of popular politics in late nineteenth-century Liverpool has been that the city features only in passing in the historiography of the ideological and organisational framework of Conservatism as a whole. This is surprising given that the Redistribution of Seats Act, 1885, radically altered the geography of elections in Liverpool, creating nine single member constituencies and making the city the largest unit of representation in parliament outside London. Consequently, just as the progressivism of Liverpool Conservatism in the sphere of social reform has long been underestimated, so too radical innovations within the local party structure have much to contribute to our understanding of the modernisation of political parties down to the First World War.

In terms of formal organisation, Conservatism in Liverpool had already taken the lead in adapting its programme to appeal to a mass electorate during the late 1880s. In a political climate in which working-class voters were numerically dominant in 89 of 95 constituencies, there was still, however, a pressing need to draw the previously disenfranchised masses into the formal organisational framework of the party.[50] Here as elsewhere, Liverpool Conservatism spearheaded modernisation and reform. From 1883, the Liverpool Constitutional Association, recognising the need for an army of unpaid canvassers, had urged Conservatives to join ward and district committees, and to engage more actively in local political mobilisation. This coincided with the arrival of Archibald Salvidge upon the local political scene.[51]

Salvidge, a self-made local brewer and publican, forged his reputation through a revival and revitalisation of the Working Men's Conservative Association. Though the WMCA had been in existence in Liverpool since the 1860s, branch membership had been in steady decline and by 1885 there were just seven poorly attended branches remaining in the city.[52] Salvidge was quick to recognise the potential of the ailing WMCA as an organisational structure through which he could make the workingmen of Liverpool a formidable political force, and he apparently resolved to secure 'a great position in Liverpool, with a big name and lots of power, [to] make the city into a real democracy and show the masses how they can rule themselves.'[53] This was not a creed that one would usually associate with Conservatism, but Salvidge's outspoken self-assurance no doubt hastened his elevation to the chairmanship of the South Toxteth branch of the WMCA in February 1889. Following his election as chairman of the Liverpool Working Men's Conservative Association just three years later, Salvidge, now infamous as Forwood's protege, quoted from the Liverpool democratic gospel:

> Follow me and I will make you JPs and city councillors. Follow me and you shall gain a majority on most of the Tory Parliamentary Divisional Councils in Liverpool, and become divisional secretaries and even chairmen. Follow me and Cabinet Ministers will court you, lord mayors be elected at your behest and Members of Parliament tremble at your displeasure.[54]

True to his word, Salvidge was determined to see the WMCA have a hand in both the selection of candidates and the framing of practical policy in Liverpool, and almost immediately upon taking up his seat on the executive committee of the Constitutional Association later in 1892, he began to press his democratic principles upon the party leadership. Remarkably, one of Salvidge's first achievements as workingmen's leader was the expulsion of the Orange Order from the formal Conservative organisation.

Salvidge's claim to be the voice of working-class Conservatism in Liverpool was initially accepted by a Tory leadership that found it increasingly difficult to placate militant Orangeism in the city. Whilst sporadic eruptions of sectarian street violence in Liverpool invariably heralded the 'Glorious Twelfth' and 'Patrick's Day', the Orange Order had begun to pose a more serious challenge to Conservatism in the city through its increasing involvement in electoral politics. The Orange Order in Liverpool, as elsewhere, was too exclusive as an organisation and too limited in its political agenda to pose a serious threat to Conservative statecraft, but when an Orangeman stood for municipal or parliamentary election in Liverpool, the Liberal Party was likely to gain from an associated adulteration of the Unionist vote. Like the historiography of popular Conservatism, Orangeism has too often been portrayed as a curiously British, plebeian deviance, characterised by Protestant fanaticism, violence, Catholic baiting, ritual and bigotry. Viewed through a Marxian lens, Orangeism has been further demonised for having obscured those nascent socio-economic solidarities that ought to have inflamed England's industrial proletariat to revolution. Recent historiographical revisions, however, have begun to explore the movement's more functional and collective role within nineteenth-century working-class culture.[55]

English Orangeism was fundamentally committed to Protestantism, the Established Church and the Union, yet the mutual and convivial benefits associated with membership were of no less significance. Certainly in Liverpool, the city's network of seventy-three male and three female lodges doubled as social centres, providing funeral, illness and occasionally unemployment insurance benefits to paying members.[56] According to Don MacRaild, the Orange Institution can be more accurately defined as a working-man's church, with prayer, sociability and mutuality being of far greater significance than any political agenda. Indeed, Orangemen 'spent more time at meetings expelling those members who had attended Catholic weddings, than they did on discussing party or political matters'.[57] Though primarily a syndicate of sociability and associationalism, the Orange tradition nevertheless reinforced an exclusive popular belief system which linked low Protestantism, constitutionalism and Conservatism. As an avenue for formal political activism, however, its role was rather more limiting and it was at precisely the moment Liverpool's Orangemen were demanding a more participatory political role that Salvidge stepped forward to promote the WMCA as a legitimate medium for political agency and expression amongst the city's working-class electorate. In 1892, the Orange Institution nominated Thomas McCracken as its official candidate for the forthcoming Everton by-election. Following Salvidge's advice, the Constitutional Association voted unanimously to expel all Orange delegates from the executive and to sever the Orange Institution's affiliation with the party.[58]

Salvidge now encouraged the city's workingmen to pursue a broader and exclusively political agenda. It was the new emphasis upon popular political agency that revitalised the WMCA in Liverpool under Salvidge's guidance, so that by 1893 its membership, invigorated by a busy programme of political lectures, debates and public meetings alongside a lively social calendar, had grown to between five and six thousand, with eighteen branches.[59]

As if to confirm the new populist style of Liverpool Conservatism and its renewed emphasis upon social reform, the first edition of Liverpool's Conservative penny weekly, the *Tory*, published in June 1892, devoted two pages to cataloguing recent legislation that it claimed the Conservative Party had introduced wholly in the interests of the British working classes. Simultaneously, Salvidge, encouraged by the warm reception he had received from the city's Tory elite and his hasty elevation within the party structure, embarked upon a campaign to attract high ranking Conservative speakers to Liverpool under the auspices of the WMCA. Among the eminent politicians who courted Liverpool workingmen were Randolph Churchill, the Earl of Dudley, and, in September 1892, Joseph Chamberlain. Populism characterised Salvidge's events, and there were two stages: one for political oratory and one for the 'Kentucky Darkies' who entertained the crowd during the intervals with music hall favourites and patriotic songs. More informally, the party began to cultivate associations with aspects of working-class culture. Both Everton and Liverpool Football Clubs were founded thanks to the patronage of 'King John Houlding' of Everton, a self made publican and Tory councillor.

It was through a powerful cocktail of social reform and class rhetoric that Salvidge and the WMCA gained the political leverage to overthrow patrician control of Conservatism in Liverpool, turning rhetoric into actions to instate a working Tory Democracy. Municipal socialism was the goal and the achievements of Liverpool's Conservative Corporation in the later decades of the nineteenth century were unprecedented. In 1897 the Tory council negotiated the purchase of Liverpool's tramways, which were electrified following the completion of a municipal generating station in 1899, which also powered street lighting for the city. Special workmen's fares made fast reliable transport throughout the city available to all. Liverpool's unique, overhead railway, or the 'docker's umbrella' as it came to be known, was a Tory achievement, as was that contemporary miracle of engineering, the Mersey Tunnel. The city's passenger railway tunnel, completed in 1886, and the vehicular tunnel opened some fifty year later in 1931, were both celebrated as triumphs of practical Tory Democracy. Lake Vyrnwy, the first large masonry dam in Britain and the largest contemporary artificial reservoir in Europe, was another ambitious Tory achievement, and has carried a continuous supply of fresh water some sixty-three miles to Liverpool since 1892.

It is a strange irony that it should be the death of the grand historical narrative alongside the decentring of class that has made it possible to begin the historical revisions that will ultimately rescue Liverpool's political past from the enormous condescension of sectarianism.

References

1. J. C. Belchem, *Merseypride: Essays in Liverpool Exceptionalism* (Liverpool, 2000).

2. S. Davies, *Liverpool Labour: Social and Political Influences on the Development of the Labour Party in Liverpool, 1900-1939* (Keele, 1996), p. 82.

3. 'In the rest of England, Scotland and Wales, the only major city to compare with Liverpool was Birmingham, which returned its first Labour MP even later, in 1924.' Ibid.

4. P. J. Waller, *Democracy and Sectarianism: A Political and Social History of Liverpool, 1868-1939* (Liverpool, 1981); R. J. Holton, 'Syndicalism and Labour on Merseyside, 1906-1914', in *Building the Union: Merseyside, 1756-1967*, ed. H. R. Hikins (Liverpool, 1973); W. Hamling, *A Short History of the Liverpool Trades Council, 1848-1948* (Liverpool, 1948); R. Baxter, 'The Working Class and Labour Politics', *Political Studies*, xx (1972). See also D. Cannadine, *Class in Britain* (Yale, 1998), pp. 2-8.

5. B. O'Connell, 'Irish Nationalism in Liverpool, 1873-1923', *Eire-Ireland*, x (1975), 24-37; B. O'Connell 'The Irish Nationalist Party in Liverpool, 1873-1922' (University of Liverpool, PhD thesis, 1971).

6. F. Neale, *Sectarian Violence: The Liverpool Experience, 1819-1914* (Manchester, 1988).

7. R. McKenzie and A. Silver, *Angels in Marble: Working-Class Conservatism in Urban England* (London, 1968); E. Nordlinger, *The Working Class Tories, Authority, Deference and Stable Democracy* (London, 1967); H. Pelling, 'Working-Class Conservatives', *Historical Journal*, xiii (1970), 339-43; F. Parkin, 'Working-Class Conservatives: A Theory of Political Deviance', *British Journal of Sociology*, xviii (1967), 278-90.

8. Belchem, *Merseypride*; Davies, *Liverpool Labour*; A. Shallice, 'Orange and Green Militancy: Sectarianism and Working Class Politics in Liverpool, 1900-1914', *North West Historical Society Journal*, vi (1979-80); J. Smith, 'Labour Tradition in Glasgow and Liverpool', *History Workshop Journal*, xvii (1984), and idem, 'Class, Skill and Sectarianism in Glasgow and Liverpool, 1880-1914' in *Class, Power and Social Structure in British Nineteenth-Century Towns*, ed. R. J. Morris (Leicester, 1986).

9. See R. Swift, 'Historians and the Irish: Recent Writings on the Irish in Nineteenth-Century Britain', in *The Great Famine and Beyond: Irish Migrants in Britain in the Nineteenth and Twentieth Centuries*, ed. D. MacRaild (Dublin,

2000), pp. 14-39; R. Swift, 'The Historiography of the Irish in Nineteenth-Century Britain: Some Perspectives', in *The Irish World-Wide: The Irish in the New Communities*, ed. P. O'Sullivan (Leicester, 1992), pp. 52-81.

10. J. C. Belchem, *Popular Radicalism in Nineteenth-Century Britain* (Basingstoke, 1996), p. 4.

11. G. S. Jones, 'The Language of Chartism', in *The Chartist Experience: Studies in Working-Class Radicalism and Culture, 1830-1860*, ed. J. Epstein and D. Thompson (Basingstoke, 1982), pp. 3-58.

12. G. S. Jones, *Languages of Class: Studies in English Working Class History, 1832-1982* (Cambridge, 1983), p. 93. See also J. Lawrence, *Speaking for the People: Party, Language and Popular Politics in England, 1867-1914* (Cambridge, 1998), ch.3; R. Gray, 'The Deconstruction of the English Working Class', *Social History*, xi (1986), 363-73; N. Kirk, 'In Defence of Class: A Critique of Recent Revisionist Writing upon the Nineteenth-Century English Working Class', *International Review of Social History*, xxxii (1987), 2-47; B. D. Palmer, *Descent into Discourse: The Reification of Language and the Writing of Social History* (Philadelphia, 1990).

13. Jones, *Languages of Class*, p. 8.

14. Neale, *Sectarian Violence*; J. Bohstedt, 'More than One Working Class: Protestant and Catholic Riots in Edwardian Liverpool', in *Popular Politics, Riot and Labour: Essays in Liverpool History, 1790-1940*, ed. J. C. Belchem (Liverpool, 1992).

15. See also Waller, *Democracy and Sectarianism*.

16. *Liverpool Albion*, 5 Dec. 1882.

17. *London Standard*, 9 Dec. 1882; *Times*, 9 Dec. 1882. For the Liberal press see R. Foster, *Lord Randolph Churchill: A Political Life* (Oxford, 1981), p.108.

18. Lord Randolph Churchill, 'Elijah's Mantle', *Fortnightly Review*, cxcvii (1883), 621. For a more detailed account of Churchill and Tory Democracy see Foster, *Lord Randolph Churchill*; R. Shannon, *The Age of Disraeli, 1868-1881: The Rise of Tory Democracy* (London, 1997); R. Quinault, 'Lord Randolph Churchill and Tory Democracy, 1880-1885', *Historical Journal*, xxii (1979), 141-165; R. Foster, 'Tory Democracy and Political Elitism', *Parliament and Community: Historical Studies*, xiv (Belfast, 1983).

19. W. S. Adams, *Edwardian Portraits* (London, 1957), p. 79; W. S. Blunt, *Gordon at Khartoum* (London, 1911), p. 414; 'Randolph Churchill: A Personal Recollection', *Nineteenth Century* (Mar. 1907), pp. 407-15.

20. *North Liverpool Times*, 25 Apr. 1885. For a contemporary account of the currency of Tory Democracy in Liverpool and evidence that Churchill usurped the mantle of Tory Democrat from Forwood, see M. Ostrogorski, *Democracy and the Organisation of Political Parties* (New York, 1902) pp. 278-281. For Forwood's involvement with Churchill and the National Union controversy, see Waller, *Democracy and Sectarianism*, pp. 48-52.

21. A. B. Forwood, 'Democratic Toryism', *Contemporary Review*, xliii (Feb. 1883), 293-305.

22. R. Taylor, *Lord Salisbury* (London, 1975), p. 73.

23. See also J. Lawrence, 'Class and Gender in the Making of Urban Toryism, 1880-1914', *English Historical Review*, cvii (1993).

24. Forwood, 'Democratic Toryism', p. 295; *London Standard*, 9 Dec. 1882; E. H. H. Green, *The Crisis of Conservatism: The Politics, Economics, and Ideology of the Conservative Party, 1880-1914* (London, 1995), p. 129. Green has shown that some of Chamberlain's most ardent supporters were Conservative.

25. Local studies include C. Pooley and C. Irish, *The Development of Corporation Housing in Liverpool, 1869-1945*, (Lancaster, 1984); C. Pooley, 'Housing for the Poorest Poor: Slum-Clearance and Rehousing in Liverpool, 1890-1918', *Journal of Historical Geography*, xi (1985), 70-88; J. N. Tarn, 'Housing in Liverpool and Glasgow: The Growth of Civic Responsibility', *Town Planning Review*, xxxix (1968-9), 319-334; I. C. Taylor, 'The Court and Cellar Dwelling: The Eighteenth Century Origin of the Liverpool Slum', *Transactions of the Historic Society of Lancashire and Cheshire*, cxxii (1970); I. C. Taylor, 'The Insanitary Housing Question and Tenement Dwellings in Nineteenth-Century Liverpool', in *Multi-Storey Living*, ed. A. Sutcliffe (London, 1974); J. H. Treble, 'Liverpool Working Class Housing, 1801-1851', in *The History of Working Class Housing: A Symposium*, ed. S. Chapman (Newton Abbott, 1971), pp. 167-220; B. D. White, *A History of the Corporation of Liverpool* (Liverpool, 1951); L. Feehan, 'Liverpool Corporation and Municipal Housing for the Working Classes, 1864-1914' (University of Liverpool, MA thesis, 1974); H. C. Morton, 'A Technical Study of Housing in Liverpool, 1790-1938' (University of Liverpool, PhD thesis, 1971), vols A, B, C. See also J. Morton, *Cheaper than Peabody: Local Authority Housing, 1890-1919* (London, 1991); A. S. Wohl, *The Eternal Slum: Housing and Social Policy in Victorian London* (London, 1977); E. Gaudie, *Cruel Habitations: A History of Working-Class Housing, 1780-1918* (London, 1974); J. Tarn, *Working*

Class Housing in Britain (London, 1971), and idem, *Five Per Cent Philanthropy* (Cambridge, 1973).

26. Housing as a Conservative political 'programme' is considered briefly in Waller, *Democracy and Sectarianism*, pp. 85-90. See also Feehan, 'Liverpool Corporation and Municipal Housing'.

27. Bohstedt refers briefly to Irish Nationalist 'co-operation with the Tories to produce Liverpool's pioneering housing programme' in 'More than One Working Class', p. 206.

28. A. B. Forwood, *The Dwellings of the Industrial Classes in the Diocese of Liverpool and How to Improve Them: A Paper Read at the Liverpool Diocesan Conference* (Liverpool, 1883).

29. Ibid.

30. *The Bitter Cry of Outcast London*, ed. A. S. Wohl (Leicester, 1970), p. 9.

31. *Royal Commission on the Housing of the Working Classes*, H. C. 1884, xxx, First Report, 13,414-17.

32. J. Chamberlain, 'Labourers' and Artisans' Dwellings', *Fortnightly Review*, new series, cciv (Dec. 1883); Lord Salisbury, 'Labourers' and Artisans' Dwellings', *National Review*, ix (Nov. 1883).

33. Forwood, *The Dwellings of the Industrial Classes*, p. 4.

34. Ibid.

35. *Programme of the Ceremony of Opening the New Labourers' Dwellings in the Bevington Street Area*, 14 June 1912.

36. 16.5 per cent of occupied dwellings at St. Martin's Cottages had a female 'head of household', and for the council's Juvenal Dwellings this figure was 26 per cent.

37. Analysis of such empirical data can of course only ever be useful as a guide; in this instance simply because the ethnic character of any group cannot be truly defined in terms of a single characteristic or attribute. There are likely to have been numerous corporation tenants in Liverpool who, though born elsewhere, considered themselves to be 'Irish'. L[iverpool] R[ecord] O[ffice], Census Office Enquiry Form, 18 Sept. 1891, Liverpool St. Martin's District, 451-3 (Ref: 2905).

38. T. Lane, *Liverpool: Gateway of Empire* (London, 1987); Baxter 'The Working Class and Labour Politics'; Smith 'Labour Tradition in Glasgow and Liverpool';

Davies *Liverpool Labour*, pp. 31-74. For a contemporary allegation see T. P. O'Connor's address to the Commons, 11 May 1892, *Hansard*, 4th series, iv (1892), 632-3.

39. *Liverpool Daily Post*, 1 Mar. 1887.

40. Ibid.

41. For a discussion of American style machine politics and the Labour/Catholic alliance during the 1930s, see Davies, *Liverpool Labour*, pp. 69-75, and idem, 'The Liverpool Labour Party and the Liverpool Working Class', 1900-1939', *Bulletin of the North West Labour History Society*, vi (1979-80).

42. Forwood, 'Democratic Toryism', pp. 293-305.

43. *Times*, 27 Aug. 1884.

44. A. Jones, *The Politics of Reform, 1884* (Cambridge, 1972), n.1.

45. Forwood, 'Democratic Toryism', p. 301.

46. LRO, Liverpool Constitutional Association, Annual Report for 1883, Constitutional Minute Book, 6/1 (Ref: 329.CON), p. 4.

47. Ibid.

48. Forwood to Churchill, 31 July 1886, University of Cambridge, Churchill Archives Centre, RCHL, xiii (1606).

49. Foster 'Tory Democracy and Political Elitism', p. 149.

50. H. M. Pelling, *A Social Geography of British Elections, 1885-1910* (London, 1967), p.419.

51. Liverpool Constitutional Association, Annual Report for 1883, p. 4.

52. In 1869 there were over 1,600 subscribing members of the LWMCA, with 12 branches across the city by 1872. *Parliamentary Papers*, viii (1868-9), 3379; *Kelly's Directory* (Liverpool, 1886).

53. S. Salvidge *Salvidge of Liverpool* (London, 1934), p.13. This account of Salvidge's early ambitions for the WMCA was in wide circulation throughout his lifetime. See LRO, Biographical Newscutting Collection, Ref: 1246; J. Smith, 'Commonsense Thought and Working Class Consciousness: Some Aspects of the

Liverpool and Glasgow Labour Movement in the Early Years of the Twentieth Century' (University of Edinburgh, PhD thesis, 1981), p.269.

54. Salvidge, *Salvidge of Liverpool*, p.15.

55. D. MacRaild, *Irish Migrants in Modern Britain, 1750-1922* (New York, 1999), pp. 199-122; E. McFarland, *Protestants First: Orangeism in Nineteenth Century Scotland* (Edinburgh, 1990); D. MacRaild, 'Principle, Party and Protest: The Language of Victorian Orangeism in the North of England', in *The Victorians and Race*, ed. S. West (Leicester, 1996); D. Fitzpatrick, 'A Curious Middle Place: The Irish in Britain, 1871-1921', in *The Irish in Britain, 1815-1939*, ed. R. Swift and S. Gilley (London, 1989), pp. 35-46.

56. Loyal Orange Institution, *A Handy Guide to the Various Lodges of the Province of Liverpool* (Liverpool, 1885); S. J. Fielding, *Class and Ethnicity: Irish Catholics in England, 1880-1939* (Buckingham, 1993), pp. 88-91.

57. D. MacRaild, 'Ethnic Political Culture and Irish Migration: The Case of the Orange Order in the North East of England, c.1885-1914', paper presented to conference on 'Varieties of Political Belief in Britain, 1832-1914' at the University of Sunderland, June 2001.

58. LRO, Liverpool Constitutional Association, Executive Committee Minute Book, 1878-98, 16 May 1892 (Ref: 329.CON. 1/1/2).

59. B. G. Orchard, *Liverpool's Legion of Honour* (Birkenhead, 1893), p. 618.